Write to Return

McGill-Queen's Refugee and Forced Migration Studies

SERIES EDITORS: Megan Bradley and James Milner

Forced migration is a local, national, regional, and global challenge with profound political and social implications. Understanding the causes and consequences of, and possible responses to, forced migration requires careful analysis from a range of disciplinary perspectives, as well as interdisciplinary dialogue.

The purpose of the McGill-Queen's Refugee and Forced Migration Studies series is to advance in-depth examination of diverse forms, dimensions, and experiences of displacement, including in the context of conflict and violence, repression and persecution, and disasters and environmental change. The series will explore responses to refugees, internal displacement, and other forms of forced migration to illuminate the dynamics surrounding forced migration in global, national, and local contexts, including Canada, the perspectives of displaced individuals and communities, and the connections to broader patterns of human mobility. Featuring research from fields including politics, international relations, law, anthropology, sociology, geography, and history, the series highlights new and critical areas of enquiry within the field, especially conversations across disciplines and from the perspective of researchers in the global South, where the majority of forced migration unfolds. The series benefits from an international advisory board made up of leading scholars in refugee and forced migration studies.

5 The Precarious Lives of Syrians
Migration, Citizenship, and Temporary Protection in Turkey
Feyzi Baban, Suzan Ilcan, and Kim Rygiel

6 The Urbanization of Forced Displacement UNHCR, Urban Refugees, and the Dynamics of Policy Change
Neil James Wilson Crawford

7 Finding Safe Harbour
Supporting the Integration of Refugee Youth
Emily Pelley

8 Documenting Displacement
Questioning Methodological Boundaries in Forced Migration Research
Edited by Katarzyna Grabska and Christina R. Clark-Kazak

9 Voluntary and Forced Migration in Latin America
Law and Policy Reforms
Edited by Natalia Caicedo Camacho and Luisa Feline Freier

10 The Right to Research
Historical Narratives by Refugee and Global South Researchers
Edited by Kate Reed and Marcia C. Schenck

11 Kingdom of Barracks
Polish Displaced Persons in Allied-Occupied Germany and Austria
Katarzyna Nowak

12 Urban Refugees and Digital Technology
Reshaping Social, Political, and Economic Networks
Charles Martin-Shields

13 Migration Governance in North America
Policy, Politics, and Community
Edited by Kiran Banerjee and Craig Damian Smith

14 Write to Return
Huguenot Refugees on the Frontiers of the French Enlightenment
Bryan A. Banks

Write to Return

Huguenot Refugees on the Frontiers of the French Enlightenment

***

BRYAN A. BANKS

McGill-Queen's University Press
Montreal & Kingston • London • Chicago

ISBN 978-0-2280-2109-4 (cloth)
ISBN 978-0-2280-2163-6 (ePDF)
ISBN 978-0-2280-2164-3 (ePUB)

Legal deposit second quarter 2024
Bibliothèque nationale du Québec

Printed in Canada on acid-free paper that is 100% ancient forest free (100% post-consumer recycled), processed chlorine free

Funded by the Government of Canada | Financé par le gouvernement du Canada | Canada | Canada Council for the Arts | Conseil des arts du Canada

We acknowledge the support of the Canada Council for the Arts.
Nous remercions le Conseil des arts du Canada de son soutien.

McGill-Queen's University Press in Montreal is on land which long served as a site of meeting and exchange amongst Indigenous Peoples, including the Haudenosaunee and Anishinabeg nations. In Kingston it is situated on the territory of the Haudenosaunee and Anishinaabek. We acknowledge and thank the diverse Indigenous Peoples whose footsteps have marked these territories on which peoples of the world now gather.

Library and Archives Canada Cataloguing in Publication

Title: Write to return : Huguenot refugees on the frontiers of the French Enlightenment / Bryan A. Banks.
Names: Banks, Bryan A., author.
Series: McGill-Queen's refugee and forced migration studies ; 14.
Description: Series statement: McGill-Queen's refugee and forced migration studies ; 14 | Includes bibliographical references and index.
Identifiers: Canadiana (print) 20240294157 | Canadiana (ebook) 20240294211 | ISBN 9780228021094 (cloth) | ISBN 9780228021643 (ePUB) | ISBN 9780228021636 (ePDF)
Subjects: LCSH: Jurieu, Pierre, 1637-1713—Criticism and interpretation. | LCSH: Court, Antoine, 1696-1760—Criticism and interpretation. | LCSH: Bayle, Pierre, 1647-1706—Criticism and interpretation. | LCSH: Rabaut, Jean-Paul, 1743-1793—Criticism and interpretation. | LCSH: Huguenots—History. | LCSH: Religious refugees—Europe—History. | LCSH: Enlightenment—France.
Classification: LCC BX9454.3 .B36 2024 | DDC 284.509/032—dc23

Those few refugees who insist upon telling the truth, even to the point of "indecency," get in exchange for their unpopularity one priceless advantage: history is no longer a closed book to them and politics is no longer the privilege of gentiles.

Hannah Arendt, "We Refugees," 1943

Contents

Figures

Preface

In 2013, I attended a meeting of the Huguenot Society of Great Britain and Ireland to hear a colleague and well-known scholar, Robin Howells, speak on the Enlightenment philosopher Jean-Jacques Rousseau's connections with the displaced Huguenot community, especially in Geneva.[1] There in the University College London's Chadwick Lecture Theatre, before the meeting commenced, an elderly man of medium stature sat in the auditorium chair next to me. We made small talk as one does at these kinds of events, and inevitably he asked if I was of Huguenot descent. I told him no, that I was researching the Huguenot refugees and the Enlightenment, hence my particular interest in the lecture that evening. The man seemed intrigued if not piqued with a kind of pride I had not yet recognized. The fact that an outsider – myself, not being of Huguenot ancestry – showed an interest in *his* history meant a lot to him. He told me of his family's flight into the English refuge following Louis XIV's 1685 Revocation of the Edict of Nantes, and of their continued attachment to the Threadneedle Street Church in London even as many had come to join the Anglican Church in the generations that followed.

The Huguenot Society's meetings were a chance for him to celebrate his heritage and to commemorate the struggles that his ancestors had experienced. Huguenot groups like the Huguenot Society of Great Britain and Ireland offer a chance for communities to invent their own traditions.[2] These societies have a history of their own, having emerged from the nineteenth century's rise in ethno-nationalism. The Huguenot Society of America was founded in New York in 1883. The Huguenot Society of London (later renamed the Huguenot Society of Great Britain and Ireland) and the Huguenot Society of South Carolina began work two years later in 1885. German Huguenots founded the Deutsche Hugenotten-Gesellschaft in 1890. Since then, the Huguenot Society of Virginia (1922), the Huguenot Foundation of South Africa (1953), the Dutch Nederlandse Hugenoten Stichting (1975), and the Huguenot Society of Australia (2003) have been created to foster further the Huguenot identity. It would be tempting to argue that the work these Huguenot societies are doing is more imaginative than anything, but what this book argues is that such inventions have lasting impacts not only in terms of identity, but also in terms of cultural heritage and politics. They play a part in a very long story of Huguenot refugees shaping their own identities. Huguenots have also actively curated their own archives and publications for over a century. Reading those archives within the context of their own ethno-national construction is key to making them productive without uncritically reproducing the same invented traditions.

While all of these institutions employ the term *Huguenot*, pronounced in myriad ways and translated as cognates into their own languages, the equivalent society in France does not use the word *Huguenot* in their title. La Société de l'histoire du protestantisme français, now situated behind a bright blue door and across from an outdoor patio in the Seventh Arrondissement of Paris, was founded in 1852 before all the other societies. In France, the term is most often used to refer to the diaspora, spatially removed from France, and to the historical Huguenots of the Wars of Religion, temporally disconnected from the present. As will become clear in this book, the missing *Huguenot* in the French society's name was an intentional, contextually driven factor for the French Calvinist community, who for the duration of the long eighteenth century (1685–1800) continued to face repression or repression's spectre. Their safety depended on the identity they projected out to French society. "*Protestantisme français*" reminds people that they are both Protestant and French, because for a time in France, to be Protestant meant one was not French, at least in the eyes of the Old Regime Bourbon sacral monarchy. Huguenots in the past and present are and have been active agents in shaping how the rest of society views their community.

This book focuses on Huguenot efforts to recast their identity anew from the 1685 Revocation of the Edict of Nantes through the eighteenth century. It was in the crucible known as the *Désert* period (traditionally defined as the period between 1715 and 1789) in French Protestant history that the word *Huguenot* became disconnected from the French Protestant community in France. Huguenots in the diaspora strengthened their Huguenot identity over the centuries that followed and especially during the rise of nineteenth-century ethno-nationalism; for those seeking repatriation, a new identity needed to be forged. The Huguenot refugee identity was capable of levelling a critique of the Revocation as well as courting the minds and hearts of those empathetic to the pain and suffering of the Huguenot community. In this period, Huguenots began to refer to themselves as refugees; soon after, the refugee identity became a common feature of the modern political consciousness. The refugee identity remained in the diaspora, but for those interested in repatriation, it proved an obstacle to emphasizing Huguenot French identity. The story told in this book is one of competing identities at a time of international mobility and nation-building.

Acknowledgments

Authors can often pinpoint the moment that a new project began. For me, that story begins in 2009, in a Parisian café on the Rue de Rivoli, where I met Rafe Blaufarb, who would become my MA adviser. I explained my interests in religion and the revolutionary era, not knowing which research topic would be feasible or timely. The literature on the French Revolution is copious and most subjects have received treatment, but what struck us both in that moment was just how little attention had been given to French Protestants in the revolutionary era. Indeed, the most extensive treatment on the subject had last been published in the 1950s. From that point forward, my project went through two advanced degrees – with my doctoral work overseen by Darrin M. McMahon and transformed from one iteration to the next. The project proved feasible time and time again, but the question of timeliness eluded me for quite some time. And then Syrian refugees began flooding into Europe, refugees from across Latin America moved through Mexico to the American border, and most recently, Ukrainians have fled their homes by the millions. That Huguenots were the first ones to apply the word *refugee* to their own displacement figured into my doctoral work on a minuscule level. My desire to say something timely with this project meant that my doctoral dissertation needed a complete rewrite if I wanted to speak to our current moment of refugee crises. After graduating in December 2014, I began to rewrite my work, and the insights that this volume bears owe much to that long, winding process and the many wonderful people who shared their expertise with me.

What I found most striking during my research actually comes at the end of this volume. French revolutionaries offered citizenship to Huguenots whether they lived in France or not. In addition, the revolutionaries passed legislation that would return ancestral lands to Huguenots upon their return. While it turned out that these plans were not all that impactful, it struck me as odd that, at a time when organized religion was under scrutiny, revolutionaries chose to codify such a gesture in order to attract Huguenots back to France. This element is woefully understudied, but those who have remarked on its uniqueness have largely pointed to the efforts of Enlightenment philosophers who advocated for the Huguenot cause, or to benevolent magistrates who sought social stability by promoting religious toleration. And yet, the efforts of Huguenots themselves have gone almost completely unnoticed. So I made it my mission to uncover how Huguenots advocated for themselves, how they shaped the minds and arguments of enlightened philosophers and magistrates alike, and how their work ultimately created the climate that encouraged revolutionaries to sponsor their return.

Forefronting the voices of Huguenot refugees meant spending a majority of my time in Paris at the Bibliothèque de la Société d'histoire du protestantisme français. Behind the library's blue door lie generations of curatorial work done for the French Protestant people and for historians interested in their story. For weeks on end, I photographed nearly every document in their collection that related to the *Désert* Huguenot leaders who kept the French Calvinist community together after the Revocation of the Edict of Nantes formally outlawed their existence. From there, I visited archival collections and libraries around the Calvinist triangle stretching from Geneva to Rotterdam to London. Once I began to process all of the photos I took, I realized that Huguenots tended to most fully explicate the meaning of their refugee identity in printed texts. Huguenots played a pivotal role in printing in the eighteenth century along France's borders, so it makes sense that one would locate the fullest discussions of Huguenot refugeedom there. I am ever grateful to librarians at the Bibliothèque nationale de France, the British Library, Florida State University's Special Collections, and Emory University's Special Collections. Of course, the tireless efforts of so many interlibrary loan officers made this book project possible too.

I have given what feels like countless presentations on this research for over a decade now. On both sides of the Atlantic, I have found scholarly communities to give me feedback, to push my analysis, and to challenge my unwitting misconceptions. In particular, Timothy Best, Jeffrey Burson, Erica Johnson Edwards, Cindy Ermus, Abraham Gibson, Carol Harrison, Lynn Hunt, Joshua Meeks, John Merriman, Ronen Steinberg, Timothy Tackett, Daniel Watkins, and Dale Van Kley all provided invaluable comments at different stages. Darrin M. McMahon has, on dozens of occasions, pointed me toward valuable insights. During the final stages of this project, I benefited from the wisdom of the participants of the Atlantic Exiles project at the University of Duisburg–Essen. Jan C. Jansen and Thomas Mareite organized a wonderful week for us in Essen and in the process helped me rework the conclusion to this project.

Colleagues in my department at Columbus State University have been a boon to me intellectually. Sarah Bowman, Jordan Brasher, Ryan Lynch, Caroline Newhall, Eric Spears, Gary Sprayberry, and Doug Tompson have helped me to craft my argument, but have also helped me create the space to research and write at a teaching-focused institution. Part of this has meant that the classroom has become a more deliberate space for me to work through my own research interests. I owe Mariko Izumi greatly for helping me think through how best to balance teaching and research. During the spring 2020 semester, right as the COVID-19 pandemic shut much of the world down, I was in the middle of teaching a course titled "Refugees in World History." My students had spent much of the first half of the semester thinking about push and pull factors that led to mass displacement, and yet none of us realized just how displaced we would feel as our campus closed and we dispersed to the online world. Periodically, over the course of that semester, I presented elements of this book to the students. Micah Arnholt, Kathryn Askerzada, Ashley Brand, Jonathan Gunn, Dustin Hudgins, Shelby Johnson, Blake Lorentz, Dylan Rice, and Lawrence Washington provided feedback that helped me draw broader connections and drill down deeper into particular sources in that very class. Other colleagues, near and far, helped me think through my arguments and provided invaluable moral support. Jessica VanValkenburgh encouraged me to keep pushing to get this work through publication.

As it takes a village to raise a child, so it takes a village to write a book. And those closest to the project often carry the most weight. My father, Robert Banks, taught high school English for much of his adult life, and he never tired of being my teacher – whether through scrawled notes in the margins of a paper or just being a sounding board. My mother, Grier Banks, never failed to show an interest in what must have seemed to be my parochial curiosities. Emily Banks, my sister, equally listened and enthusiastically prodded me on. Tiffany Sirignano-Banks saw this book born from a dissertation and offered valuable support.

My daughter, Cecilia Banks, was born in 2018, and reworking this project in her formative years proved challenging in all kinds of ways. Raising her forced me to rethink my purpose in writing this book. I hope this book stands as a testament to what perseverance can produce. I dedicate this book to her. I cannot wait to see what she manages to do in life. She will certainly always make her father proud.

Write to Return

Introduction

> The main Calvinist families were assembled, especially those that were believed to be the easiest [to convert]. They renounced their faith in the name of others; and the obstinate were handed over to the soldiers, who had all license except that of killing. However, there were several people so cruelly mistreated that they died. The children of refugees in foreign countries still cry out over this persecution of their fathers. They compare it to the most violent that the Church suffered in the early days. It was a strange contrast, that from the bosom of a voluptuous court, where reigned the gentleness of manners, the graces, the charms of society, there arose orders so hard and so pitiless.[1]
>
> Voltaire, *Le Siècle de Louis XIV*, 1733

Scholars of refugee history or policy often begin their analyses with the United Nations High Commissioner for Refugees (UNHCR)'s 1951 *Convention and Protocol Relating to the Status of Refugees*. The Convention's definition of *refugee*, which has now become the international legal definition, is "someone who is unable or unwilling to return to their country of origin owing to a well-founded fear of being persecuted for reasons of race, *religion*, nationality, membership of a particular social group or political opinion."[2] If not the UNHCR's definition, scholars tend to point to Hannah Arendt's understanding of refugees as peoples existing in a legal purgatory of "statelessness," or as having lost the protection of any given state.[3] Before the publication of *The Origins of Totalitarianism*, in which Arendt laid out her theory of statelessness, she had already come to terms with the complicated identity of refugees in her 1943 essay "We Refugees." Arendt was a Jewish philosopher who fled Nazi Germany and eventually made her way to the United States in 1941, where she found herself enmeshed in a refugee community that was at once established and in flux. Two competing factions of refugees emerged in the community. Arendt saw both the political utility of the term *refugee* and how it divided refugee communities desperately trying to create new homes for themselves.

Even older definitions exist that help us to understand the transhistorical emergence of refugees as an identity as well as a political category.[4] Denis Diderot, the compiler and chief editor of the compendium of Enlightenment thought the *Encyclopédie* (published from 1751 to 1772), defined *refugees* as Huguenots "whom the Revocation of the Edict of Nantes forced to leave French soil and to look for sanctuary in foreign nations in order to hide from the persecutions that a blind and rash zeal made them endure in their own country."[5] Diderot was a fierce critic of the French monarchy and sacral absolutism, which justified persecution of religious minorities. In the years surrounding the infamous anti-Calvinist legislation of the "Sun King," Louis XIV, Huguenots in southern France fled the country or went into hiding, taking refuge abroad or in the rural French countryside. While estimates vary, around two hundred thousand Huguenots fled France in the 1680s. Diderot's definition summoned the Huguenot refugee community as a means to critique the French state. Diderot, though, was not the inventor of the refugee identity. He drew inspiration from Huguenots themselves.

Seventy years before Diderot provided his definition, Claude Brousson used the term *refugee* to give meaning to the suffering the Huguenot community faced. Like the Ancient Israelites of the Old Testament, the Huguenots saw themselves as chosen by God to wander in their own torturous *Désert*. Brousson was a Calvinist lawyer turned preacher during the era surrounding Louis XIV's Revocation of the Edict of Nantes in 1685. Brousson, like many others, fled Toulouse to Holland. Filled with dread, Brousson returned to the kingdom that had expelled him to preach to those threatened by the *dragonnades*, the king's paramilitary force. Brousson became a wanted man with the considerable bounty of six hundred louis d'or placed on his head. For many Catholics, Brousson's person represented not only financial gain, but also the last breath of the Calvinist heresy in the country. They hunted Brousson, but he evaded them with the help of his network. He slipped his hunters repeatedly, travelling along a network of Calvinist households. When Catholic soldiers nipped at his heels, he hid in grottos, up mountainsides, and in old barns. On one occasion, they were hot on his trail when he dove into a well. At the bottom of the well, a crag in the rock created a space just big enough for him to hide his body. One of the Catholic soldiers who pursued him, suspecting Brousson lay concealed in the well's dank depths, lowered himself slowly, but in the darkness, the soldier failed to catch sight of the renegade Reformed preacher.[6]

The earthen well safeguarded Brousson just as France's frontiers had done for generations of Huguenots since the Reformation. The plateaus of the Massif Central, with the Cévennes Mountains on the eastern edge – cut off from the Alps by the power of the Rhône River – provided Calvinists with a rural refuge inside the boundaries of the French kingdom. From the early years of the French Reformation, Calvinists had found these lands integral to their survival. The distance from Paris proved useful. Their Swiss refuge lay just beyond France's borders, and well-worn paths used by Calvinists and smugglers crisscrossed France's frontiers, making the kingdom's borders porous.[7] This geography and these trails offered Calvinists a way to stay in France after the Revocation and still remain connected with the rest of the Huguenot diaspora. These networks facilitated Brousson's missions into France, but they also aided the transmission of Protestant writings, like Pierre Jurieu's *Lettres pastorales* or some of the illegal writings of the Enlightenment later in the eighteenth century. Calvinists cut through the geomorphology of the Alps, the southern plateau, and rugged landscapes in between to connect those Huguenots implanted beyond France's borders in the Protestant international – spanning from London through the Netherlands to Lausanne – with the Calvinist community still in France. But in some ways, they also used the landscape not just as a mode of defense against the Catholic dragoons hell-bent on their conversions, but as a means to assert their rights to worship. The soil of their refuge took on symbolic importance.

Brousson appropriated the landscape, drawing on the cultural understandings of Christianity. In his 1695 publication, *La Manne mystique du Désert, ou Sermons prononcez en France dans les Déserts & dans les Cavernes Durant les ténêbres de la nui & l'affliction les années 1689, 1690, 1691, 1692, & 1693*, Brousson likened the persecution of Calvinists in France to the biblical persecution of the Jews. The story of Jewish persecution and their languishment in the Egyptian *Désert* provided a pivotal narrative for sustaining the community. Ultra-Catholic Bourbon rule became the Babylonian Captivity.[8] Louis XIV was Nebuchadnezzar. Yet through it all, the Huguenots still maintained the position of the people of God, a prized identity, which simultaneously satiated those who might have been lured into conversion and promised a future where their persecutions would finally end, when the king's clemency would be won, and the Calvinists could repatriate literally to France and figuratively from the remoteness of their *Désert*. Brousson was eventually captured on September 18, 1698, in the Béarn region of southwestern France. He was executed in his own imagined *Désert*. His biblical allusion stuck.

The *Désert* has come to denote the period of Calvinist illegality in France. The period begins with the Revocation of the Edict of Nantes in 1685, or with Antoine Court's efforts to reorganize the Church after the Revocation in 1715. The former chronological marker emphasizes the persecution of the Protestants, and the latter draws our attention to the intentional efforts to reestablish the Huguenot community in France. The traditional ending of the period is either the Edict of Versailles (more commonly referred to as the Edict of Toleration) in 1787 or the start of the French Revolution in 1789. Historians normally split the *Désert* period in two. The period between 1685 and the early 1760s denotes the exercise of state violence against those Calvinists remaining in the country. This also corresponds to a generational shift within the larger Huguenot diaspora outside of France, which witnessed acculturation and a decline in attachment to France as their ancestral home. In

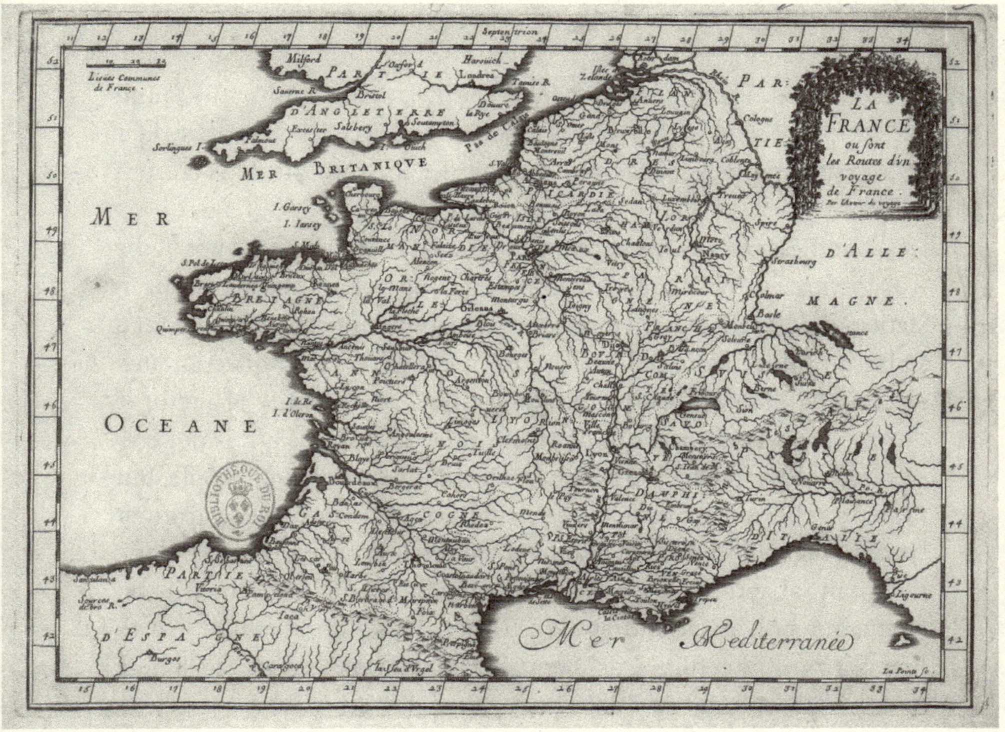

Figure 0.1 A map of seventeenth-century France.

1762, Voltaire popularized and publicized the plight of French Calvinists by seeking justice for the wrongly executed Calvinist Jean Calas, as well as the Calvinist Sirvens who were persecuted for their daughter's death the same year.[9] This case appears as the bookend to the first period and the start of the second. Beginning in the 1760s, a shift away from the violence of the preceding period inaugurated a sort of tacit tolerance, which led to Louis XVI's formal proclamation of tolerance in 1787. In this definition of the *Désert*, Huguenots played the role of the victim – of outright persecution in the first period, and of a tolerance that is only tacitly accepted and not formally guaranteed in the second. Hindsight tells us that the period from the 1760s to 1787 was a period of relative peace, but for the Huguenots on the ground, in the refuge, the return to the first period was profoundly and likely imminent. Even in 1787, when Huguenots sang psalms in honour of Louis XVI, they used guarded language. They moderated their excitement for fear of a return to bloodshed. Having left the *Désert* in 1787, Huguenots still found metaphorical sand in their shoes for years and even decades after their legal restitution as subjects, and later under the revolution, as citizens of France.

What these brief sketches of the Huguenot origins and the use of the word *refugee* show is that the term *refugee* is not and has never been static but, like refugees themselves, is always in motion, searching for a stable meaning, a safe refuge away from the violence that necessitated its conception in the first place. While mobile, the identity of a refugee during this period was born on the frontiers, insofar as it was not created by a state for the purposes of surveilling or policing people, but rather was born from the Christian tradition of those crossing frontier spaces. Huguenots lived on France's frontiers – both internal and along their natural and built borders. While this study focuses primarily on Huguenot polemical and apologetic arguments for their return to France from the refuge, I deliberately use the word *frontier* to signify spaces both internal and external to France.[10] As will become clear, Huguenots crossed borders regularly. France's borders existed mostly on maps and Huguenots could regularly cross those imaginary lines for safety as they saw fit.

Huguenot refugees occupied similar frontier spaces to those occupied by the leading lights of the French Enlightenment, and the two groups influenced each other. This point belies the idea that Huguenots were passive in their self-advocation and that they depended solely on the philosophical and legal writings of their non-Huguenot contemporaries. Huguenots published Enlightenment tracts in Geneva and Holland. Voltaire lived in Ferney, not far from Geneva or the Franco-Swiss border, for around twenty years. Rousseau had come out of the Calvinist community of Geneva as well. Huguenots infiltrated the world of the salons, academies, and masonic lodges that hosted spheres of Enlightenment sociability. French Enlightenment philosophers in all their cosmopolitan travels came in contact with Huguenots regularly. Huguenots influenced Enlightenment ideals of religious toleration, but they also adopted forms of political argumentation from the philosophers too. As Jeremy Adelman and Stephen Aron argue, frontiers denote a "meeting place of peoples in which geographic and cultural borders [are] not clearly defined." Huguenot refugees and French Enlightenment philosophers participated in "intercultural relations," which "produced mixing and accommodation as opposed to unambiguous triumph."[11] In this frontier middle ground, Huguenot refugees mobilized their refugee representations and refuted anti-Huguenot polemics launched by Catholics in such ways as to influence prominent Enlightenment philosophers. The most obvious point of commonality was embedded in the term *refugee* itself. The refugee identity acted as both a salve for those suffering persecutions and as a critical barb against the French Bourbon monarchy that had expelled them. In the former, Huguenots found meaning in their suffering and stayed the Reformed course. In the latter, Huguenots challenged the sacral absolutist claims of the monarchy – imagining their power as anti-Christian. The critique of the Bourbon state is clear in Diderot's definition of *refugees* in the *Encyclopédie*. The choice of Huguenots, especially those in France, to abandon the term *refugee*, then, should not be surprising either as they tried to find space within the French state.

Early modern European history was rife with religious and political turmoil, which led to the displacement of entire communities. Jews, Muslims, and various splinters of the Protestant Reformation made up expelled groups throughout the period. Twenty thousand Jews were expelled from towns in France and Germany in the fifteenth century. Eighty thousand Jews were forced out of Spain in 1492. That same year, the *Reconquista* in Spain saw thousands of Muslims pushed southward on the Iberian Peninsula. Two hundred thousand Muslims who remained in Granada faced an ultimatum that was all too familiar to the Huguenots: conversion or exile. The Protestant Reformation witnessed Anabaptists fleeing Eastern Europe, *spirituali* fleeing Italy, Marians exiled from England, Catholics from the Netherlands, and so many more. The seventeenth century experienced an escalation. Three hundred thousand Muslims fled the Iberian Peninsula from 1609 to 1614, and around two hundred thousand Huguenots left following the Revocation. These were forced migrations, but many more groups left under their own volition to carve out spaces for their religious freedoms.[12]

And still others were ripped from their homelands and forcibly transported as chattel. European slavers transported over two hundred thousand enslaved Africans in the sixteenth century, 1.8 million in the seventeenth, and six million in the eighteenth. The early modern period inaugurated an "age of refugees," which set the stage for subsequent periods of dispossession and mass displacement.[13]

Huguenots were not the first to fashion themselves as religious refugees, even if they reinvigorated and appropriated the term for themselves. One of the strongest expressions of this theme of "self-conscious *religious* exiles" came from the English Puritans. Those who called themselves Pilgrims adopted a similar model as the Huguenots, who drew from the Israelites fleeing Egypt to embolden their numbers. The Pilgrims in North America saw themselves occupying the Light on a Hill, as chosen people, just as Huguenots attempted to forge new Edenic worlds outside of France.[14] Rhetoric of martyrdom, too, pervaded the period. Since salvation was at stake and true believers willingly died for their beliefs, it should not be surprising that such religious resolve would manifest itself in biblical allusion.

Where Huguenots and Pilgrims differ in this early period is the extent to which they developed political arguments for their inclusion back home. This book is therefore as much about inventing a refugee identity as it is about the ways Huguenots developed a political discourse of sentimentalism concomitant with the French Enlightenment. This sentimentalism left a mark on refugee discourse that continues to this day. Representations of emaciated bodies, children removed from their families, women fleeing persecution across arid landscapes, men held captive and forced to perform manual labour, and the deceased refugee body all share a similar cultural meaning meant to cut through the political, religious, economic, and environmental reasons for purging an entire portion of a population. In arguing less for a religious understanding of suffering and shifting to one based on a political and sentimental footing, Huguenots shaped the understandings of displaced peoples through the nineteenth century and to this day.

We should give credit where credit is due. Huguenot refugees politicized their plight in new ways, but they also benefited from their timing. That the Enlightenment birthed new forms of governance, religious organization, and economic modalities – as well as new excesses of empire-building, scientific racism, and total war – seems clear.[15] Theodor Adorno and Max Horkheimer recognized the dialectic of the Enlightenment amidst the most disastrous war in human history, World War II, which witnessed the flight of over ten million refugees in Europe and forced world powers to charge an international body with drafting the original 1951 United Nations *Convention and Protocol Relating to the Status of Refugees.*[16] In linking their legacy with the Enlightenment, Huguenot refugees imprinted a version of their refugee narrative in the so-called Western imagination. As the age of empire waxed into the nineteenth century, refugee groups were effaced in historical narratives in favour of imperial spread and immigration analyses. Yet the cultural construction of refugees remained; and when the World Wars broke out and the ugly head of nationalism showed its face in Europe again, the legacy of the Huguenot refugees remained, malleable as it was, to serve new refugees and those who sought to defend their cause.

Historiographical Crossroads

While Claude Brousson lived during the apex of the Revocation's storm, second-generation Huguenots, like the Chevalier Louis de Jaucourt, had other opportunities to remain legally in France. Jaucourt was born in 1704 to aristocratic Huguenot parents who refused to renounce their faith, but did acquiesce to hide their faith in public. Jaucourt, at a young age, lived with relatives in Geneva under the *Désert* name Louis de Neufville. Huguenots regularly adopted new names to conceal their true identity and protect their families. After attending university in Geneva, Jaucourt attended Cambridge University before studying medicine at the university in Leiden. In Holland, Jaucourt became embedded in the intellectual culture of the refuge and began to write. Although he received his Doctor of Medicine degree in 1730, he never practiced medicine, choosing instead to enter the world of letters, supported by the Huguenot refugee community and especially Huguenot publishers. After his father died in 1736, he returned to Paris and began cultivating relationships with the aristocratic elite, including

Malesherbes, who was the Directeur de la Librairie and therefore integral in the eighteenth-century censorship process. Malesherbes's work made it possible for the *Encyclopédie* to be published and disseminated in France.[17] Jaucourt wrote 17,395 articles (approximately 28 per cent of the total) for the bastion of Enlightenment thought, the *Encyclopédie*; his sister-in-law Suzanne-Marie de Vivans, also descended from Huguenot ancestors, likely authored a couple of articles attributed to an anonymous woman. Their influence shaped Diderot's definition of the term *refugee*.[18] Jaucourt depended on the work of those in the Huguenot diaspora, especially the writings on toleration by Jean Barbeyac, a displaced Huguenot legal theorist; but Jaucourt also recognized that certain arguments around the notion of an "erring conscience" were outmoded, and the contemporary reader in times of "enlightened morality" would be better served by reading Montesquieu.[19] Jaucourt died during a time of de facto toleration in France in 1779.

As Jaucourt's life story shows, there were ample opportunities for Huguenots to encounter French philosophers and shape the French Enlightenment, but also to recalibrate certain Enlightenment ideals for confessional purposes. This latter point is important as much of the historiography on Huguenot interactions with French Enlightenment philosophers imagines a unidirectional relationship between philosophical defenders and benighted Huguenots. It was through these networks that Huguenots began to influence prominent Enlightenment philosophers, like Diderot and especially Voltaire, to support their cause. In the historiography, it has become increasingly accepted to talk about the Enlightenment as indebted to its religious counterparts and forebears rather than as in opposition to them.[20] That being the case, it is time to revisit what has been described as the "unnatural alliance" between French Protestants and the French Enlightenment. Historians like John Woodbridge, David Bien, and Geoffrey Adams argue that common anti-clericalism made persecuted Huguenots and French philosophers bedfellows; but historians like David Garroich and Graham Gargett have since shown that Huguenots adopted more enlightened principles, and French Enlightenment philosophers held softer, more favourable opinions of Protestants, than was previously understood.[21]

In pursuing their own religious toleration, Huguenots forged cosmopolitan bonds through epistolary and printing networks, joining in what historians like J.G.A. Pocock have termed a Protestant Enlightenment.[22] Enlightened Protestants – Huguenot and not – generally espoused a faith based on theological moderation and religious toleration. These Protestants could recite doctrines, but did not apply them stridently to their day-to-day lives, nor in their interactions with other sects, thus allowing for a multi-religious community to exist. Some promoted a kind of progressive revelation, or the belief that the Old Testament contained older Truths, and the New Testament contained clearer Truths, which also had the benefit of crafting a theology that promoted progress and reason over doctrinal absolutism. Jesus became a moral teacher in their writings, more so than a redeemer of the lessons of the Old Testament. As a teacher and a guide, Jesus's body took on new meaning, as did his suffering, which Protestant Enlightenment thinkers readily identified with the suffering of the Huguenot population at the hands of a perceived corrupt Christian power in the form of the papacy. As Helena Rosenblatt shows a theologically informed and politically shaped sentimentalism emerged in Protestant Enlightenment writings, especially in the latter half of the eighteenth century.[23]

Historians writing about various denominational and national Enlightenments have forced historians to revisit the classic paradigms of Ernst Cassirer and Peter Gay, who placed secular ideals – new pagan sciences, as Gay argued – over religious ones.[24] What has emerged, then, is a complicated and diverse field of "enlightenments," which has undercut what was once understood uncritically as an Age of Reason. Was there a monolithic Religious Enlightenment that connected Christians and Jews together through a shared vision of theological moderation and religious toleration, as David Sorkin has argued? Literary critics and historians like Dan Edelstein emphasize the narratological nature of the Enlightenment as a reflexive story told about their philosophical break with the past. Most recently, Jeffrey Burson describes a "culture of enlightening" that cut across various Enlightenments in the vein of *l'histoire croisée* tradition, which emphasizes social and discursive entanglement.[25] Regardless of the model, what becomes clear is that there was no inevitable rise of secularity during the Enlightenment period; instead, as Charles Taylor argues, secularism is best understood as a process of constant recalibration between the sacred and the profane.[26] Certainly, Huguenots were informed by their religious beliefs and could cast themselves as French first. Even Pierre Bayle, who appears in this study as the arbiter of a more secular approach to Huguenot refugeedom, owed much to his Calvinist upbringing.

This study makes use of two specific Enlightenments – a Huguenot or Protestant Enlightenment on the one hand, and the French Enlightenment on the other – and recognizes the usefulness of the historical entanglement paradigm of Jeffrey Burson and Dale Van Kley.[27] Such an approach to the Enlightenment makes room for conflicting arguments in the production of knowledge. The Protestant Enlightenment was not a unitary phenomenon, nor was it static. Similarly, the Protestant Enlightenment's encounters with voices most commonly associated with the French Enlightenment were not uniform or without tension. Much of these intellectual interactions were also shaped by received knowledge that was greatly informed by Catholic anti-Huguenot arguments, born out of the age of confessionalization stretching from the Reformation through the seventeenth century. Chapter 1 outlines the most significant anti-Huguenot arguments used to justify the Revocation of the Edict of Nantes and the expulsion and forced conversion of the French Calvinist population. It also offers a theory of verisimilitude for how to understand such cultural constructions in the context of the demographic realities of the Huguenot diaspora of the early modern period.

Much of the twentieth-century historiography on the Huguenot diaspora focused on their political ideals, especially on those derivations from the monarchomach tradition that put Huguenots on the defensive and led them down the path toward theories of popular sovereignty.[28] Huguenots played central roles in the shift toward historical rhetoric in religious controversies. Elizabeth Israels Perry, in her book on the late seventeenth-century debates between Catholics and Protestants known as the *Controverse*, argues that the "sterility of the debates [between the two camps] on remaining theological issues" drove controversialists on both sides to "renew their attacks" against the other on the field of history. Both sides "painted vivid pictures of the violence of the Reformation" and the Wars of Religion, and by doing so put historical suffering on the political table.[29] In politics, history, and theology, Huguenots lobbied for their interests, shaping their relationship to the state, and in the process offering new visions of what the French state might look like. The state was not a ready-made category in the seventeenth and eighteenth centuries. In fact, historians of the absolutist tradition have come to show just how beholden so-called absolutist regimes were to provincial powers, especially aristocratic ones, who controlled the military as well as the purse strings of the kingdom.[30] It was thus possible for Huguenots, operating from France's frontiers, to encourage state policy to reorient itself and recalibrate its relationship to religion over the course of the eighteenth century. If we follow J.G.A. Pocock's early definition of the Enlightenment as a "series of programs for reducing the power of either churches or congregations to disturb the peace of civil society by challenging its authority," then the political and historical challenges that Huguenots launched make it clear that they deserve to be studied alongside the French Enlightenment of the period.[31]

Understanding the French absolutist regime in this way helps us comprehend how someone like Jaucourt could remain in France as a Huguenot, maintain his contacts with the refuge, and publish in the *Encyclopédie*. Historians of Huguenots during this period have generally moved away from the political and intellectual debates in their work in favour of social and cultural histories, emphasizing survival, acculturation, and generational assimilation. David van der Linden's work is particularly good at exploring the Huguenot experience in the Dutch refuge, where, he argues, "Huguenot exiles who suffered gloriously for their beliefs were few and far between." Van der Linden shows that Huguenot refugees in the Netherlands "struggled to make ends meet," "sought reassurance in their Bible that leaving France had been the right decision," and mobilized a "triumphant" understanding of Huguenot history to renew their "sense of purpose and belonging." Van der Linden shows, too, that Huguenots who failed to make it in the refuge returned to France, to their familial networks, and old stopping grounds – some converting and others concealing their religious identities.[32] Regional histories have reinforced not only the varied experiences of Huguenot refugees, but also the common threads that linked each community, especially epistolary, business, and familial networks.[33]

Shifts toward cultural and world history have meant that Huguenots have received a fair amount of attention in recent years. In these analyses, the focus is on social considerations, family networks, and communities seeking out Edens in far-flung lands, with little concern for those Huguenots aiming to return to France.[34] To some extent, this book argues that we need to return to the political theories of the dispersion and to explore them anew through the lens of political culture – a lens that takes into account the insights of social and cultural histories of the refuge. In this book, then, I am more interested in capturing Huguenot self-representations against the cultural background, informed by Catholic and philosophe alike. In particular, revisiting Huguenot writings of their refugee experience from the Revocation forward reveals three prominent arguments.

First, the idea of suffering shifted from a theological principle predicated on eschatological belief to one of political significance within the Huguenot community over the course of the seventeenth and eighteenth centuries. This swing occurred during the *Controverse* and can be seen in the writings of Huguenot theologian Pierre Jurieu, covered in chapter 2, and Huguenot philosopher Pierre Bayle, whose ideas are explored in chapter 3, in particular. Jurieu, like Brousson, insisted on the divine design behind Huguenot toil, whereas Bayle emphasized the political character of Huguenots, offering a vision of Huguenot suffering driven by religious belief but controlled by political mechanisms. Of great significance to this Jurieu-Bayle refugee clash was the role of revolution and the justification of violence in the name of the faith and the suffering. For Jurieu, Huguenots needed to take up arms and participate in the English Revolution of 1688. He saw it as a precursor to a revolution in France, which would be in fulfillment of prophecy. Bayle sought to disconnect the Huguenot diaspora from revolutionary action. For him, revolution was a political action adopted by religious leaders.

Second, theological arguments did not disappear, but in the context of the French political realm and French Enlightenment, Huguenots sought out less theologically exclusive rhetoric in favour of arguments that fostered religious toleration. In chapter 4, I explore how Antoine

Court argued for the restitution of the Huguenot synodal system as a means to strengthen the kingdom through a discourse on patriotism. For Court, religious toleration of the Calvinists would only strengthen the royalist body politic. As patriot discourse emerged to undercut Catholic absolutism in the eighteenth century and furthered the emergence of nationalism, it proved a vital argument in favour of Calvinist tolerance. Thinking through systems of belonging, of community, and of the body politic also proved a valuable antidote to Catholic claims of errant Calvinist individualism fuelled by freedom of conscience. As Charly Coleman has explored, anti-individualist strains of thought in the eighteenth century were vehicles of enlightenment thought nearly as prevalent as individual rationality.[35] The body metaphor meant the emergence of a thoughtfully articulated sentimentalism in the writings of Rabaut Saint-Étienne. In particular, chapter 5 explores his *Le vieux Cévenol* (first published in 1779 and reissued several times in the 1780s). In this work, Saint-Étienne mobilized a similar examination of Huguenot suffering, this time in the vein of sentimentalism, which he argued was innate to humanity. Saint-Étienne's sentimentalism depended greatly on Rousseau's writings. Both men had been educated in Switzerland, where religious thinkers had been developing theories of sentiment for decades. Yet for all the universal sentimentality that Saint-Étienne insisted upon, religious toleration's limits became increasingly apparent, leading him to demand religious liberty at the outset of the French Revolution of 1789.[36]

Third, all of these varied depictions of Huguenot refugees fostered the development of sentimental discourse that increasingly influenced the late French Enlightenment. As Lynn Hunt maintains, the emergence of human rights discourse depended on the rise of Enlightenment sentimentalism. Hunt encourages us to explore the emotive regimes of the Enlightenment in search for a kind of "imagined empathy" that promoted human rights discourse, as opposed to nationalism.[37] While Court fostered a patriotic discourse, his writings overwhelmingly leaned on Huguenot histories replete with suffering, rather than of heroic defenses of the king and kingdom. Michael L. Frazer argues that moral sentiments defined a parallel Enlightenment tradition of sympathy that continues to inform political practice today.[38] A focus on the political culture of the Huguenot diaspora encourages us to revisit the long eighteenth century political rhetoric anew, seeing the origins of not only patriotism and nationalism, but also universal, innate sentimentalism and Huguenot rights discourse from a religious vantage point. Under these twin peaks, Huguenots pursued religious toleration and their return to France.

Moreover, studying Huguenot refugee self-reflections helps us to explore the trans-historical origins of refugee culture, especially the emergence of the role that sentimentalism and empathy play in refugee politics today.[39] B.S. Chimni argues that the "legal definitions of 'refugee' have always been partial and designed to serve state policy."[40] A refugee's statelessness is determined by categorical utility to the nation-state, when defined in legal terms. One solution to this, proposed by historian Peter Gatrell, is to think about refugees as transnational agents, not just victims cast from a national system, void of the ability to act or shape the historical processes they participated in. Shifting our analytical lens to the transnational forces us to challenge the domain of the nation-state, supplanting it with another regime, which Gatrell calls "refugeedom" translated from the Russian concept *bezhenstvo*. He defines it as "a matrix involving administrative practices, legal norms, social relations and refugees' experiences, and how these have been represented in cultural terms."[41] At the heart of the problem of refugee studies, then, is the definition of a refugee and the relationship of that definition to the state and citizenship. Gatrell's is one solution of many attempting to rectify power imbalances through linguistic recastings. Other historians have preferred to use the phrase *refugee regimes* to draw attention to the discursive agency refugees could mobilize for their own cause.[42]

Labelling people as "refugees" has been a historical practice dominated by the twentieth century and the nation-state, in part because historians and refugee studies practitioners have maintained that the period following the World Wars inaugurated a new era of refugee crises. Simply put, issues of scale cut historians off from the eras before the twentieth century. Philip Marfleet recognizes that "refugees did not appear as a meaningful category of persons until the mid-twentieth century."[43] This meaningfulness is largely derived again from the utility of the refugee label as a legal category to nation-states. In her analysis of

Huguenot refugees, Emma Haddad argues for a break between the early modern Huguenot case and the twentieth century, primarily because early modern states did not develop international means to regulate statelessness. This was not needed, she argues, because Huguenot refugee numbers failed to reach a critical threshold in comparison to the scale of twentieth-century crises, and Huguenots tended to bring wealth with them, thus limiting their need for state financial assistance or housing in the form of camps.[44] Such a focus on the twentieth century and the "meaningfulness" of the category of "refugee" inherently reifies its legal utility and the power of the nation-state that fills the negative space, allowing us to imagine an image of the refuge figure. However, in focusing on the twentieth century's legal apparatus we forefront the nation-state instead of the displaced, and therefore negate the refugee's agency or ability to shape said state.

If we want to decentre the nation-state from our analysis of refugees, then we need to rethink the centrality of the twentieth century to our analyses of refugees as a category as well. In this book, I want to follow Frank Caestecker's lead in pushing us to think "beyond the administrative category of policy-making and use an independent category of 'refugee' to understand what happened on the ground."[45] This requires rigorous contextualization and a focus on the historical actions of refugees as they constituted their refugeedom and imagined their refugee identity against such a matrix. A trans-historical focus, then, on Huguenots, refugee identity, and the role these played in the emergence of what might be deemed secular statecraft helps us to provincialize the state and centre those Huguenots on the frontiers of the French kingdom.

Methodological Considerations from the Frontiers of the French Enlightenment

Readers will likely recognize that this book is based primarily on printed sources. Printed sources offer the fullest explanations of what "refugee" identity meant to Huguenots. In many cases, printed works articulate more fully what these same individuals wrote in letters or delivered in front of their congregations. Given the role that Huguenots played in the seventeenth- and eighteenth-century printing trade, especially from the Netherlands, London, and Switzerland, there are ample sources written by Huguenots advancing their refugee concerns. I have consulted archival documents in several countries and draw on these also. In trying to understand the arguments for repatriation that Huguenots advanced over the course of the long eighteenth century, archival records or absence thereof can produce obstacles that obscure the image of the Huguenot refugee or efface them altogether. Most records regarding Huguenot repatriation after the Revocation reflect the power structures that led to their disenfranchisement in the first place. The monarchy and the Catholic Church stood to gain by misrepresenting Huguenots in France and just beyond the frontiers. This dynamic, to draw on the work done by Marissa Fuentes, is a violence upon the Huguenot community and requires us to read against the grain and search out the voices of the Huguenot population specifically.[46]

Nowhere is this archival violence more explicit than in the case of Huguenot women. Jeanne de Lartigue (1692?–1770) was a French Calvinist from a wealthy family and the wife of the French philosopher Montesquieu. Like many Calvinists in the wake of the Revocation, Lartigue's family did not flee France, but instead remained behind and chose a strategic marriage for their daughter – a marriage that would allow her to maintain her faith and guarantee her family's wealth at a time when *dragonnades* targeted Calvinists, seizing their landed and material properties in the name of the state and the Catholic Church. Lartigue wed Montesquieu in 1714 for these reasons, and Montesquieu agreed to the marriage because Lartigue came with a sizable dowry and her family's properties neighboured Montesquieu's. Montesquieu went on to publish two of the best-known tracts of the French Enlightenment, *Lettres persanes* (first published in 1721) and *De l'esprit de loix* (first published in 1748). Both works bear the mark of his marriage to the Calvinist Lartigue. The difference between Catholics and Calvinists, for example, took on a remarkably familial character in both texts. Protestants made better parents because they did not send their children to convents or monasteries. This translated into a more industrious Protestant labour in Montesquieu's mind, because their children's labour was not sacrificed in the name of the Church. Similarly, Montesquieu praised Protestants for not abandoning the "rights of propagation" like Catholic parents did when they sent their children into cloth.[47] It is easy to read Montesquieu's discussions of religion as anticlerical and specifically anti-Catholic, but they can also be read as indicative of the positive relationship and semi-dependent relationship Montesquieu had with Lartigue, who he regularly left in charge of his affairs on their estate when he travelled.[48]

Such an interpretation is absent from the historiography on Montesquieu. This is largely attributable to the fact that while Lartigue did not recant her faith, she did keep it silent. Scant mention of her exists in the archival record (save some documents that reflect her domestic and maternal roles in life), and even less exists in the extensive corpus of her husband Montesquieu. It would be very easy to interpret her archival silence as gendered and thus indicative of her domestic role. Certainly historians have taken this stance, imagining Lartigue as "better known for her goodness than her beauty, for timidity than her charm, and for her virtue than her loveliness."[49] Émile de Perceval described Lartigue as "an exemplary mother, silent, discreet, and modest."[50] And yet, we have no firm evidence for these assertions. Instead, if we contextualize Lartigue against the backdrop of the *Désert* and the diaspora, a stronger argument recognizes the possibility that Lartigue deliberately manufactured her archival silence, most likely through erasure or the deliberate destruction of her paper trail. The archival record of the *Désert* and the diaspora needs to be read again against the backdrop of its production. And this production, as the vignette on Lartigue shows, needs to be understood as both an effort to maintain the security of the Calvinists themselves, but also as heavily informed by gendered power within the Calvinist community itself. Most sources used by historians of the *Désert* can be categorized into two forms: unintentionally produced when Calvinists came into contact with the Catholic state apparatus as it existed, and intentionally produced by Calvinists – most often from outside of France. Lartigue's story is shown primarily through the former. Her marriage certificate, the baptismal records of her children, documents related to the purported bungling of a property transaction Montesquieu blamed on Lartigue, and her death certificate are the firmest pieces of evidence for her existence – all of which were created about her, not by her. Lartigue did not leave a record and the most likely assumption is that she did so intentionally.

In an effort to examine constructions of refugee identity, one has to come to terms with this gendered imbalance in the sources. In an effort to thoughtfully consider the "gendered violence" of the archive, as Marisa Fuentes has done, we need to recognize the links between "archival disappearance" and "historical representation." Fuentes argues that the most effective way to work against such silences – whether unintentional, in the case of the enslaved women she studies, or intentionally silenced, as I suggest is a possible explanation for Lartigue's archival absence – is to read against the grain or "along the bias grain to eke out extinguished and invisible but no less historically important lives."[51] Lartigue used Montesquieu's wealth and clout to shield herself from possible persecution. But concealment was not the only avenue open to Calvinist women in the *Désert* or the diaspora. For especially those women who turned toward prophecy and apocalypticism, the post-Revocation era offered an opportunity to act on their own interests and to express their own faith. Mita Choudhury examines the French scandal that surrounded Catherine Cadière, who had accused her Jesuit confessor of seduction, heresy, and bewitchment in the 1730s. Choudhury argues that religious mysticism "represented a feminized form of spirituality because it defied the boundaries between the rational and the emotional." "Female mysticism" became "a mutant product of female intellect." Choudhury pushes beyond such facile and gendered-political interpretations to show that mystical women exercised "an authoritative position within their immediate social world by placing them so close to the divine."[52] Huguenot gendered mysticism made regular appearances in the wake of the Revocation. Jurieu's wife, Hélène Jurieu, left Rotterdam in 1713 after her husband's death to join the Prophets of the Cévennes who had relocated to London. Similarly, Antoine Court's mother introduced Court, the future leader of the Church of the *Désert*, to the clandestine meetings of the Prophets of the Cévennes, where he encountered mystic women prophesying and inciting violence. Rather than reproduce the actions of mystic women as backwards, it is more beneficial to see this as one of the few modes of agency available to

Huguenot refugees during this time period and as actively shaping Huguenot representations of their community.[53]

In the case of Huguenots from the Revocation to the French Revolution, it is possible to find Huguenots exercising their voices and leaving intentional marks on the archive, but this does not mean we should take them at face value; instead, we should continue to read along the bias grain. Each of the texts examined in this study were produced under strain. The political and historical theorist James C. Scott argues that those subjugated often develop a "public transcript," which conceals a "hidden transcript." The public transcript reflects the efforts of the group to save face and "conceal" their "loss of power." The public transcript is produced from the interaction between "subordinates and those who dominate." Scott argues that "women's power can be exercised only behind a veil of properties that reaffirm men's official rule as powerholders" and men oftentimes have "control of the public transcript."[54] To understand the ways that Huguenots moulded refugee discourse in the long eighteenth century, we need to work toward uncovering the hidden transcript, which I show can be done through both contextualization and close textual readings.

Women were integral to the intellectual production of these texts, despite their voicelessness and representational absence in important Huguenot polemical and apologetical texts. Women appear in these writings, not as leaders or arbiters of their own faith, but as wives, sisters, and mothers and as victims in an era of persecution. Only rarely did women of Huguenot ancestry actually forefront their experiences. Rarity should be read not as unimportance but rather as a marker of their persecuted status.[55] Their status in relationship to paternal authority is key, because it reinforces the gendered authority of the Church of the *Désert* and diaspora. As is especially the case in Antoine Court's writings, women's more radical impulses toward prophecy and mysticism needed to be counterbalanced by male authority. Fostering a strong, paternalistic Calvinist Church in France, according to Court, would only strengthen the king's control over the fatherland.

Who were the Calvinists who produced archival records intentionally then? Calvinist men in positions of power and authority, most often far from the long arm of the French legal system. These men led the reestablishment of the Church of the *Désert*, providing for it both paternal authority and security, at a time when security was always under threat. Jurieu, Bayle, Court, and Saint-Étienne each figured into this period of Huguenot history at critical junctures and each promoted a definition of Huguenot identity. Many of the tracts published by these men were anonymous. Contextualization, then, is very important in order to ascribe a text to a particular author, but also to unpack the culture of anonymity that existed in the early modern publishing world. Much of the *Encyclopédie* was left with unattributed authorship – a fact that may have encouraged Jaucourt's participation in its creation.[56] Anonymity was a defensive tactic, and reading against the grain of the text and the context gives us clues into the debates raging within the Huguenot community over their exile and possible repatriation. Choosing to publish many of their tracts anonymously also explains why Huguenots rarely reached out to public opinion in the eighteenth century as a source of authority, instead choosing to safeguard their pursuit of religious toleration with pleas to the king. As scholars like Juergen Habermas, Keith Michael Baker, and Arlette Farge have shown, appeals to public opinion pervaded French society from the court and the Parlements to the courtyards and coffee houses.[57] Huguenots mostly avoided talk of public opinion in their writings, but their publications themselves were efforts to speak to a public sphere built on multiple forms of sociability that shaped public opinion.

***

How did Huguenots shape their refugee identity, and how did this identity translate to Diderot in the eighteenth century? How did the word *refugee* become synonymous, especially in Western Europe, with *Huguenots* in the eighteenth century? While researching this book, I visited archives in France, Switzerland, the Netherlands, England, and the United States and learned that the most explicit discussion of refugee identity is found in printed polemics and apologetics of these thinkers. Consequently, this book offers a targeted re-reading of these works in pursuit of proffering an answer to the central *problematique* of this study (how did Huguenots shape their refugee identity in a time of Enlightenment and promote religious toleration in France?), while recognizing that each of these men existed in their own context, and that context was shaped by less-known men *and* women.

This study offers close contextual work in two ways. First, chapter 1 offers a demographic study of the Huguenot diaspora within France and beyond its borders. It examines how demographic realities of the Huguenot community might be read against common anti-Huguenot arguments of the period. This is necessary because for all their explicit discussion of refugee identity, the danger is that focusing on these authors too intently and uncritically can lead to the effacement of the rest of the refugee community they represent. Chapter 1 is not solely a contextual chapter; it also offers an argument for verisimilitude in order to understand anti-Huguenot arguments. Catholic polemics against Calvinists carried with them tissues of truth that turned into self-fulfilling prophecies. Catholics often emphasized Huguenot individualism as a means to colour their business acumen as the result of greed and their republicanism as the manifestation of errant political anarchism and disloyalty to the king. In the post-revolutionary world of the nineteenth and twentieth centuries, similar narratives emerged that painted Calvinists as arbiters of modernity – as capitalists and republicans par excellence. Chapter 1 makes the argument that Catholics actively invented a vision of Calvinism conducive to later visions of modernity, but in a way that was reinforced by the demographic realities they were privy to – that they could see. Huguenot aristocrats converted or left France during the seventeenth century. Huguenot farmers largely stayed in France and sought refuge in the land they worked. Huguenot urbanites turned to business when most other bureaucratic, medicinal, and military positions closed to them. Catholics saw prosperous Huguenots and imagined their prosperity as a result of their greed. As I argue, this demographic verisimilitude established a cultural understanding that would continue to colour Calvinism for generations and ultimately inform the German sociologist Max Weber, who argued that the earliest capitalist tendencies owed much to Protestant ascetic traditions.[58] Similarly, if Calvinist synodal systems appeared more republican during the time period than Catholic ecclesiastical structure, and if Calvinists largely found refuge in Switzerland and the Netherlands, which had republican forms of governance, then it made sense for Catholics to colour this as the result of innate republican sentiment. These representations mattered. Huguenots and their defenders had to respond to them. They had to defend the Reformed against them before they could launch alternative demographic narratives of the Huguenot population.

To establish a contextual baseline for the subsequent chapters, chapter 1 focuses specifically on the demographic realities of the Huguenot diaspora and the Church of the *Désert* within France as they related to prominent Catholic arguments against religious toleration. Chapters 2 through 5 each focus on a particular theologian, philosopher, or pastor, and each of these chapters begins by placing them within their own intellectual and social networks in order to provide a close reading of their texts, as well as to attempt a sketch of the hidden transcripts of their respective Huguenot refugee communities. In chapters 2 and 3, I examine the *Controverse* writings of two well-known Huguenots. The first, Pierre Jurieu, was a Huguenot theologian known for his millenarianism and support of the English Revolution of 1688. Jurieu's construction of the refugee identity was grounded in the Bible and the religious geopolitics of the Revocation era. His most staunch critic, the philosopher Pierre Bayle, the subject of chapter 3, imagined a refugee coloured by their political place in early modern Europe – one that was free from religion, or at least made religion a private matter. In chapters 4 and 5, we see the emergence of a refugee identity increasingly predicated on sentimentalism and the empathy that their suffering might spark in others. Antoine Court and Rabaut Saint-Étienne, both pastors in the *Désert*, inaugurated this shift toward sentimentalism in the late eighteenth century, which proved vital in pushing the French crown to institute religious toleration in 1787. It also shaped French Revolutionary discourse, leading the revolutionaries to call Huguenots to return to the country, to accept citizenship regardless of place of birth or baptism, and even to reclaim ancestral lands. Rather than a traditional conclusion, the reader will find a coda at the end of this book that attempts to bring the lessons of this book to the present, both for the state of France and for our twenty-first-century world. As we live in an age of refugees, it is important that we recognize their complex origins.

1

Self-Fulfilling Prophecies of the Huguenot Diaspora

To understand why Calvinists invented a refugee identity for themselves in the Revocation era, it is necessary to establish the context from which they positioned themselves as such. By 1685, Louis XIV had come to believe – or at least pretend to believe – that most Calvinists had converted or left the country. In the Revocation of the Edict of Nantes, promulgated that year, he insisted that, "with God's aid, ... the greater part of our subjects of the said R.P.R. [*Religion Prétendue Réformée*, or 'So-called Reformed Religion'] have embraced the Catholic faith." The document continued to argue that since the majority of Calvinists had converted, the Edict of Nantes had "been rendered nugatory." Louis XIV and his ministers could then think of "nothing better, in order to obliterate, wholly, the memory of the troubles, the confusion, and the evils which the progress of this false religion has caused in the kingdom, ... than to entirely revoke the said Edict of Nantes."[1] Not only had Louis XIV issued an order that would lead to the flight of two hundred thousand Huguenots from France, he also sought to expunge them and the Wars of Religion from France's memory.

Representation and reality are linked and shape one another. Louis XIV saw a diminishment in the Calvinist population as a direct result of his own policies. In his *Mémoires pour l'instruction du dauphin*, dictated and written in the 1660s, Louis XIV presented the dauphin with the power of "restrictions," which would eventually create the conditions for effacing Calvinists from France. He stated, "I believed, my son, that the best means to gradually reduce the Huguenots in my kingdom was not to pressure them at all by any new rigours, to recognize the privileges they had gained under previous reigns, but also to grant them nothing further, and even to restrict them within the narrowest limits that justice and propriety would permit."[2] Restrictions, he hoped, would win conversions and precipitate the demise of the Calvinist faith in France. From 1650 onward, the Council of State issued orders prohibiting Protestants from taking collections, holding services in undesignated spaces to discuss congregational matters, and even singing psalms at public executions. The last National Synod met in 1659–60; the synods were ended at the behest of Louis XIV who maintained that the cost for such assemblies was too great. In 1670, the number of Protestants able to attend a wedding or baptism was limited to twelve. The crown restricted Protestants' choice of work – several occupations from linen-draper to midwife were declared off limits, the latter out of fear for the child's baptism. The General Law of 1666 granted permission to local curates to visit any dying individual under the assumption that they might want to convert to Catholicism in their last hour, regardless of the wishes of the sick or their family. Where laws were not enough, the King approved a plan to purchase conversions. The *Caisse des Conversions*, the brainchild of the ex-Huguenot Paul Pelisson, granted bishops access to ecclesiastical and state funds for the purchase of conversions at the cheapest rate possible in 1676. As many as ten thousand abjurations were recorded in the first three years.[3]

The French Protestant pastor and refugee Jacques Fontaine noted in his memoirs to his children that prior to 1685, Henri IV's monumental Edict of Nantes had already been eroded in the face of continued Catholic intolerance and a series of royal ordinances aimed at destroying both the faith and civil status of Protestants.[4] The nineteenth-century republican historian Jules Michelet noted that "the entire century gravitated towards the Revocation."[5] Louis XIV's Revocation of the Edict of Nantes rested on what Peter Sahlins calls the "fiction of a Catholic France" and sought to ring the final death knell of French Calvinism.[6] The Revocation prohibited the practices of Protestant cults. Protestant churches were demolished. All pastors unwilling to convert to Catholicism were to leave the kingdom in a fortnight or take the degree of Doc-

Figure 1.1 A depiction of the demolition of the Temple de Charenton in October 1685.

tor of Laws. All seminaries were forbidden. Any Protestants who had fled the country had to return to France to avoid forfeiting their property to the State. The Edict of 1715 formally proclaimed the "fiction of a Catholic France" to be a French reality, and the declaration of April 9, 1736, required all subjects to register baptisms, marriages, and deaths with the Catholic clergy.[7] The destruction of Calvinist temples, the program of forced conversions, and the violence of the *dragonnades* that followed all presumably began with the king's false notion that "the better and the greater part of our subjects of the said R.P.R. have already embraced the Catholic faith."[8] The best argument for effectively outlawing Calvinism in France – expelling more Huguenot refugees into the diaspora – was to deny their very existence and manufacture a demographic reality that suited his Gallican goals.

So, to defend their own interests, Huguenots needed a new identity, or rather a very old identity that could simultaneously respond to popular representations of Calvinists during the Revocation era and make the case for their return. This chapter focuses more on the former, the legal and sociodemographic realities and the anti-Huguenot arguments connected to them. The phenomenon of demographic verisimilitude is at the heart of the controversy surrounding Huguenots. As Calvinists hid themselves on France's frontiers or fled the kingdom entirely, their place in French society shifted and made room for caricature that validated long-held Catholic tropes mobilized to justify Calvinist persecution. Certainly, the king rarely if ever came into contact with communities of Calvinists. His Catholic ministers undoubtedly insisted on the narrative of Calvinist conversions as well to placate the king. Louis XIV's belief that most Calvinists had already converted would have seemed plausible. Yet what Louis XIV read as his regime's success in the realm of religion was the by-product of the demographic, legal, and systemic cultural shifts brought on by his regime's own efforts to curtail Calvinists. Calvinists went underground. They converted when doing so to safeguard their property, their families' well-being, and ultimately their faith, which they could rekindle in the *Désert*.

Tracing the French Calvinist Frontier

To understand why certain priests, pastors, philosophers, legists, and others chose to represent Calvinists in a particular way, a cursory understanding is needed of the basic demographics of Calvinists in France at the time of the Revocation, and beyond in the diaspora; the legal restraints placed on Protestants; how Protestants responded to these laws; and how they subsequently organized themselves. Representations may be things of the imagination, but our thoughts are always guided by experience.[9] No strict barrier existed between discourse and practice, myth and reality, or between the fiction of a Catholic France and the nonfiction of internally displaced Calvinists and Huguenot refugees abroad. This chapter is a look at how the Catholic Church and state persecuted the Calvinist minority, but also how the lowly Huguenots responded, survived, and attempted to shape the perception of their community.

The term *Désert* demarcated a spatial location as much as a time of persecution in French Protestant history. The Calvinist *Désert* persisted in Upper and Lower Languedoc, stretching east from the Garonne River and the city of Toulouse to the Mediterranean Sea, and then north past Montpellier and along the western bank of the Rhône River. The Calvinist population had long harboured itself in Dauphiné, Midi, and to the west in Poitou and Saintonge. Other smaller enclave communities persevered in Normandy, in the environs of the Parisian basin, and in the Loire Valley.[10] The Cévennes region where Camisard violence broke out in the early eighteenth century (roughly 1702–10) had historically been a place where the Protestant ethos seeped potently into a population protected from direct royal influence by distance and landscape.[11] In several villages and small towns, Protestants constituted the majority of the population. For example, prior to the Revocation, Calvinists numbered ten thousand in Montauban, a substantial town in the Midi-Pyrénées region with no more than sixteen thousand inhabitants in total.

The geographical incidence of Calvinism was not a fluke but rather the result of a complex historical process. In the first half of the sixteenth century, Reformation doctrines reached many of the communities across France, but as the Wars of Religion commenced, a discernible space in the south of France, now known as the "Calvinist crescent," emerged.[12] Several factors influenced the positioning of the Calvinist churches in southern France. Some historians argue the social geography of Calvinism was influenced by the proximity to Geneva and its Calvinist seminary, yet this does not explain the communities in Normandy or the larger populations in Languedoc.[13] Other similar refuge points existed, like the principalities of Orange or Béarn, not to mention the Channel Islands, London, Sedan, or, after 1572, the Netherlands. Protestantism did not necessarily follow the book trade, despite several book publishing powerhouses appearing in Protestant areas like Geneva, Neufchâtel, Rotterdam, Amsterdam, and London. Literacy was of considerable importance to the growth of the Calvinist community, but literacy records from the early nineteenth century do not indicate a higher degree of literacy in the south as compared to the north of France.[14] Rather, as Mark Greengrass has argued, the Calvinist concentration in the south can best be explained as an "amalgam of ... the consequences of noble patronage, its small towns, with their proud elites of notaries, schoolmasters, city worthies and strong artisanal networks reaching out into the countryside, and the relatively light weight of the royal official presence."[15]

The position of Calvinist communities on the periphery made them difficult to control and to quantify. In addition, the demographic study of the Calvinist population has proven to be problematic, in part because numbers from the period often reflected their compiler's political position. A higher figure could simultaneously be interpreted as a justification for oppression and as an indication of the level of suffering. In 1679, the crown amassed a series of Catholic clerical reports on the numbers of the Reformed, which, collectively, placed the number of Protestants at 1.7 million, just shy of the two million mark maintained by the Archbishop of Paris over a decade later in 1690. Eight years earlier, the Protestant pastor and publicist Pierre Jurieu also placed the number at two million, yet their objectives differed greatly – one sought to arouse anti-Protestant sentiment, while the other wanted to highlight the resilience of the Reformed community. In 1686, Louis XIV put the number at nine hundred thousand "infected" souls, as if to signal the early successes of converting Protestants to the Catholic faith.[16] In his more recent demographic study, historian Philip Benedict places the number of French Calvinists before the Revocation somewhere between eight hundred thousand and one million people.[17] Benedict proposes a modest, yet capacious gap of two hundred thousand individuals to account for imprecise and uneven availability of local census records, baptismal records, and regional histories across France. Calvinists often concealed their numbers – both from the Catholic Church to avoid unwanted proselytizing or sectarian violence, and from the crown and local authorities to evade taxes. Such a practice undoubtedly makes it difficult to achieve a desired level of demographic accuracy.

Following the Revocation, population estimates remained in flux and reflected the variety of political and sometimes polemical aims of their authors. Rippert de Montclar, the Jansenist *procureur général* of the Parlement of Province, estimated more than three million Protestants lived within the kingdom as of 1755. He made this claim in his *Mémoire théologique et politique au sujet des mariages clandestines des protestants de France* – the first in a long line of studies that eventually influenced Louis XVI to promulgate what became known as the Edict of Toleration in 1787. The Abbé de Caveirac, a Catholic apologist for the Counter-Catholic Reformation and the Wars of Religion, responded to Rippert de Montclar's claim in 1756 with a drastically lower estimate of four hundred thousand. The estimates of Rippert de Montclar and Caveirac represent the two extremes on the spectrum concerning the remaining Calvinist communities after the Revocation.[18]

All who followed settled on figures in the middle, but some like Marie Jean Antoine Nicolas de Caritat, Marquis of Condorcet blatantly inflated the number in response to their contemporary political climate. In 1778, Condorcet argued that around one million Protestants remained on French soil. Almost a decade later, during a surge of intellectual support for the Protestant cause, he published alongside Rabaut Saint-Étienne, the most prominent Protestant pastor at the time, a work that doubled the estimated number of supposed Calvinists to two million – a number he increased again to three million in 1790.[19] Such conjecture reflected personal political objectives, but ultimately failed to present an accurate, verifiable assessment of the Protestant population still in France. In the nineteenth century, Protestant historians compiled testimonies of eighteenth-century pastors and other scant Calvinist church records, which placed the number of Protestants in 1760 at 593,307 – an approximate 40 per cent reduction in the total population since the Revocation.[20] If the Protestant population grew between 1760 and 1789 at a pace similar to the rest of the country, then there may have been as many as seven hundred thousand Protestants in France on the eve of the French Revolution. Calvinists constituted only 1 to 2 per cent of the country's total population.[21]

France's frontiers were porous to Huguenots, just as France's interior provided *Désert* spaces for Calvinists to survive. During the Wars of Religion, Huguenot leaders like the Admiral of France Gaspard de Coligny had openly supported a Huguenot Atlantic trade in the hopes of proving the utility of the Protestant merchant class to the Catholic king. In this way, the Atlantic oceanic world provided hope for pragmatic politics in the sixteenth century as well as a colonial space to find refuge from the persecutory policies of the French regime. Often, the secular interests of the state (or their explicit Catholic religious interests) closed political doors for the Huguenots, who then carved out transatlantic spaces for their religious imperatives. They created Edenic communities capable of manifesting a kind of Calvinist utopia far from the long arm of the French Catholic state.[22]

A Huguenot Atlantic existed during the first wave of migration in the sixteenth century, but it was a world not of settlements, families, or entire congregations, but of Huguenot explorers, privateers, and fisherman. Early efforts to settle in Brazil and La Florida failed spectacularly, in large part due to interreligious and interimperial conflicts. Where Rio de Janeiro now sits, the French colony of France antarctique became a haven for Huguenots in the mid-1550s. Assisted by the French vice admiral Nicolas Durand de Villegaignon, Huguenots soon found refuge in the short-lived Franco-Brazilian colony. Villegaignon named the principal fort Fort Coligny after one of the colony's benefactors and later de facto leader of the Huguenot population in France Gaspard de Coligny. In 1555, Villegaignon sent the first fleet to the Brazilian colony with a hundred Protestants or so in tow. Within a couple of years, religious tensions between Catholics and Calvinists came to a head, and in 1557, Villegaignon expelled the Calvinists from the colony. Many jettisoned out into the Atlantic World again, while others settled with the indigenous Brazilian Tupinambá people for a period of time, only to return to France the following year. In 1560, the Portuguese turned their sights on the French colony, disbanding the remaining French Catholics within a couple of years and levelling Fort Coligny in the process.[23]

In 1562, Coligny also sponsored a French Huguenot colonization experiment in Spanish Florida. Led by René Goulaine de Laudonnière, French Huguenots settled Fort Caroline, near modern-day Jacksonville. Just south, the Spanish founded St. Augustine. Famously, Huguenot artist Jacques Le Moyne produced an illustrated narrative of the Florida expedition, which was published in 1591.[24] Soon after its founding, the Spanish sought to colonize the French settlement to the north. Three years later, a thousand colonists, many of which were Huguenot, were systematically slaughtered by the order of Menendez de Avilés.

Later in the seventeenth century, Huguenots turned to the Atlantic World to find "Edens" for their spiritual communities as well as to find economies where they could flourish; and most often they found their religious pursuits most suited to the Anglo-Dutch-American spaces where other once-persecuted Protestant sects had also found toleration.[25] Huguenots relayed through the Netherlands and England in order to funnel out into the wider world. At the time of the Revocation in 1685, Huguenots spread to Ireland, New England, New York, Virginia, and the Carolinas. Congregations with transatlantic mercantile, religious, and intellectual ties emerged in the 1680s and 1690s. The London Threadneedle Street Church made recommendations for pastor positions in Boston and Charleston, while Huguenot merchants exiled from Dieppe, Rouen, La Rochelle, and other Huguenot trading centres in France used their familial and religious community connections to trade between Europe and Boston, New York, and Charleston.[26]

Religious networks were key, but so, too, were familial and intellectual communities that spanned the Atlantic World and across empires. The Faneuil family had members in the English colonial cities of Boston and New York City, as well as in London and Amsterdam. Similarly, the Simond family, known best for the prominent role their patriarch Pierre Simond played in Dutch South Africa, developed business interests with a Swiss-Huguenot community in Purrysburgh, South Carolina, along with merchants in parts of Georgia and the English West Indies.[27]

The English colonies offered Huguenots ample refuge. Early efforts to settle in what is today South Carolina were met with Spanish violence. Jean Ribaut settled Charlesfort on Parris Island, South Carolina in 1562, only to fall three years later in 1565. In the seventeenth century, Huguenots founded communities in New Paltz, New York. In 1680s, Huguenots settled again in the Carolinas, Cape May, New Jersey, Rhode Island, Boston, and several other places along the English colonial east coast of North America. Under the protection of the English empire, Huguenots founded communities, harnessing the Protestant tradition of England to shield themselves from French and Spanish Catholic violence. Many of these early settlers were craftsmen and merchants, but life in North America often forced them to learn new skills that would help them survive. Many became farmers, slowly adopting the customs of their environs and the languages of their neighbours. All of this gradually led the march toward acculturation, which, in turn, led to the decline of the Huguenot identity in the Americas as second- and then third-generation Huguenots increasingly abandoned their ancestral identity.

The failed sixteenth-century experiments in Brazil and Spanish Florida did not stop later generations of Huguenots from carving out spaces south of the English colonies in the seventeenth century. Many continued to participate in overseas business and colonial ventures, returning to Brazil, Florida, and even parts of New France. A short-lived colony in Tortuga failed in the 1640s, but Huguenots continued to make up a sizable portion of the populations in Guadeloupe and Saint-Christophe. Despite the efforts of the Bourbon throne to make the French "New World" homogeneously Catholic, many Huguenots lived clandestinely even in New France. Huguenot merchants and some farmers turned their sights to the Caribbean and West Indies, Surinam, and Africa.

The West Indies were key for Huguenots. Sugarcane and the entire plantation economy that surrounded it offered a boon to Huguenots seeking economic opportunity and the diversification of their wealth. Families created banking and trade networks that connected the islands to Brazil and back to the Netherlands and France. In 1664, when Jean-Baptiste Colbert founded the French Compagnie des Indes Occidentales, he openly requested assistance from Huguenot merchants with trading relationships in the region and access to capital. The relative tolerance that Huguenots had in the Antilles soon subsided with Louis XIV's colonial slave reform known as the Code Noir (1685), which delegitimized many of their marriages and firmly placed Huguenot merchants outside of the French law. The Code Noir *only* made provisions for the Catholic Church and Catholic subjects and ordered Jewish inhabitants of the islands to vacate immediately.[28] The Revocation that followed cemented the illegal status of Huguenots sailing under French flags in the Antilles. Jesuits acted as the long arm of the Bourbon law in the Antilles, forcing conversions and breaking up Huguenot communities. Huguenots were faced with the same choice in the Antilles as they were in the French *Désert*: convert or practice clandestinely.[29]

Regardless, sugar remained king in the Antilles, and Huguenots continued to finance their clandestine communities from it. Most of this sugar production depended on slavery. Jean Barbot's slaving voyages from North and South Guinea were well-known. A member of the Compagnie du Sénégal, Barbot was a Huguenot who left France after the Revocation of the Edict of Nantes. He settled in England where he wrote his *Description of the Coasts of North and South Guinea*. In this text, Barbot details his two voyages – the first in 1678–79 and the second in 1681–82.[30] Barbot's compilation describes the coastal economies of West Africa, particularly from Senegal to what is today Benin, Nigeria, and the island of Príncipe, noting especially what African traders accepted as payment. Historians in the last couple of centuries have noted that much of Barbot's writing was copied from other studies on West Africa, but his *Description* still constitutes a significant source from the period.[31]

A well-known Atlantic World case of Huguenot migration was the Dutch Cape Colony in South Africa, which was established in the seventeenth century and began receiving Huguenot immigrants near the end of 1687. Approximately 180 Huguenots arrived in the South African colony and composed nearly a quarter of the "white" settler population. Labeled "free burghers" by the Dutch colonial state and given plots of land, these Huguenots established farms and provided foodstuffs to the Dutch East India Company and its agents. Religious tensions and Dutch-Franco linguistic boundaries soon emerged, forcing the most prominent Huguenot pastor, Pierre Simond, from the colony in 1702. Those who remained became acculturated, safeguarded the land given to them by the Dutch state from the pastoral Khoikhois peoples, and eventually set the stage for the later apartheid racial restrictions.[32]

Displaced Huguenot communities were equally marked by division, and generational change hastened the deterioration of the international Calvinist community abroad; second-generation Huguenots in the Netherlands, England, the German states, and Switzerland found acculturation preferable. The language, customs, and religious institutions of their new diasporal homes encouraged Huguenots to identify increasingly with their refuge and less so with the persecutions of their parents. This compounded with the lack of resources many Huguenot communities faced when relocating. Walloon communities in the Netherlands, where the French language was in high standing, offered a path to acculturation with fewer obstacles, but in places where French was not an acceptable lingua franca, second- and third-generation Huguenots found conversion and integration to be the only routes to peace and prosperity.

A Calvinist Capitalist Ethic in Early Modern France and the Atlantic World?

While the diversity of experience of migration and exile around the Atlantic World defies uniform analysis, a common thread throughout is the Calvinist role in developing global trade networks. The persecution of Huguenots encouraged Huguenot perseverance, which oftentimes came in the form of trading networks as conduits to refuge. Yet many at the time did not see this as a demographic reality, as a kind of political economy born from perseverance; rather, they saw Huguenot theology as linked to business acumen or avarice. Louis XIV's anti-Huguenot policies and shifting Huguenot demography shaped those arguments used against Calvinists in the Revocation era and afforded opportunities – perhaps drawing some Huguenots into mercantile markets – that Huguenots might seize in their own defense especially during the Enlightenment, as arguments for social utility began to challenge patriarchal privileges.

Early modern France and the French Atlantic statesmen and church officials made arguments similar to that of the German sociologist Max Weber, who in *The Protestant Ethic and the Spirit of Capitalism* argued that the Calvinist belief in double predestination shaped a culture of inner-worldly asceticism. This severe self-discipline encouraged the development of "modern capitalism." "[T]he idea of a duty of the individual to increase his wealth," Weber argued, drove Protestant faiths like Calvinism. This wealth was the "result and manifestation of competence and proficiency in a vocational calling." In Weber's mind, a truly modern capitalist "strives systematically and rationally in a calling for legitimate profit."[33] Calvinists interpreted this success as a sign from God that they were of the "Elect" and would ascend to Heaven at the end of their lives. Many scholars have interpreted and critiqued Weber's argument of a Protestant elective affinity, as expressing a direct and singular connection between Protestantism and capitalism or capitalist wealth.[34] My argument is that the Weberian thesis had genealogical origins in seventeenth- and eighteenth-century Europe. What Weber interpreted as a link between religious asceticism and capitalist success was the demographic outcome of persecutory policies developed in Catholic countries during the Protestant Reformation and exacerbated by Louis XIV's Revocation of the Edict of Nantes.

This connection between the Protestant community and industry or early commercial capitalism began, in part, as a response to the centralizing measures enacted by Louis XIV and the pressures placed on the Protestant aristocracy to convert to Catholicism. French aristocrats played a seminal role in distributing and sponsoring Reformation tracts early in the sixteenth century, but the Wars of Religion had forced many aristocratic leaders to flee, and those prominent Calvinist families who remained witnessed their heirs choose conversion over continued persecution. The ancestors of the nineteenth-century liberal Benjamin Constant had left their aristocratic landholdings in France for Geneva during the Reformation. Later, Constant's grandfather became an army officer in Holland, and several other relatives held prestigious social positions or fancied themselves as intellectuals.[35] Those noble families remaining into the seventeenth century encouraged the growth of Protestant communities through their patronage and protection, but with the growth of the intendant office and the reified bond between church and state with the promulgation of the Gallican Articles in 1682, many Protestant families rushed to convert to Catholicism in order to maintain their local power and to remain on their ancestral lands with their kin.[36] As Carolyn Chappell Lougee shows in *Facing the Revocation: Huguenot Families, Faith, and the King's Will*, "the number of middling provincial nobles who remained Protestant down to the Revocation and then struggled to make their inherited religion viable under transformed circumstances" was too great to allow monolithic assertions about the nobility's "shallow religious commitment" in the face of losing their "material advantage" to go unchallenged.[37]

Without the aristocracy to support the Protestant community following the Revocation, communal leadership fell to bourgeois merchants with connections to the global refuge, the manufacturers, and the men of letters. Urban, industrious Protestants were a distinct minority. In Nîmes, the second largest silk-producing city and the capital of Calvinist France, around 13,000 Protestants remained in 1787 out of a population of 43,000. Their numbers had diminished greatly since the Revocation. Around 1,100 Protestants resided in La Rochelle in 1787, whereas 7,500 had been recorded following the promulgation of the Edict of Nantes nearly two hundred years earlier.[38] These Protestant families chose to abandon France to protect their non-landed, mercantile interests. Their urban footprint and absence left a strong impression on the population and therefore exacerbated the scale and extent of their perceived loss. Similarly, the number of Calvinist merchants who chose to flee France in order to guard their commercial wealth in many ways affirmed the imagined Calvinist penchant for commerce and finance as much as the economic presence of Calvinists in urban spaces.

Despite the preponderance of work on Huguenot mercantilism and the Protestant international, the Calvinist ethic argument depends on a notable agrarian shift within the Calvinist community and their respective silence. As Burdette Poland correctly showed, one of the greatest consequences of the Revocation was "to heighten the importance of the peasant element in French Protestantism and to make Protestantism in France basically a rural phenomenon."[39] There are no statistics for the total number of French Calvinist farmers who remained in France, and therefore no way of knowing what percentage of the overall population was composed of those ascetic agrarians. There is also no way to know whether their asceticism reflected any intentional theological consideration or simply reflected their lack of material wealth. In the decade that followed the Revocation of the Edict of Nantes, the bishop of Nîmes complained about the roughly fifty thousand Calvinists in his bishopric who were too great a distance away to be adequately shepherded to the Catholic path. Because of this complaint and the resulting fervour for forced conversions in southern France, a new bishopric was established in Alais (i.e., Alès). A couple of decades later in 1737, the number of Protestants remained steady, and the vicar of Alais noted that "scarcely any families have been genuinely converted, and we have noticed several perversions among those which have been traditionally Catholic."[40] The *Désert* kept Calvinist families safe while they weathered the storm of the Revocation.

The question, then, is one of demographics and interaction. Shop-owning city-dwelling Calvinists lived under the nose of the Catholic Church. Calvinist merchants trading at French Catholic ports used their mercantilism to evade dragoons. They amassed fortunes capable of courting prominent Catholic families who would use their own religious privilege to provide safety in exchange for wealth. These interactions fuelled the Calvinist connection to financial industry, more than any innate Calvinist propensity for capitalist accumulation. It was not a Protestant ethic but rather a Protestant synthetic, or a proposition informed by observation.

Already at the time of the Revocation, many questioned the economic loss of the Huguenot population to foreign kingdoms. Ultra-Catholics celebrated the final triumph of the Catholic faith, while the more secular thinkers lamented the loss of capital. Sébastien Le Prestre de Vauban, author of *La Dîme royale*, courtier to the king, and military engineer responsible for many of the stalwart fortifications in France, questioned the implications of the Revocation and the qualities of the Protestant population. Vauban prepared his memorandum entitled *Mémoire pour le rappel des Huguenots* in 1689 only to revise it again in 1691 and 1693. Implicit in his argument was that the Huguenot population was somehow more adept at economic production than their Catholic neighbours and that economic benefit should outweigh religious homogeneity. He lamented the loss of eighty to one hundred thousand people of all professions, but most of all the hundreds of army officers and thousands of trained sailors and soldiers – the cost of which threatened the military supremacy of louisquatorzean France. In addition, the lost capital, commerce, and manufacturing skills, largely unknown outside of France, he added, would inevitably "cause the ruin of the most considerable part of [French] commerce."[41] Vauban correctly characterized the majority of Huguenot refugees as industrious or employed in commercial trades. These migrants were mainly craftsmen, weavers, stoneworkers, gunsmiths, ironworkers, architects, and merchants. They were also active intellectual leaders, many professing to be philosophers, artists, sculptors, writers, lawyers, and pastors. Included among those who sought refuge through the Threadneedle Street Church in London were 440 weavers and lace-makers, 79 leather workers, 66 metal workers, and 56 wood workers. The French state employed 27 in the navy or army; 110 were employed as merchants or served in some official capacity at sea either as captains or fishermen; 62 reported they had some medical preparation ranging from surgical and medicinal knowledge to barber training; 25 were schoolteachers, students, or booksellers; and 11 were reported to be lawyers or notaries. Only 24 listed themselves as "gentlemen" or "gentlewomen," thus showing the disproportionate ratio of aristocrats to artisans.[42] For Vauban and many others, the Huguenot diaspora represented not only a loss for France, but also a gain for other rival nations. The loss of such a significant number of industrious Huguenots provided the historical fodder for later French thinkers like the philosophes concerned with political economy, and even later the socialist Saint-Simonians who sought to raise the importance of engineers over aristocrats.

How significant in economic terms was the loss of the Huguenots? As with estimates of those Calvinists still in France after the Revocation, much of the historiography has been based on educated guesswork. One of the most famous French Protestant leaders in exile, Antoine Court stated that more than eight hundred thousand had left, only to later revise his number to two million.[43] Caveirac asserted in 1758 that only fifty thousand Protestants had fled over the French borders, while the Duke of Burgundy reported in 1710, with unfounded confidence befitting his personality, that only 67,732 Huguenots had emigrated.[44] Most who have written on the subject since the Revocation have placed the number between five hundred thousand and 1.5 million.

The most thorough investigation of the number of expatriated Huguenots and the effects of the Revocation on the economy remains Warren C. Scoville's *The Persecution of Huguenots and French Economic Development, 1680–1720*.[45] Scoville accumulated estimates from foreign countries where Huguenots were reported to have settled, ultimately coming to a figure of approximately two hundred thousand. His number is strikingly lower than other estimates. Scoville carefully compared reports of the numbers of Huguenot refugees in various areas as groups of Huguenots were often counted in multiple cities. For example, local authorities recorded transient migrants in Switzerland on their way to the German states, where they were most likely counted as well. Based on numerous estimates from leading intellectuals and government officials at the time, Scoville estimated that forty to fifty thousand Huguenots had settled in England, five to ten thousand in Ireland, fifty to seventy-five thousand in the United Provinces (mainly in Holland), thirty thousand in the German states, and sixty thousand in Geneva and the Swiss Cantons, of which only around twenty-five thousand remained for more than a year. Many of the Huguenots who finally settled in North America, the Channel Islands, South Africa, Constantinople, Denmark, or Sweden probably first emigrated to England, the Swiss Cantons, or Holland before relocating a second or even a third time. Previous authors had registered the effect of the Revocation on the French economy by the number of Huguenots that left France. Scoville, on the other hand, recognized that although proportionately, only 1 per cent of the population left France in the late seventeenth and early eighteenth centuries, their concentration in certain industries may have caused a larger impact – perhaps one large enough to explain the economic decline during the last two decades of Louis XIV's reign.[46] Ultimately, Scoville reasoned that to give such an argument primacy over all others would fail to give the necessary credence to the ravages of Mother Nature, the economic weight of Louis XIV's wars, the ill-effects of Colbert's mercantile system, and the continued, if flawed, centralization of the Bourbon successors. French Catholics readily resumed businesses and markets vacated by Protestants, thus reducing the Revocation's economic effects.[47]

The myth of Calvinist business proclivities prospered in France and abroad despite the elasticity of the French labour market in large part because it provided a discursive middle ground from which to counterbalance the King's attachment to the Catholic Church. Over the course of the seventeenth century, Protestants had become renowned for their industrious work ethic to the point that opponents of the Revocation emphasized the economic effects of anti-Protestant policies. At this point, it might be tempting to describe an affinity between early commercial capitalism and Calvinism as primarily the by-product of a shifting political culture that valued work over privilege. For many of the philosophes, the commercial interaction between groups would increase wealth if the barriers of prejudice were broken down. On the other side, some Catholics believed Protestant "immoral" or irreligious dealings had led to their commercial success. As many aristocrats formally converted to Catholicism around 1685 to safeguard their propertied interests, many felt the presence of the urban Protestant bourgeoisie to a greater degree. Without the opportunity to purchase positions in service of the crown or to safely acquire large expanses of land, Protestants could only follow the avenue left open to them – business.[48] Louis XIV's anti-Protestant policies gave the tortured Protestant populace a nudge in the direction of early mercantile capitalism.[49]

The Self-Fulfilling Prophecy of the Republican Refuge

By the seventeenth century, several definitions of *république* existed in France. The first was drawn from *res publica*, or any legitimately constituted body politic – such was Jean Bodin's meaning in *Les six livres de la République* (*The Six Books of the Republic*), first published in 1576, whose title is often translated into English as *The Six Books of the Commonwealth*. The second use of the term referred to specific states where government was held by many rather than by a single sovereign – the United Provinces, Venice, and Geneva are often mentioned. In this definition, very little differentiation existed. The third definition of *république* falls under the category of "civic republicanism," which stressed the moral duty of the individual, even individual self-government, as an antidote to the licentiousness, corruption, and tyranny of an absolutist state. A fourth definition related to the so-called Reformed republicanism, which stressed both their approach to ecclesiastical governance and their political propensity toward republican forms of governance. Catholics mobilized such arguments to insist on the disloyal character of Huguenots to the monarchy in France. Following the Revocation, as Huguenots fled to Geneva and the Netherlands – both places governed by forms of republicanism – French Catholics saw their prophecies self-fulfilled.

There is a tendency in existing historical works to relegate the role of religion in early republican thought. Claude Nicolet's canonical study *L'Idee republicaine en France* is perplexingly teleological at times. He makes the argument that republicanism is a *mot voyageur*. Republicanism in the French social imaginary shifted in meaning over time, but in its "movement," the idea of republicanism remained remarkably disconnected from religious forces that shaped it, in Nicolet's account.[50] In his article on anti-republicanism in the seventeenth century, Arthur Herman argues that in the "Huguenot Republic" myth, there "is a picture of participatory politics that is the exact reverse of its modern image."[51] For Herman, this image is reflective of Catholic and monarchical fears driven by a widespread belief that republics are not motivated by civic idealism or popular politics, but rather are manipulated by cabals organized to serve the interests and ambitions of great nobles. In the historiography of French republican thought, religious visions of republicanism are unilaterally imagined as antithetical to more modern (read: secular) republican forms. While a range of republican practices existed in reality and in theory – from aristocratic and oligarchical on one side to democratic on the other – all stood in direct opposition to theories of sacral absolutism and claims to Catholic dominance over France.

It should be unsurprising to find Catholics levelling claims of republicanism against the Reformed Church as a means to discredit Huguenot loyalty to the Catholic monarch. Huguenot monarchomachs during the French Wars of Religion had espoused explicitly anti-monarchical ideals and advanced prototypical social contract theories as a basis for their popular sovereignty leanings. Calvinist insistence on freedom of conscience in religious matters spilled out of their temples into the streets, breeding a type of politics rooted in individualism. Individual freedom wrought division and destroyed Catholic and monarchical order. As this chapter has shown, this republicanism was rooted not simply in flights of polemical fancy, but in social reality. This is not to say that the Reformed were, in fact, inherently republican, but that their diasporal movements and social organization in France gave Catholic theologians the material to evidence such claims of republicanism.

On the macro-geopolitical level, this Calvinist-republican cultural construction reflected the displacement patterns of the Huguenot diaspora. Extending from the Swiss lands to the Dutch Republic to the English Commonwealth, the Huguenot diaspora benefited from regimes with republican political structures, if not republican governments in name; this seemed to prove their polemics and evidenced their arguments for religious intolerance. For French republicans, at the end of the eighteenth century and following the revolutionary tumult, the loss of Calvinists to republican spaces and their perceived republicanism coalesced into adamant calls for their return to France (see chapter 5).

Either from the frontiers or from within, Catholics feared the establishment of republican states within France. The size of the Calvinist population in the south and their perceived republicanism made them a target of the centralizing tendencies of Louis XIV's regime. The "state within a state" rhetoric reflected the continuing power of provincial elites and the delicate balancing act French monarchs kept in order to limit the number of contestations to their own power.[52] The Huguenot leaders during the Wars of Religion had shown their ability to rally forces from the provinces to attack Catholics, and for many Catholics at the end of the seventeenth century, the Edict of Nantes had frozen these "quasi-republican" spaces in the French kingdom and could melt at any moment, heating up another War of Religion. In his *Histoire du Calvinisme*, the French Jesuit Louis Maimbourg argued that Calvin's "great revolution" overtook the established "religion and state in Geneva" and threatened to commence in France as well: "Strangers had introduced ... a republican space established inside the kingdom." These spaces represented the "greatest monument to heresy" for Maimbourg.[53]

Republicanism was not innate at the earliest outset of the French Calvinist Church, but rather a by-product of hostile relations between the Catholic Church and the budding Reformed faith. Since the early years of the Reformation, Calvinists organized themselves in a system of secret conventicles and not-so-secret synods, both of which were necessary to evade state and church censorship and to establish some semblance of uniform church practice and doctrine. These consistories took seemingly republican forms – an outcome of alliance formation amongst a group of dissidents. From the 1560s onward, Huguenots used their synodal structure to organize, targeting urban governments first in order to safeguard the nascent faith. What emerged was a concerted effort not necessarily to establish republics, but instead to build strongholds, which could then be used to influence the monarchy or to take it over. Huguenot leaders, like Admiral Coligny and Prince Condé, were royalists, not republicans. So, the establishment of pseudo-republican, Huguenot strongholds was not the principal aim of these early Huguenot leaders, but a necessary by-product of the pursuit of place and toleration within the kingdom. Only after the establishment of these Huguenot cities did republican ideals start to seed and become more prevalent amongst Huguenots. La Rochelle, Montauban, and other Huguenot strongholds functioned like republican city-states from the sixteenth century onward, making treaties with the crown wherein they balanced toleration of Calvinism with the political and economic needs of the crown. La Rochelle, arguably the most stalwart Huguenot "republic," maintained its autonomy into the seventeenth century, eventually buckling to the superior military power of the Catholic state during the siege of 1627–28.[54]

Catholics found their republican prophecy further evidenced by the writings of Pierre Jurieu, which I explore in chapter 2. At the core of the debate surrounding Jurieu's republicanism was the role of the individual – in religion, in politics, and in society. The freedom of conscience espoused by Calvinist theologians like Jurieu was translated to republican politics and theories of popular sovereignty. Jurieu was by no means the only Huguenot to earn the label "republican," nor was he a standard-bearer. In fact, during the *Controverse*, he was an aberration. From the early seventeenth century on, especially during the period between 1630 and 1660, Huguenots had very few reasons to resort to republican ideals to justify rebellion. Fidelity to the king, especially after the Edict of Nantes, was the north star of the French Calvinist population. Even through the Revocation of the Edict of Nantes, even as Calvinist writers began directly attacking the Catholic Church for the plight of their people, the king's body was rarely the explicit target; he may have been a target by association, but rarely were polemics lobbed at Louis XIV directly. Even during the Fronde (a French civil war between 1648 and 1653), when the king's constitutional powers were checked by the Parlements in France, the Huguenots maintained their royalism. Frondeurs did not spark fears of republicanism in Calvinists in France. Instead, the civil war in England and the execution of Charles I led to a recrystallization of the Calvinist-republican stigma, which in turn only strengthened the "desperate royalism" characteristic of the period.[55] It is against this backdrop of political moderation and loyalism that Jurieu stands in stark relief. The English Revolution of 1688 became the cause to draw Jurieu out into the light as the republican Theologian of Rotterdam.

***

The "fiction" of a Catholic France was precisely that – a fiction, wrought from the perceived realities of the early modern period. Elements of this fiction – the licentiousness of the greedy Calvinist "evidenced" by Calvinist business success in France and around the Atlantic World and the anarchical politics of the so-called republican Reformed – propped up Catholic calls for the forced conversion of the Calvinist population, for reigniting the sectarian violence of the Wars of Religion, and ultimately for the expulsion of a second wave of Calvinists from France into the wider refuge. Through their persecutions, Catholics found "evidence" for their initial claims. This verisimilitude or demographic perspective proved vital to the regenerating cycle of persecution that Catholics churned from the Reformation years through the Revocation and into the *Désert*, which would only be challenged by the Enlightenment and the French Revolution that followed. While such fictions were destructive for Huguenot communities, Huguenots ultimately made them constructive in their attempts to promote religious toleration and find their place in France. Huguenots had to respond to these fictions, to shape their own narratives, and to invent new political tactics in order to alleviate their suffering. From this Christian crucible emerged the modern refugee identity.

2

Millenarian Refugee: *Pierre Jurieu*

Catholics called Pierre Jurieu the "Goliath of the Protestants."[1] Jurieu was one of the most prolific and fiery writers of the Huguenot refuge. A Huguenot theologian based in Rotterdam, Jurieu's millenarianism and refugee politics intertwined to imagine the Huguenot population as new age Israelites reenacting the persecutions of the Hebrew Old Testament, under the thumb of the Babylonian Captivity of a French Catholic variety. In short, Jurieu saw himself more as a David than a Goliath. Yet in the second half of the seventeenth century, biblical politics took on new meaning, as a wave of Huguenot refugees fled France in the face of the intolerance of Louis XIV (a Nebuchadnezzarian figure) and his Revocation of the Edict of Nantes. Old Testament met New Testament for Jurieu in critical ways. The persecution the Huguenots faced signalled the coming of the fall of the anti-Christian Empire and the rise of Jesus Christ's one-thousand-year reign. As the word *refugee* was mostly used to refer to the Ancient Israelites, it only made sense for Jurieu and other like-minded Huguenots to seize the moniker for their moment and invent an important strand in the history of the refugee concept in the process.[2]

On 9 July 1681, Louis XIV, by way of royal decree, suppressed the Calvinist Academy at Sedan. The crown transferred its buildings to the Jesuits and expelled two of the most vocal Calvinists, who would also shape the next century's discourse on the Huguenot refugees and religious toleration. The first was Jurieu.[3] The second was Jurieu's colleague and friend turned fierce critic, noted Pyrrhonian skeptical professor of philosophy, and leader of the Republic of Letters, Pierre Bayle (the subject of the following chapter). Both men fled France for the Netherlands, taking up positions at the newly founded École Illustre in Rotterdam. Despite their similar expulsions, Jurieu and Bayle reacted to the Sun King's intolerant *arrêts* and subsequent Revocation in remarkably different ways: one reified the moral supremacy of Calvinist doctrine, and the other abandoned organized religion and morality, radically reconceiving the social and political order to allow for religious toleration. The ensuing polemical debate, which ensnared much of the refuge and *Désert*, was neither positive nor profitable for the Huguenot community as a whole. The dissonance between Jurieu and Bayle evidenced the Catholic equivalence between Protestant religious dissidence on the one side and political anarchy on the other.[4]

Jurieu had few illusions that Louis XIV would reverse his Revocation, whereas Bayle insisted religious moderation and displays of loyalty would encourage the king to return to the tolerant religious and political climate of Henri IV and the Edict of Nantes. Essentially, their programs revolved around the question of allegiance. Should the Huguenot identify by cult or by kingdom? In his *L'esprit de Mr Arnaud* (1684), Jurieu insisted that one's absolute duty was to God and his or her religious brethren.[5] Jurieu's spiritual absolutist perspective terrified Bayle. He feared for those still in France, where the dragoons were tearing homes and families asunder. In response to Jurieu's writings, Bayle anonymously penned *Avis aux réfugiez sur leur prochain retour en France* in 1690 and continued to rail against Jurieu in his famous *Dictionnaire historique et critique*, first published in 1697.[6] *Avis* sparked a vituperative attack from Jurieu. The back-and-forth only finally came to a close in December of 1706, when Bayle died suddenly from cardiac arrest.

While the debate between Jurieu and Bayle was caustic and often perceived as casuistic, it was productive in other ways. Through their heated exchanges, the category of refugees became politicized in new ways, indeed inventing what we might consider the modern refugee. The debate over Huguenots prefigured debates over religious toleration, the legitimate use of violence, and the contours of monarchical power more generally, as well as the religious or areligious character of revolutionary thought. As John Christian Laursen notes, Huguenots in the refuge often "mixed theology, philosophy, science, law, economics, and philology with political thought."[7] While defending their Huguenot brethren or launching attacks at those who they perceived as false leaders, Huguenot political theorists, historians, and theologians broached several subjects integral to the politics of religion during the early Enlightenment period.

French Enlightenment philosophers often thought of Bayle's writings as inspiring early Enlightenment calls to reason, whereas Jurieu's scriptural approach may strike readers as decidedly unmodern.[8] The category of refugees was born through this dialectic. Jurieu imagined refugees as religious cast-outs persisting through God's tribulations in pursuit of a safe haven. Bayle cast them as political actors capable of proving their loyalty by formally renouncing their superstitions and hailing the power of the tolerant, secular state. Implicit in both positions was a basic critique of the power of the French king and the Gallican state. In the Huguenot diaspora, such recalibrations were actively debated, imagined, constructed, and deconstructed in ways that allowed those who followed to imagine a world free from religious intolerance and violence – a time when one could envision a reduced if not eliminated role for the Holy See of Rome.

Another by-product of this intra-Protestant *Controverse* was the birth of enlightened Protestant apologetics. In the post-Revocation world, it became necessary to imagine a post-Protestant identity. While this did not mean disavowing faith entirely, it did mean striking new balances between emphasizing and de-emphasizing the particularity of Protestantism. Other leaders, either in the refuge or the *Désert*, contributed to this apologetical redefinition of French Calvinist identity. Élie Benoît, Elie Merlat, Antoine Court, and others used history, like their Catholic counterparts, to make the case for Protestant subjecthood. In doing so, they renounced republicanism as the political pipe dream of a few in favour of monarchism, strengthened by a Protestant populace untethered to the powers of the papacy. Alongside claims of their ultimate loyalty, they courted the king's favour by emphasizing their business acumen, abandonment of superstition, and general rejection of those doctrines that made the Camisard Wars possible at the beginning of the eighteenth century. In short, their apologetics relied on the secular concerns of the state, not the eschatological duties propagated by certain religious patriarchs.

Jurieu's religiously grounded writings created a vibrant strain of Protestant particularist thought that Catholic controversialists would continue to point to over the coming century. In the nineteenth century, too, republicans with a desire to trace the ascendency of modern French republicanism would point back to Jurieu to argue that Protestantism and republicanism went hand in hand. In their minds, Jurieu was not simply a man trapped by his times, but a visionary, whose political predilections for republicanism seemed to materialize during the French Revolution for some.

In *La crise de la conscience européenne, 1680–1715*, Paul Hazard argued that a shift occurred in the late seventeenth century, which forever changed the intellectual landscape of the Europe. "One day, the French people, almost to a man, were thinking like [Jacques-Bénigne] Bossuet. The day after, they were thinking like Voltaire. No ordinary swing of the pendulum, that. It was a revolution," Hazard argued.[9] For him, a dialectical development pushed this revolution in thought. Shifting attitudes toward religion and rising humanistic concerns were causal factors, and both were at play in the rhetoric of Huguenot writers at the time, but Hazard succumbed to teleology, anticipating the rationality of Voltaire, rather than paying due diligence to the sentimentality of those Huguenots living through the Revocation's storm. At the core of Huguenot rhetoric was the call for sentiment with the plight of their suffering. It was at the core of the historical tracts detailing the shedding of Huguenot blood, and it was explicit in the choice of the term *refugee*, as in a new age Israelite, born from the fires of the Wars of Religion rather than Egyptian enslavement, to denote their diaspora.

While Jurieu's and Bayle's stories are intertwined, this chapter contextualizes Jurieu in order to understand the religious underpinnings of the religious refugee identity that Huguenots adopted to embolden their confessional identity. In several of Jurieu's writings, but most prominently in his *Lettres pastorales adressées aux fidéles de France qui gemissent sous la captivité de Babylon*, the refugee identity was used to tie persecuted Huguenots in the refuge and the *Désert* together.[10] His

Lettres pastorales also reveal how quickly the shifting phantasmagoria of the refugee experience manifested itself in radical religious thought, in prophetic claims, and in calls to action justified by millenarianism. Through the *Lettres pastorales*, the central text of this chapter, it becomes clear how powerful such apocalyptic and prophetic claims were to the persecuted population and how they keyed into Jurieu's political agenda, especially against the backdrop of the English Revolution of 1688. In separating Jurieu as well, I aim not to present a tidy linear narrative out of the religious refugee into the political one, but rather to expose this hotbed of refugee rhetoric and how it produced multiple visions of refugeedom. Jurieu's refugee formed a palimpsest for subsequent generations to seize and make their own – each subsequent iteration bearing the marks of previous images.

Finding Refuge in Rotterdam

Born in Mer, in the Orléanais province, in 1637, Jurieu came from a long line of ministers. His father and his grandfathers on both sides had both been ministers in the Reformed Church. Jurieu's mother, Esther Du Moulin, was a daughter of one of the most prominent Calvinist families in France. Pierre Du Moulin had served as chaplain to the Duchess of Bar after the death of her brother Henri IV, and had found favour with James I of England. He was also related to André Rivet, who had been tutor to William II of Nassau, and Samuel Bochart, a French Calvinist humanist who was renowned for his understandings of ancient languages as well as being the tutor of Wentworth Dillon, later Earl of Roscommon. In short, Jurieu's family tree had roots across Europe – roots which would facilitate his rise within the Calvinist Church in France, as well as the recreation of his intellectual network once he fled France to Rotterdam.

Jurieu's education and early career embodied a kind of religious cosmopolitanism too. He studied at the Academy of Saumur in England with his uncles Pierre Du Moulin, an Anglican, and Louis Du Moulin, a Nonconformist, whom he would later take to task for questioning the authority of the Reformed synods.[11] It is possible that Jurieu received ordination in the Church of England, but there is no definitive proof for or against this claim. Between 1661 and 1664, Jurieu occupied the curate position under his father at Mer, and later took his father's place upon his passing. He married his cousin, Hélène Du Moulin. They never had children. His parish came under pressure due to a lawsuit, and at the same time, the Parlement of Paris decided their temple had been illegally built. It was demolished and relocated. He spent some time in the parish of Vitry-le-François before leaving to go to the Academy of Sedan. When the Academy was shuttered to the Protestants in 1681, Jurieu fled to the Netherlands. Jurieu likely had to leave France, turning down an offer to join the church in Rouen, because of his pending *La Politique du clergé de France* (1681).[12] In Rotterdam, he became a minister of the Walloon Church and a professor at the École Illustre. He spent the rest of his life there, living in the Hoogstraat near his church. After his death in 1713, Hélène left for England, joining the Prophets of the Cévennes, leaving her brother-in-law, the Huguenot preacher Jacques Basnage, to deal with her shares of the Jurieu estate.

Jurieu's rebellious spirit resulted from several overlapping trajectories in the seventeenth century. At the time of his schooling, the Jansenists had challenged the Catholic Church, and Huguenots mostly had emphasized their continued royalism. Huguenots even remained out of the Fronde, hoping not to draw any undue attention to the Calvinist aristocracy. The English Civil War (1642–51) seemed to catalyze Catholics to question Protestants' allegiance to the French throne. Given Jurieu's connections to and time in England, it is possible that his willingness to critique the French state came from this cross-Channel experience. Despite Calvinist attempts to plead their loyalism, the 1660s witnessed the rise of anti-Calvinist policies with Louis XIV, who began his personal rule in 1661, after the regency period. Tensions with Spanish and the Dutch died down with the successive Peace of the Pyrenees (1659) and the Peace of Nimwegen (1678–79), which allowed Louis XIV to focus on cleaning the French house of religious dissenters, namely the Calvinists. National synods were banned after 1659. The General Assembly of the French Clergy encouraged the King to gradually strip the Calvinists of all privileges not strictly protected by the Edict of Nantes, until the *dragonnades* commenced their hostilities toward the Calvinists in 1681, the same year that Louis XIV issued an *arrêt* expelling the Huguenots from the Academy of the Sedan, where Jurieu held a faculty position like his grandfather before him. Through all of this, a "desperate royalism" existed in France, captured best by the writings of Elie Merlat, whose *Traité pouvoir sur les absolus des souverains* insisted that Louis XIV's temper toward the Calvinists could be cooled, if only he could be convinced of the loyalism of the Calvinists. Jurieu was not a desperate royalist.[13]

Especially after the death of the Calvinist moderate controversialist Jean Claude, Jurieu became the most significant defender of the Protestant religion, if not, as Bossuet had it, "the only defender of the Protestant religion."[14] Jurieu's fiery disposition and ability to produce both polemic and news for the refuge community, combined with his theological and political acumen to recast the Huguenot population's sufferings and his extensive network across Europe, allowed him to assume this role. His works were published in French, English, German, Dutch, Hungarian, and Italian. As his fellow Huguenot Élie Benoît remarked: "Jurieu seemed incapable of getting tired or exhausted and especially during those three unfortunate years 1683, 1684, and 1685, he wrote so many books. It would seem that he needed less time to compose them than it took the Reformed to read them. His writings made their way into France with some difficulty, but were sought after, read, benefited from, dreaded by those seeking to convert Calvinists, who always found them in their way and who could not deny their brilliance."[15] He was outspoken, argumentative, and convincing. Jurieu found his audience and used his voice to polemicize the works of Catholics like Antoine Arnauld, Pierre Nicole, and Jacques-Bénigne Bossuet as well as Protestants like Louis Du Moilin, Claude Pajon, and Pierre Bayle.

In all things, Jurieu intertwined religion with politics. While the political context of the Revocation and the English Revolution of 1688 undoubtedly influenced Jurieu's writings, these were political events to be inscribed on a religious temporality. During the formative years of the Revocation, Jurieu undoubtedly read more widely, in both sides of the *Controverse*'s literature, but also drew rather ecumenically from other thinkers as far ranging as the skeptics on one side, and the millenarians on the other, especially Joseph Mede, the English millenarian and Arminian theologian of the early seventeenth century. Gottfried Wilhelm Leibniz insisted Jurieu's apocalypticism was in many ways a carbon copy of Mede's interpretations.[16] In the opening of his *L'Accomplisssement des propheties ou la deliverance prochaine de l'Église* (1686), published the next year as *The Accomplishment of the Scripture Prophecies: Or the Approaching Deliverance of the Church* (1687), Jurieu remarked that his vision of end times was strongly rooted in scripture and influenced by "the Exposition of Joseph Mede, whom I formerly look't upon as a man inspired for the Interpretation of the Prophecies."[17] Jurieu's prophetic claims resounded well with two different groups. First, French Protestants in both the diaspora and in the *Désert* were enthusiastic supporters of Jurieu. This should not be surprising given that, if not directly in the *Accomplissement*, then explicitly in the *Lettres pastorales*, Jurieu was talking to them. Second, Dutch and English Protestants of various stripes were receptive to Jurieu's millenarianism. Jurieu's book took off once it appeared in English, passing along Dutch and English trading routes across the Atlantic Ocean to places like the desks of Boston minister and millennialist himself Increase Mather, who read the book in 1686, and the Virginia frontier planter William Byrd, who requested a copy of Jurieu's *Scripture Prophecies* in 1690.[18]

In the 1680s, Jurieu witnessed a decisive shift in the intellectual climate of the Huguenot community. The Revocation era sparked a new round of criticism of both the state and the Catholic Church. Calvinists began to respond by promoting religious toleration – a derogation of the Calvinist's claims to religious truth according to Jurieu – and appealing to reason – the cause of religious splintering, undercutting the unity Jurieu believed the Reformed Church needed in order to face down the Bourbon threat. Jurieu's response to early rational claims about the natural law of man and religious toleration led to his retrenchment in the Old Testament, where the role of the prophet cut across any perceivable divide between religion and politics. And while he often refused to claim this prophetic role, "he virtually anointed himself" in the process. From this position, he could seize the authority to interpret the New Testament's apocalyptic texts for political purposes as well as provide a program for salvation to those facing the eschatological crises faced by the Calvinist community within the French kingdom and in the diaspora.[19] Richard Popkin long ago argued that millenarian thought needs to be viewed within the contexts of rising intellectual movements related to science and skepticism in the seventeenth century, both of which Jurieu abhorred. Jurieu's millenarianism then provided a "third force" to challenge the orthodox forms of knowledge, most closely guarded by the Catholic Church.[20] An important component of this millenarian thought was its ability to apply biblical allusions to contemporary events and to embolden confessional allies to launch critiques of Catholic orthodoxy from a biblical basis. To understand Jurieu's millenarianism as a third way, we need to reassess Jurieu's mobilization of the Bible for political purposes. Rather than focusing so closely on Old Testament constructions of prophecy, I argue we need to pay attention to Jurieu's construction of the persecuted Huguenot refugees, a mirror of the exodus and persecution of the Jewish population. His millenarianism, inspired by his interpretations of the New Testament's apocalyptic text, rested on this assertion that the Huguenot refugees were a new chosen people. Any persecution of Huguenot refugees, then, was seen as a tragic and sacrilegious act, which proved the basis for empathizing with the Huguenot population.

Huguenot Refugees in their Babylonian Captivity

Both Jurieu and Bayle were refugees, forced from France for their faith. But what it meant to be a refugee differed greatly between them. One of the most prominent issues facing the construction of the refugee identity at the end of the seventeenth century was its relationship to the Israelites and their exodus from Egyptian enslavement, their Babylonian Captivity, and eventually their pursuit of peace. An immensely powerful allusion, this biblical narrative mirrored in rough form the Huguenot experience for many. And in holding this mirror up, the Huguenot began to realize a victim narrative, which could be levelled at the French absolutist power. For some, God chose them to suffer tribulations, to wage a holy war in His name, and to realize a peaceful, religious utopia. Such was the driving force behind Jurieu's refugee rhetoric, and such a comparison reified the importance of faith in his works. Yet such an analog was dangerous and incongruous in Bayle's mind. By placing the Huguenot atop a pedestal, aside the Israelites, the Huguenot refugees resigned themselves to persecution for millennia to come at a time when religious particularism and identity should be effaced – at least in the mind of the Philosopher of Rotterdam, Bayle.

At the heart of the construction of the modern refugee was the appropriation of the narrative of victimization. Catholics devoted thousands of pages to demonizing the Calvinist population, historicizing their transgressions against the French state, and justifying the violence perpetrated against them. It was the Huguenot's job to reverse this narrative, turning the politics of the diaspora away from a rhetoric of the perpetrator to one of the victim – a narrative that would inevitably promote a secular power and state-building, while continuing the anti-Catholic rhetoric of the preceding century. Jurieu emphasized the victimization of the Calvinist population by an unjust ruler – whether his transgressions against the Calvinists were the fruits of his own sectionalism or the machinations of Catholic ministers, the "agents of Satan" who "breathed in his ears."[21] With the construction of this victimization, Jurieu further sounded the clarion call of war. The king reversed Henri IV's supposedly perpetual edict of religious peace. Calvinists had an obligation to resist. Bayle, too, emphasized the victimization of the Huguenot population. Far from emphasizing an equivalency between the violence perpetrated by Catholics and Protestants, Bayle placed greater pressure on the Huguenot population to make the necessary overtures to win the Catholic king to the side of toleration.

No religious refugee story stood out more to the Calvinists than the exodus of the Israelites. For Jurieu, the persecution of the Huguenot refugees both reflected the Babylonian captivity of the Jewish population historically and fulfilled a prophecy made calculable from the scripture. In 1686, Jurieu began to write and publish his *Lettres pastorales adressées aux fidéles de France qui gemissent sous la captivité de Babylon* from his exile. Despite the efforts of the police, the remaining Calvinist communities in France distributed Jurieu's pastoral letters. Jurieu's goal was simple. As the subtitle of his letters indicates, Jurieu imagined the Calvinists as trapped, "moaning under the captivity of Babylon," just as the Jews of Moses's time were captured in Babylon: "Rome is the spiritual Babylon of which God spoke. *Leave Babylon, my people* ... The papists are the Gentiles who tread on and oppressed the Church of God; their Images are the idols of ancient pagans and their saints stand in the stead of ancient Gods."[22] This comparison between Rome and Babylon makes its way into the *Lettres pastorales* repeatedly to encourage Calvinists to resist the Catholic Church's efforts to convert them. Just as God told the Jews to leave Babylon, so, too, must Calvinists remember to leave the modern Babylon. Rebuking the writings of Bossuet, Jurieu insists that the "Pope is the Antichrist, Papism is anti-Christianity, and the Roman Church is the true Babylon that Saint John described in his version of the Apocalypse,"[23] and that "the beast is the Empire of the Roman Catholic Church."[24] Conversion was the same as willingly submitting oneself to the servitude of a spiritual Babylon. While the religious motives for such discourse are apparent, it is also important to note how such comparisons erected an image of Calvinists as the persecuted chosen people, necessary in order for later writers to imagine Calvinists as primarily victims of a closely knit church and state.

His conceptions of apocalypse and Babylon were interlinked. Jurieu worked through a rather complex calculation of the Apocalypse. He argued that the "beast began his empire with the dismemberment of the Roman Empire into ten kingdoms." Here, Jurieu draws from the day-year principle, which normally takes the mention of 1,260 days or 42 months in Daniel and Revelation to be predictions of the coming of the Apocalypse. Days translate to years in Jurieu's Huguenot formulation. Jurieu then pinpoints three different transition points in the decline and fall of the Roman Empire. The first was 360 CE, the point at which Jurieu says, rather vaguely, that "superstition and tyranny began to enter the Church" and the "barbarians began to accost the Roman Empire." In 430 CE, religious superstition and the invocation of Saints had begun to beset the Church, ravaging the true Christian sensibility. His last prophetic chronological pinpoint appears in 450 CE with the full fall of the Roman Empire. The first "beginning" then corresponded with 1620 (1,260 years after 360 CE) and what Jurieu imagined as the waning of papal power in Franc. The second "beginning" then led Jurieu to believe that 1690 would see the greatest check against the power of the spiritual Babylon. The final ruin of Babylon and the coming of the Apocalypse would come in 1710.[25] Perhaps even more important than his prophecies is how he read his contemporary moment as a proof of his divine calculations.

Jurieu interpreted the persecutions of French Huguenots under the reign of Louis XIV and especially with the coming of the Revocation of the Edict of Nantes as a sign of the deterioration of the Catholic Babylon. This persecution could then be mobilized to encourage Calvinists to take up arms and to overthrow priests and princes in the name of their church. Drawing a historical lesson, Jurieu notes that the Babylonian empire had to be destroyed by the sword of the Spirit that lay in the mouth of the Son of God. Jurieu emphasized the biblical need for God's chosen refugees to "leave" Babylon; in this way he attacked the Catholic Church and bolstered the boundaries between the two Christian sects. Yet, while the Catholic Church may have represented Babylon, France – the geographical and political expression – could emerge from the spiritual Babylon.

It is against this backdrop of the Huguenot refugees as a chosen, persecuted people that we can understand Jurieu's antipathy toward religious toleration. Accepting Calvinist claims of doctrinal truth meant Louis XIV's persecution of the Protestant sect was a crime against truth and God. Jurieu did not explicitly denounce the state's persecutions against other religious minorities, because they did not have a justified conscience or claim to religious truth. In his *La Politique du clergé* (1687), Jurieu rebukes Bayle's arguments for religious toleration by arguing that freedom of conscience and truth were undeniably bound, and moral equality could only be found between truth and conscience that reflected that truth.[26] Jurieu's belief in the absolute nature of Calvinist claims to truth and conscience bled into his millenarianism and apocalyptic propheticism. It also reinforced his commitment to the English Revolution of 1688 and the Dutch stadtholder William of Orange, who appeared as a defender of the downtrodden.

The *Lettres pastorales* reaffirmed Calvinist faith by transposing this biblical narrative onto the Huguenot plight, but Jurieu also used them to document and report the suffering of Huguenots at the hands of the *dragonnades*. This documentary approach was meant to strengthen Huguenot resolve as well as the narrative of their persistent victimization. Huguenots of different provinces or those beyond France's borders could empathize with the plight of their coreligionists. Suffering was sacred. For Jurieu, perseverance in the face of suffering was an attribute of godliness. Jurieu did not need to reinvent the wheel entirely. Ever since the Reformation, Calvinists had fortified their consciences with the language of martyrdom.[27] Calvinist suffering evidenced their election. God "intended to use these people as a vanguard to create a new world – an Eden, a Canaan – on the ashes of the old Antichristian empire." Simultaneously, they seized "the emotional center of European geopolitics in the late 1600s."[28]

While Jurieu never developed a theory of sentiment, it is easy to see how this approach encouraged later Huguenots to turn to sentiment as a political approach toward toleration of their sect in France. In general, this cataloguing of the atrocities faced by Huguenots was common in Reformed writings of the *Controverse*. If exposition of theological truth could not convince Catholics, then claiming the moral high ground and establishing the narrative of victimization could prove useful. Elizabeth Israels Perry traced the development of historical analysis within the *Controverse*, which witnessed the ascendency of historical justifications for intolerance on both sides – Catholic and Protestant. This turn toward historical methodologies as means to claim the moral and historical high ground established a firm basis for historical writing during the Enlightenment.[29] Perry does not explore the ways that such historical writings formed the basis for later sentimental writings, though, as I explore in chapter 5 on Rabaut Saint-Étienne, who regularly cited Benoît.

Juxtapositions of the pain and suffering of the Huguenots against the "happiness of deliverance" were potent.[30] Jurieu, in his *Lettres pastorales*, highlights the violence of the *dragonnades* alongside espousals of his apocalyptic thinking. The *dragonnades* attempted to squash the spirit of the Huguenots in order to convert them, but "the spirit of life, this is to say, courage, heart, conviction will return."[31] Jurieu used his pastoral letters as well as his sermons to mould the religious feelings of his followers. Huguenot exile sermons regularly used pleas to the emotional side of the flock in order to "confirm refugees in their faith and to explain to them the mysteries of the Christian religion" – this despite the frequent typecasting of Calvinism as stern and unfeeling.[32] Common affective understandings of their exile proved integral to establishing an "emotional community" for the Huguenots, but this emotional rhetoric also proved instrumental for Jurieu, who was in the process of constructing and reaffirming the Huguenot refugee position as one under both physical and emotional threat.[33]

While affect figured significantly in Jurieu's work, detailing the suffering of Huguenots was not done merely for the historical record, but rather because it might leave a mark on the moral consciences of the persecutors. Jurieu described "the fear and dread that the persecutors" felt when faced with scenes of tortured Huguenots. The reciprocal relationship between the persecuted and the persecutor is sentimental in nature. "The fear comes from seeing the faithful oppressed," he wrote; "[t]his is the sense of Prophecy."[34] Forced conversions had affective effects. Jurieu published a story from 1687 of a woman named Jeanne de Baille, the wife of a surgeon named Esaye Viridet. A Jesuit priest named Langeron forced Baille to convert to Catholicism. When forced to sign her conversion declaration, she "fell as if she had died, the only movement was a swift convulsion of her right arm," which had been holding the quill given to her by the priest. Fearing she would lose her children, she stood back up and took the quill up again. But as soon as she had formed "the first letter of her name," she fainted again and remained in that state for "more than six hours." Jurieu noted that the Mayor who had been present for the entire affair claimed he would have paid "a lot of money" to have not witnessed the episode and that it took him "five days to recover from the emotional [trauma] of the incident."[35] Women regularly appear in the *Lettres pastorales*, paired with their suffering children, or depicted as motivated to convert for fear of their children's fates.

While in Holland, the Calvinist lawyer and preacher Claude Brousson had certainly read Jurieu's work. In the summer of 1686, the two men had become friends. They also worked together to lobby the Elector Frederick William of Prussia, as well as William of Orange and his Grand Pensioner Fagel, on behalf of Huguenot refugees in 1687–88. Shortly after, in the Netherlands, 250 Huguenot pastors began receiving 400 to 600 florins from the Dutch Estates as pensions.[36] Shortly after, when William of Orange became William III of England, Brousson saw what he believed to be the fulfillment of Jurieu's prophetic claims. Like Jurieu, Brousson could not "separate his religious vocation from his role as a political negotiator."[37] In his most prolific text, Brousson borrowed and extended the biblical metaphor of Jurieu. In his 1695 publication, *La Manne mystique du Désert*, Brousson describes the suffering of the Huguenot population as akin to that of the Ancient Israelites at the hands of their Babylonian oppressors, adopting the emotional language of the persecuted. On four separate occasions in the text, he refers to the Huguenot "sentiment of our misery," as he describes the "so-called justice" doled out by the Bourbon throne before God's Throne. Just like Jurieu, Brousson likens the Babylonian Captivity to the French monarchy and the Catholic Church more specifically. The coming destruction of the new Babylon was fast approaching.[38]

Millenarianism and Religious "Revolution" in the Refuge

Alexis de Tocqueville described the French Revolution of 1789 as a political revolution with all the trappings of a "religious revolution."[39] Yet in the late seventeenth century, the idea of a revolution, political or cultural, was always viewed in religious terms. Even in purely astronomical terms, the revolutions of Earth on its axis, revolutions of Earth around the Sun, or the moon's revolution around Earth were all products of God's design.[40] Like most issues caught up between Catholics and Protestants of the time, whether revolutions were good or bad was a matter of whether they were the by-product of God's work or were the machinations of unbelievers. Pierre Jurieu saw revolution as both written in scripture and justified by it, just as the tribulations of Huguenot refugees were inscribed with scriptural significance. The intertwining of two linked concepts – revolution and refugees – was intentional and reflected exercises of state power that made both thinkable.

Revolution was innate to religious change for Jurieu. Christianity had been born through revolution and had built its vast empire through revolution. Without using the term, Catholics represented counter-revolutionaries, extinguishing the light of the Ancient Church with dogma and falsehoods. For Jurieu, then, a second coming of the revolution the early Church represented was both needed and a part of God's design.

> I considered the present posture of the World, and it seem'd to me, as if all things were prepared for some great Revolution … Nevertheless, we see that by secret methods, which men perceive not, he opens the way to his greatest works. For Example, the Fall of Paganism by the preaching of the Gospel, and the conversion of the Heathen World, was a great Revolution. God prepared all things for this great Event many ages before it came to pass, by admirable means, of which no man then knew the tendency and design.[41]

God prepared revolution, according to Jurieu, and the minds of human beings were the vehicle to revolutions. Jurieu argued that recent returns to scientific knowledge had lifted the veil of ignorance that the Catholic Church had pulled over the eyes of the Roman Empire. Similarly, the exploration of far-flung lands "East and West" made possible by new technologies like the compass, and even the indelible pursuit of riches which God had embedded into the character of human beings, resembled the first missions to convert the pagans of Europe.[42] But the "Fall and declension of the Papacy" represented the final sign "of that great work which God is making way for." "The Paganism of Popery" had preserved the falsehoods of both pre-Christian paganism and those cultures it encountered across Europe. Jurieu rehashed many Reformation-era critiques of the Catholic Church's impurities, its corruptions, its "popish superstitions," and its "Invocation of Saints with contempt."[43]

So much of Jurieu's understanding of revolutionary action and the Huguenot refugee diaspora, especially in the Netherlands, was bound up with the fate of William of Orange. Jurieu's political position wavered over the course of the 1680s. At the fulcrum of his pivot was the English Revolution of 1688. Jurieu understood the rise of William of Orange as the expression of God's elect; his successful overthrow of James II symbolized God's favour and therefore signalled Huguenots to band behind his military power. For Jurieu, the promise of salvation overrode all. His Calvinist faith was universalist; the rise of the stadtholder to the throne of England was a political expression of this universalism. William had crossed one border, invaded a kingdom, and overthrown the Catholic king. In Jurieu's mind, William could easily do the same in France with his Anglo-Dutch-Huguenot army.

On the other side of the debate, Jurieu's militant religious politics, too, lost popularity following the Glorious Revolution's failure to spread to France.[44] Jurieu never abandoned his religious outlook on life. Toleration was impossible, because religion and politics had always been bound together. "All history has aspects of sacred history" for Jurieu, as Labrousse noted. Religious and political dissent were synonymous. Religious plurality undermined the control of the state. To tolerate religious minorities was to seal the fate of the state to perpetual violence. Christianity had only risen from the ashes following the fall of the Roman Empire by aligning with secular powers, and those secular powers used religious affiliation to bolster their own claims to profane power. All of this was bound up in his reading of Revelation, which promised a resolute end to the persecution of the Calvinist people.

Catholics who stood in opposition to Jurieu and the English Revolution of 1688 did not couple revolution and refugees favourably. In his *Histoire des révolutions arrivées dans l'Europe en matière de religion*, Antoine Varillas saw the "revolutions" of the Reformed to be violent, destabilizing expressions of false beliefs and fanaticism.[45] Malicious men and women participated in revolution, guised in the name of Reformed religion, but their motives betrayed their true beliefs, and so it was within the power of the sovereign king to excise such men from the kingdom. Sentimental refugees they were not. They were cancers to homogeneous faith and the sacral absolutism of the state, according to Catholics like Varillas. Jurieu saw in revolutionary action the designs of God, not of ungodly men and women.

While Jurieu's express purpose in the *Accomplishment of the Scripture Prophecies* or the *Lettres pastorales* was not to incite violence, he did seek to dismantle divine right political theories and justify a rough vision of popular sovereignty. Perhaps due to the quick succession of their publication, Jurieu never fully constructed a sound political theory of popular sovereignty. As R.J. Howells notes, Jurieu "tends to move between broad juridical or Christian propositions about individual self-defence, and constitutional arguments from law positive."[46] Yet Jurieu's insistence on the primacy of religious conviction and the duty of the individual to challenge the king's persecutory policies did reorient the post-Revocation Protestant apologetics in the direction of emphasizing both the rights and the duties of the individual. While few after the Camisard War in France turned to Jurieu for political guidance, his discussions of popular sovereignty altered the ways that Calvinists defended their faith and made claims of loyalty to the absolutist regime.

Concepts of political and cultural revolution underscored Jurieu's millenarianism. A devoted defender of freedom of conscience and the fallibility of humankind, Jurieu made sure to preface his prophetic calculations with a brief reflection of his own imperfection.

> Behold therefore, what I assert, namely, that this is the last persecution, which Antichrist must raise against the Church, and that we are near the end of the twelve hundred and sixty years (which is the Period of his Empire,) and that in the beginning of the next age, this Empire must see its end. If I should be mistaken nine or ten years, and that this Empire should (instead of ending in the year 1710, or thereabouts) run on until the year 1720, I do not think that any could justly treat me as a false Prophet, and accuse me of rashness ... Time is preparing for me a mortification sore enough. Let us leave Providence to work: it will discover who is guilty of rashness and fond credulity.[47]

And then, he began to lay out his calculations. With each justification, Jurieu drew explicit links between Biblical symbolism and stories on one side and contemporary events that Huguenots faced on the other. Unlike Mede's millenarianism, Jurieu's understanding of the coming Apocalypse was always expressly political.

Specifically, Jurieu was focused on calculating the fall of the Antichrist before the coming of Jesus Christ's one-thousand-year reign over Earth. The Antichrist, according to Jurieu, was the Pope, whose house had fostered corruption and idolatry and renewed pagan practices through saint worship. The first four hundred years of the Ancient Church were one of purity, the period that Protestant Reformers sought to recreate. Around 450 CE, the period of antichistianism commenced that would last exactly 1,260 years, concluding around 1710 or 1715, depending on the projected end date of the Ancient Church: "At the sounds of the Last Trumpet, the last blow must be given to the Babylonish Empire & at the same time shall begin the reign of Jesus Christ, to which is assign'd a Period of 1000 Years." In all of this and based on his understanding of the Huguenot refugee diaspora as a new age chosen people, Jurieu interpreted events in biblical terms and in terms of the coming fall of the Antichrist. The Revocation of the Edict of Nantes held great significance in his writings. In this "present persecution that the Church suffers, agree with those of the last persecution which the Church must suffer from the Beast according to the Text of the Revelation."[48] In Revelation, Jurieu saw the Revocation as executing the true Reformed Gospel; its resurrection would come as the "two Witnesses." He wrote, "The Reformation shall within a few years rise again in FRANCE; after that, it shall be established by Royal Authority. France shall renounce Popery and that Kingdom shall be converted."[49]

The Protestant William of Orange's revolution against the Catholic King James II also seemed an instrument of the coming Apocalypse. Jurieu wrote as much in his *Lettres pastorales*, a couple of years after the revolution in England. In linking the Huguenot cause to the supposed Protestant revolution in England, Jurieu deliberately linked his religious politics with his prophecies. One key example of Jurieu's millenarian prophecies concerned the splitting of the western Christian Church into three parts – the "Papists, Lutherans, and Calvinists." He paid very close attention to other Christian groups in this categorization, even going so far as to note that the Anglican Church (of which William of Orange would be the head in short order) always opened their doors to Calvinists, while both Lutherans and Catholics ceased all communion with the Reformed population. Both of political importance and, perhaps, reflective of Jurieu's own attachment to the Anglican Church, Jurieu's prophecies fit into the religious diplomatic landscape quite well.[50]

Revolution met Revelation and reflected an unbreakable bond between faith and politics for Jurieu. The religious refugees were at the core of his prophecy, as the chosen ones who, through their tribulations, would survive the suffering of the Antichrist's collapse and whose faith and perseverance would be rewarded. Simultaneously, then, Jurieu designed his apocalypticism as a means to critique the French state and to offer a much needed salve to the Calvinist population in France and in the diaspora.

* * *

A considerable revamping of the historical study of modernity has emerged over the last couple of decades. Scholars now readily recognize the "theological origins of modernity" that the "unintended Reformation" sparked in Protestant countries, but also in predominantly Catholic ones.[51] Theology, persecution, and revolution combined to set the stage for Jurieu's firebrand. Refugees stripped from their ancestral lands, persecuted, tormented, forced to travel great distances or hide in hinterlands, found agency through Revolution, but also found their actions justifiable in theological terms. Millenarianism embedded with early revolutionary thought. It provided one half of the dialectical creation of modern revolutions as well as political refugees – both of which the next chapter on Bayle explores. But it is impossible to appreciate that secular turn, or the continued presence of non-secular understandings of both refugees and revolutionaries, without first acknowledging the power of theologians like Jurieu.

"Those who dissented from received culture and creed," Alan Charles Kors notes, "had been formed by received culture and creed."[52] While Huguenot leaders who followed Jurieu tended to rebuke his revolutionary zeal and apocalypticism as a by-product of the age of confessionalization and as indicative of the trauma caused by the Wars of Religion and the Revocation era, they borrowed many of the basic understandings of refugees from late seventeenth-century Calvinists like Pierre Jurieu. The concept of "refugee," the Church of the *Désert*, and allusions to the Ancient Israelites continued to abound as a means to maintain the Huguenot Church across the eighteenth century. Focus on the suffering of Huguenot bodies, too, proved an integral legacy of Jurieu's work as well. The evolution of exegesis on the Truth of Calvinist doctrine witnessed the rise of historical analyses, which inevitably forced theologians, philosophers, statesmen, pastors, and their ilk to forefront human suffering in new ways, turning tortured bodies into metaphors for the kingdom and later the nation. Revolution was a medicine for the tortured body of the Protestant international for Jurieu, and indicative of the final excising of the Catholic cancer as detailed, or so he argued, in scripture. This amputation caused more harm than good according to Bayle, whose thought we move on to now.

3

Political Refugee: *Pierre Bayle*

For Pierre Bayle (1647–1706), unlike Jurieu, the refugee identity that Huguenots needed to assume was based not in scripture, but rather in a kind of politics that called religious truths into question. Both Huguenot refugees imagined their refugee community as a victim of a state, but they disagreed greatly over the level to which Huguenots themselves were responsible for their own exile. For Jurieu, Huguenots were proverbial victims, a kind of rekindling of the Old Testament refugeedom of the Ancient Israelites melded with the prophecies of the Apocalypse from the New Testament. For Bayle, Huguenots became victims, sans scripture, but from a new political script that increasingly became commonplace in the late seventeenth-century *Controverse*, where the morality of sectarian violence was increasingly understood in human terms rather than through claims to doctrinal truths. Huguenots were flawed. For Bayle, it was time for Huguenots to recognize those flaws, distance themselves from those who would interpret those flaws through fanaticism, and call upon King Louis XIV to welcome back his Calvinist children to France. In this chapter, I focus on Bayle's *Avis important aux réfugiez* in which he put forth his vision of the refugee identity most directly.

Bayle was a Huguenot by birth and was educated in the Reformed tradition, but he was not devout like Jurieu. It is impossible to discern Bayle's conception of refugee identity without first recognizing the oscillations of Bayle's own faith – a historiographical subject of great debate. Was he an orthodox Calvinist, a "Catholic-Calvinist," a covert Socinian, an early Deist, indifferent to theology altogether, or a crypto-atheist hostile to theological, dogmatic thought?[1] Over the course of his life, he likely dabbled with each of these. He grew up in a small French Calvinist community just beneath the Pyrenees Mountains in a time of religious and political tumult. Persecuted for his Reformed faith, like many in seventeenth-century France, Bayle fled the region. He converted to Catholicism in 1668 while attending the Jesuit college of Toulouse, only to abjure and return to the Calvinist fold two years later in 1670 at Mazères. He studied theology in Geneva and became a private teacher until he found solace, however briefly, in the Protestant Academy of Sedan. In 1681, Louis XIV issued an *arrêt*, closing the school and turning its property over to the Jesuits. Bayle fled again, this time from France into the Huguenot diaspora, landing in a position at the newly created École Illustre in Rotterdam, the Dutch Republic. In Rotterdam, Bayle wrote some of his most important tomes – those texts others took as evidence for his errant, apathetic, or hostile attitude toward organized religion.[2] Most famous for his *Nouvelles de la république des lettres* and the *Dictionnaire historique et critique*, Bayle's writings proved canonical for eighteenth-century secular rationalists as well as those few overt atheists.[3]

The religion of the Philosopher of Rotterdam, Bayle, is difficult to ascertain, or even to describe in terms conventional to his life. Those who bypass the problem often refer to Bayle as a "Protestant" philosopher or a "Huguenot" exile, defined by his Reformed heritage more than any explicit religious conviction. His debt to the Calvinist intellectual tradition does not necessarily make him a devout Orthodox, just as his challenging Calvinist doctrine and communal performance does not incontrovertibly make him a prototypical atheist. Bayle's true religious beliefs may be undiscoverable, but what we can say for certain is that his intellectual work, tireless erudition, and devotion to skeptical thought denuded the mysteries of more established faiths, moderate or fanatical, and undoubtedly fashioned his own thought. As Richard Popkin correctly noted, Bayle's devotion to study and the systematic exposition of his thought allowed him to maintain an "unemotional religion of the heart."[4] Pierre Jurieu, once Bayle's friend and later his fierce critic, levelled charges of religious "indifferentism" at him in 1687.[5] How did Bayle come to develop such an unemotional, skeptical approach to religion?

The Revocation of the Edict of Nantes and the expulsion of Huguenots like himself produced Bayle's skepticism of religion. Élisabeth Labrousse and the Cambridge School contextualists would point to the traumatic role of the late seventeenth-century confessionalization, the vitriolic, theological debate between Catholic and Protestant, his expulsion from France, the deaths of loved ones he suffered, and the subsequent intellectual community of the Huguenot diaspora. Bayle's understanding of the Huguenot refugees coloured his philosophy moving forward. It proved vital for his questioning of faith and of religious power politics. And Bayle's clashes with the Calvinist theologian Jurieu also fundamentally shaped Bayle's philosophy, as Jurieu stood as a premier example of the by-products of aligning one's politics with one's religion.

French state-sponsored religious oppression led Bayle toward a kind of religious "indifferentism" or an "unemotional religion of the heart," but his philosophy was also the by-product of a volatile period of war and revolution – revolution which for many remained best explained in confessional terms.[6] In 1688, the Dutch stadtholder and Protestant William of Orange overthrew the English Catholic King James II. Many interpreted the English Revolution of 1688 as the result of the same religious divisions that drove the Wars of Religion. Catholics associated the revolutionary violence of the English Revolution with Huguenot theology, and Jurieu, a vocal supporter of William of Orange and the Revolution, only entrenched such associations in Catholic minds.

For many, including Bayle, the English example became a testing ground to imagine politics free from religious fervour and to reflect on the trauma of the Wars of Religion. He rebuked the religious narrative of 1688, disconnecting any kind of religious mentality from political action. While many Huguenots had supported William of Orange, Bayle found a way to cast their actions as purely political. Bayle did this most thoroughly in his *Avis important aux réfugiez*. Published anonymously, but thoroughly proven to have been written by Bayle,[7] the *Avis* controversy encouraged Huguenots to distance themselves from the Williamite

Revolution if they hoped to ever return to France. Bayle represented the Huguenot population as essentially loyal to the French crown. One way he did this was through exploring the political origins of the English Revolution in 1688 as well as the so-called Siamese Revolution of 1688.[8] Bayle used this comparative approach to disentangle religion from revolutionary action altogether, especially since the latter Southeast Asian revolution occurred without the influence of Protestants at all.[9]

While Bayle employed a discussion of revolutions in order to ameliorate the Calvinist political self-image, he also began to imagine a new form of political action – the "secular" revolution. In *Scripting Revolution: A Historical Approach to the Comparative Study of Revolutions*, Keith Michael Baker and Dan Edelstein advance a narratological understanding of modern revolutions.[10] Comparative frameworks of revolution often hinge upon cultural and contextual differences, making it difficult to draw useful parallels; but Baker and Edelstein argue that in 1789, a script of revolutionary change emerged that would be reused and recycled in subsequent revolutions. Revolutionaries, they state, have always been "extremely self-conscious of (and often highly knowledgeable about) how previous revolutions unfolded. These revolutionary scripts offer frameworks for political action."[11] The script that emerged was replete with acts and actors – old regimes and new social orders; learned elites mobilizing masses in the name of high-minded, universal ideals, which, in turn legitimized acts of violence. This internecine conflict sought to level social inequalities but seemed heinously unequal to those who had previously occupied socially privileged positions. And this script was not cast in stone, but instead could be reordered; the details may have been slightly rewritten, but the basic arch of this revolutionary narrative legitimized their actions. For Baker and Edelstein, this script was largely developed in the 1789 revolutionary crucible. The secular element of the modern narrative of revolutions had commenced generations earlier during the *Controverse*, when discourses surrounding revolutionary action were only just starting to take the stage.

Bayle's philosophical position on refugees and revolution reflected a much deeper appreciation for freedom of conscience, an intellectual position he owed to his Calvinist theological upbringing. This attachment to freedom of conscience led Bayle to divorce religious conviction from revolutionary politics, but the same tradition of freedom of conscience led other Protestants at the time, like Jurieu, toward revolutionary millenarianism. It is impossible to divorce the evolution of a secular revolutionary script from the religious contexts of its creation. Alexis de Tocqueville distinguished the French Revolution of 1789 from all preceding political revolutions, noting that it shared more in common with the "religious revolutions" of the sixteenth century.[12] Tocqueville stops at the level of analogy, but work by historians like Carl Becker and Dale Van Kley have teased out the primacy of Christian theology, community, and controversy in their studies of early modern France.[13] Their work challenges the ascendant rise of secular modernity, and by extension those revolutions said to be the crucibles of the modern world, by retraining our attention to the realm of theological debate. Bayle's theology, as difficult as it is to categorize and characterize, owed much to Calvinist freedom of conscience, and by guarding that freedom of conscience he advanced a secular interpretation of revolutionary politics, which could then make room for freedom of religion and also the return of the Huguenot refugees to France.

Caught in the Crossfire of the *Controverse*

From his childhood, Pierre Bayle was torn between the Calvinist and Catholic Churches. He was born in the small French village known then as Carla, since renamed Carla-Bayle to celebrate the hamlet's philosopher. Near the Spanish frontier and in the sight of the Pyrenees Mountains, a Calvinist enclave developed during the sixteenth century. Bayle's father was a Calvinist pastor and as such sent Pierre to a Calvinist school. Later, Bayle moved to the Jesuit college at Toulouse. Engrossed in controversial literature, Bayle soon converted to Catholicism. Not long passed before Bayle became a *rélaps*, an individual who returned to "heresy" following conversion. Such oscillations at such an early age sent Bayle down a dangerous road both in the eyes of the French legal system, which did not look kindly on Calvinist conversion, and in the theological landscape of the *Controverse*, which demanded polarization in the years leading up to the Revocation of the Edict of Nantes in 1685. Bayle weathered the rising storm in Geneva, studying philosophy and theology. In 1674, Bayle returned to France, holding positions as a tutor in Paris and Rouen. In 1675, he took up a professor position at the Protestant Academy of Sedan. He taught at the school until 1681, when the king's *arrêt* closed the school. He moved to Holland and held a position at the École Illustre of Rotterdam, joining the French Calvinist church in the city as well. Soon, his father and brothers died in France in 1684 and 1685, due to the religious persecutions. The intolerance of the Catholic state in France and the deaths of his kin made it impossible for Bayle to make amends with the Catholic tradition and in the process called into question what lingering attachments to Calvinist theology he might have harboured.[14]

The Huguenot diaspora was extensive even by the time that Bayle left for the Netherlands. A first wave of migrants had left France over the course of the sixteenth and seventeenth centuries. They had funnelled out to a crescent of kingdoms where their faith was tolerated – spanning from the Swiss cantons in the south, north through the western German states, into the Netherlands, and across the North Sea to England. They either settled anew in these spaces, founding new religious communities, or used Europe's expanding colonial networks to settle around the Atlantic World. Many of their early experiments in North and South America were faced with continued Catholic violence – often perpetrated by the Spanish or the Portuguese.[15] Huguenots had often used this oceanic space to distance themselves from the French state or to emphasize their economic worth to the French state, but in many ways this increasing connection between Calvinists and mercantile capitalism may have underscored Louis XIV's misunderstanding of the numbers of Calvinists still in the country by the time of the Revocation. A second wave followed in the 1680s, largely as a response to the Revocation of the Edict of Nantes. As few as two hundred thousand Huguenots fled France at the end of the seventeenth century. Estimates vary greatly, with some placing the number closer to one million or more.[16]

Bayle owed much to the toleration of his new home in Rotterdam – a city which had become a multireligious hotspot by the 1680s. Here, Bayle sunk even deeper into the literature of the *Controverse*, especially debates over religious authority, rite, and doctrine. He was especially shaped by those arguments, coming from both Catholic and Calvinist camps, that adopted "arguments from history, essentially secular arguments."[17] Theologians and polemicists shifted away from overt exegetical arguments. They adopted and developed a new religious historiography and historical methodologies to deride their opponents and to verify their faith's claims to absolute truth and Christian authority. Bayle often defended his positions using historical argument, but he also drew from Catholic as well as Calvinist historical writings of the Christian Church, the Reformation, and the Wars of Religion. Holland and the printing industry of Rotterdam and Amsterdam facilitated the anti-Catholic histories of the Huguenot diaspora as well as the religious criticism and philosophical works of Bayle. While dialectical in their confessional agendas, the arguments developed on both sides during the *Controverse* pushed Bayle toward more secular interpretations of religious expression and toleration.[18]

Relative freedom of print made the rigour of the Dutch wing of the *Controverse* possible. It made the debates between Jurieu and Bayle printable. Jurieu's *La Politique du clergé de France*, published anonymously in the Hague in January 1681, offers a prime example. In it, Jurieu presents a dialogue between two Catholics discussing the political motivations behind the persecutions of the French Calvinists and the corrupt nature of the Catholic Church. The text emphasizes the imperfections of humans spoiled by power rather than the temptations of the Devil.[19] Jurieu continued on to defend the loyalty of the Calvinist population. The following year, Louis Maimbourg published *Histoire du calvinisme*, in which he emphasized the anarchical character of the Reformed faith, placing the entirety of the blame for the Wars of Religion on the Calvinist community.[20] Maimbourg's history became the target of Bayle, who published a tract refuting Maimbourg in July 1682. Written in just two weeks' time, Bayle's *Critique générale de l'Histoire du calvinisme de M. Maimbourg* was wildly successful – running through three editions in the following three years.[21] Rejecting Bayle's rather apologetic character, Jurieu responded to the entire debate with his book, titled *Histoire du calvinisme et celle du papisme mises en parallèle*. Jurieu took Maimbourg to task for every point and flipped the confessional script, exposing the faults of the Roman Catholic tradition.[22] While both Bayle and

Jurieu opposed Maimbourg's history, they differed in the political message of their respective works. Bayle emphasized the need for Calvinists to atone for their part in the religious violence in order to set a precedent for religious toleration; whereas Jurieu continued to lambaste Catholics as perfect examples of persecutors driven by profane considerations rather than sacred ones.

Jurieu's developing apocalyptic world view and vision of the English Revolution further divided the Huguenot camp and drove Bayle to adopt an indifferent position on religion. As Hubert Bost notes, "the eschatological theories of Jurieu worsened a situation that was already deleterious."[23] In the Revocation, Jurieu believed he had decoded a chronology for the Apocalypse, which drew on Saint Augustine's *The City of God.* Despite opposition within the Huguenot refugee and Walloon church in Rotterdam, Jurieu continued to push his apocalyptic prophecy in his *Lettres pastorales.* Published every two weeks between 1686 and 1689 – the year of the supposed end of times – Jurieu's *Lettres* recorded and spread the news of Calvinist sufferings in France. The Glorious Revolution in England affirmed Jurieu's prophecy. James II's coronation as a Catholic in a Protestant country confirmed the corruption of the Catholic Church and their eternal pursuit of power. William of Orange, a Protestant, was crowned the king of England three and a half years after the Revocation of the Edict of Nantes, validating Jurieu's apocalyptical calculations. For Jurieu, William was the instrument of God's divine will – the "anti-Louis XIV." Jurieu was not the only Huguenot to risk this explicit political theology. Others readily identified the Pope as the Antichrist, William of Orange as the Saviour, and England as the Promised Land.[24] Antoine Arnauld had compared the king of England to Absalom, who took vengeance on his evil relative. William became a new David – an "envoy of God."[25] The biblical metaphors further reified the particularist character of the Huguenot population in the political narratives of the latter half of the seventeenth century. For Jurieu, Huguenots were the chosen ones, the refugees, and their participation in the English Revolution of 1688 was predetermined by God. Other Huguenot leaders – like Élie Benoît and La Combe de Vrigny – did not share the same theological bent as Jurieu, but they did agree that the time to strike the Huguenot militant iron was upon them. Huguenot ministers Gédéon Huet, Isaac Jaquelot, and Jacques Basnage and the jurist Henri Basnage de Beauval also rejected the bellicosity of Jurieu in favour of Bayle's call to temper the Huguenot support of the English Revolution.[26] For Bayle, who did not hold back his pen, Jurieu's millenarianism would certainly seal the Huguenot diaspora's fate, cutting off any chance the Bourbon throne would welcome them back. Bayle was not alone.

In many ways, it makes sense to think of Bayle and Jurieu as complete opposites. Jurieu and Bayle had been colleagues and friendly at the Academy in the Sedan, but the tumult of entering the Huguenot diaspora, Bayle's growing disenchantment with religion or at least his willingness to criticize millenarian thought, and Jurieu's radicalization and early prophecies made the two bitter opponents. Bayle, the Philosopher of Rotterdam, and Jurieu, the Theologian of Rotterdam, became intellectual rivals after taking up positions at the École Illustre. Bayle became known for his unemotional exposition, whereas Jurieu made his name with his flair, force, and pension for histrionics. Both men engaged with the *Controverse* community through polemics, targeting Catholics like Arnauld, Maimbourg, and Bossuet as well as their coreligionists such as Leclerc, Jaquelot, and Pajou. Both came to their respective positions after facing the persecutory storm of Louis XIV and those Catholics who sought to deride the Calvinist Church through historical polemics. Jurieu chose to meet polemic with polemic, whereas Bayle sought to diffuse the impact of the Glorious Revolution of 1688 on Huguenots' politics after the Revocation by insisting that Huguenots played a limited role.

For many Catholic controversialists, 1688 reeked of the history of the Wars of Religion. Anarchical Protestants, driven to destruction by freedom of conscience – the inevitable end of their theological encounter with the political world – ripped the rightful king from his throne and propped up a false idol, like all those false preachers of the Reformation era. It was common to associate Protestantism with violent social and political upheaval from the Catholic camp. Varillas, a member of the Bibliothèque du Roi and at one time the official historian of the Duke of Orléans, received a royal pension and wrote a number of so-called secular histories of Francois I, Charles V, and Anne of Austria. After losing his pension, Varillas sought assistance from the Assembly of the Clergy, who promised funds on the condition that he produce histories of heresy, following the success of individuals like the Jansenist Pierre Nicole. Varillas produced two books post-haste in the 1680s: *Histoire de l'hérésie de Viclef, Jean Hus, et Jerome de Prague* (1682) and *Histoire des révolutions arrivées dans l'Europe en matière de religion* (1686–88). Celebrated by some as the "Hero of True History," others emphasized his lax standards and loose relationship with historical realities.[27] Voltaire later referred to Varillas as a "noble author" who "took the greatest liberties" with his subject.[28]

Varillas was one of the earliest authors of a "revolutionary script." He detailed the complex plot that culminated in the Protestant Reformation. His historical narrative reads more like a novel, replete with morally deprived characters and secret societies. A cabal of insidious men, seeking their own gain, plotted the downfall of the Church and the state. Under the reign of Francois II, these *comploteurs* sought to overthrow the regime through a "concerted and secret conspiracy." These individuals, under the cloak of darkness, met to raise false idols – mortal men, like the Czech martyr Jan Hus. Hussites convened in Prague to swear oaths in the name of their fallen leader, soon dissembling under a guise of Crusaders against superstition and idolatry.[29] As such, they manoeuvred into places of prestige and social prominence. From there, they cast aspersions on the most sacred elements of Catholic dogma, in favour of their own interpretations of religious doctrine. They took advantage of the openness of Francois I, the great patron of the arts and letters. Soon those of weak resolve and intellectual ineptitude turned their backs on the universal Catholic religion and pursued modes of social upheaval. The English Revolution only seemed to evidence these claims for many Catholics. Similar, albeit much tempered, accounts of Protestant violence pervaded the Catholic side of the *Controverse*. Pierre Arnauld, Louis Maimbourg, and Jacques-Bénigne Bossuet, as well as other Catholics, harnessed this same style narrative; such a narrative, in many ways, remained as a kind of Counter Enlightenment staple, on which Darrin McMahon has written.[30]

Both Huguenots and Catholics imagined a kind of Protestant particularism. Religion was the premier identity, a kind of base from which all actions could be understood. For Bayle, this particularism forced him to consider universal principles, which could unite all religions or, for his more atheistic tendencies, tear them all down. Increasingly, from within the Huguenot community, debates emerged which depicted religion as a category – as capacious enough to include multiple religious communities and systems of belief – rather than a claim to absolute truth.[31] It was at this moment in the early modern period that the Reformed was replaced by the revolutionary, both in Protestant and Catholic camps, just as the *Controverse* saw exegetical analyses wane and secular histories rise. The revolutionary "script" Bayle came to write would be free from scripture and thus allowed him to bolster his so-called indifferentism and his unemotional examination of faith, as well as make the case for the return of Huguenots to France.

Bayle's Advice to Huguenot Refugees

In 1690, Bayle anonymously published *Avis important aux réfugiez* – a prescriptive text written in the hopes of returning Huguenots to France following the Revocation (1685).[32] Authored under the pseudonym Monsieur C.L.A.A.P.D.P.[33] and published by the fake publisher Jacques le Censeur, Bayle chose to self-identify as a recently converted Catholic in France. Such a position – as a "*nouveau converti*" – would have simultaneously lent him credence, at least on the titular level, with the Reformed community and with the Catholic French king. His pamphlet condemned outright the anti-Catholic, anti-monarchical tirades of the Huguenot population as well as the recent adoption of popular sovereignty as a political principle by leaders like Jurieu. Huguenots mobilized the latter ideology to support William of Orange, and thus to indelibly link their community to the English Revolution, but it was also being used to bolster a brand of republicanism, which appeared to Bayle more opportunism than strategic choice. The titular advice of Bayle, then, was for the *réfugies* to reject the Glorious Revolution, those errant expressions of republican sentiment, and to strengthen their resolve in the French king, who would recognize their loyalty and invite them back to the country.

In the wake of the English Revolution, a number of opprobrious and libelous pamphlets emerged in opposition to William of Orange. In February 1689, the anonymous *Réponse d'un nouveau converti à la lettre d'un réfugié* caused the greatest stir. Likely authored by Bayle, the *Réponse* anticipated many of the themes of the *Avis* – including the injurious nature of the Huguenot's alliance with those leading the "present invasion of England."[34] Bayle reminded his readers in the *Réponse* and in the *Avis*, specifically those Huguenot supporters of William, that any attempt to justify violence on behalf of their faith or even of future religious toleration would prove the double-edged sword. Either rulers would view Huguenots as entrenched in their violent ways and use such arguments to further religious violence or would undoubtedly be taken up at a later date by Catholics in Protestant kingdoms to unseat Protestant kings.

Bayle never acknowledged authorship of the *Réponse d'un nouveau converti* or the *Avis*. He attributed the former text to Paul Pellisson-Fontanier, the French author who had famously abjured Calvinism and converted to Catholicism in 1670. After Jurieu embroiled Bayle in public controversy over his authorship of the *Avis*, Bayle further dissimulated and insisted that the author was Pellisson-Fontanier or perhaps Daniel de Larroque, the Calvinist pastor who returned to France in the 1690s and also adjured his faith. Bayle had several options as the diaspora and its displacement had begun to take its toll on the Huguenot intellectual elite, forcing many to convert and return to France. Bayle's own history of adjurement and position within the community in Rotterdam made him keenly aware of the precarious path many French Protestants confronted when faced with the state's persecution.[35] Even after his death, Jacques Basnage continued to defend Bayle against defamation. But it is also worth noting that Bayle's use of anonymity underscored the real danger and active controversy that still fuelled the *Controverse*. It was within this chrysalis that Bayle developed his unemotional heart and religious skepticism. It was also this culture that forced him to reconceive revolutionary action as secular and separate from the Protestant *mentalité* that many Catholics insisted linked the Reformed to all forms of anarchical violence.

Bayle faced a puzzle created by the reaction to his polemic. How could he defend a position of nonintervention (clearly stated in the

Avis), while maintaining that he was not the author of the position? The answer came in the form of discrediting Jurieu's argument and apocalyptic viewpoint. That Jurieu was the target of this anonymous, supposed *nouveau converti* is certain. From his position in Rotterdam, Bayle would have easily faced Jurieu's millenarianism. In the text of the 1692 second edition of the *Avis*, he forcefully wrote: "The year 1689 has come to a close without so much as a memorable event. You promised us bells and whistles in that year; that the Catholic Church would face its demise, especially in France; that one would only see … miraculous revolutions, and all that, in a word, would [make 1689] the most climatic year in world history … the year 1689 has not fulfilled your predictions."[36] For Bayle, the English Revolution was an example of the general dynastic war that had embroiled Europe for a millennium. It was not the embodiment of any divine intervention marking the Apocalypse. Bayle used the word *revolution* repeatedly in his *Avis*, so what is notable here is the adjective "miraculous," which was intended to take aim at the religious significance of the event that Jurieu claimed. Bayle noted in the same section that the rhetoric employed by those millenarian preachers only served to enflame the "prejudices" and the "superstitions of the masses," as well as to play upon the "population's credulity."[37]

Bayle sought to right the misinformation of the Protestant millenarians by emphasizing that such a misstep would forever close the road back to France. Satire – the "fake news" of the seventeenth-century *Controverse* – only entrenched Louis XIV's resolve in his Revocation.

> Allow me to warn … those refugees in various countries: it is necessary to quarantine yourselves before setting foot in France, in order to purify yourselves of the bad air which you have breathed in the places of your exile and which has infected you with two very dangerous and quite odious diseases: one is the spirit of satire, the other a certain republican spirit which introduces anarchy into the world, the greatest scourge of civil society. Here are two points on which I take the liberty of speaking to you as a friend.[38]

Such was a rebuke of Jurieu's political theology, but it also strongly resembled the anti-Huguenot political rhetoric of the *Controverse* period as well. As Mara van der Lugt emphasizes, Bayle's position on the apocalyptic, pro-revolutionary positions of Jurieu owed greatly to his developing abhorrence for violence in general.[39] In this volume, he encourages Huguenots to withdraw their support from William and the Glorious Revolution of 1688, and specifically to abandon the notion of popular sovereignty that John Locke and others used to justify revolutionary action.

Implicit in this call, then, was his rebuke of the common Catholic narrative of the time that Protestant freedom of conscience led to anarchy and revolutionary violence. While doing this, Bayle "secularized" the revolutionary experience and further developed his own skepticism. In his 1692 edition of the *Avis*, Bayle added a curious discussion of the 1688 Revolution in Siam, wherein the Buddhist military leadership overthrew the king who had fostered a kind of Catholic diplomacy with France, French Jesuits, and the papacy. The distinguishing feature of the Siamese Revolution– or at least the element that was most important to Bayle – was the *absence* of Protestant actors. If a revolution could happen without the Reformed, then Catholic claims concerning the Reformed's connection to revolution could not stand.

The so-called Siamese Revolution of 1688 was worlds away, but reports, letters, and books on the incident soon came to Rotterdam.[40] Bayle certainly never came into contact with any of these revolutionaries; Bayle's encounter with the revolution was secondhand. In a letter written to the prolific epistolary writer Abbé Claude Nicaise at the end of October 1691, Bayle indicated that Pierre-Joseph d'Orléans's *Histoire de M. Constance, premier ministre du roi de Siam, et de la dernière révolution de cet état* had recently been republished in Rotterdam.[41] D'Orléans was a Jesuit priest, preacher, and historian, trained in Paris, Tours, and La Flèche in the late 1660s and early 1670s.[42] Like many in France, d'Orléans was fascinated with the 1688 Revolution in Siam, the letters of Father Guy Tachard,[43] and the career of Constantine Phaulkon, a Greek traveller, counsellor to King Narai of Ayutthaya, translator, and interlocutor between the Thai and French powers.

Phaulkon was executed in 1688 for "treason" – or so said those driving the coup against the French-allied king. D'Orléans martyrized Phaulkon for facilitating French trade in southeast Asia. By 1690, the Jesuit Marcel Le Blanc and a number of military officers produced firsthand accounts of the disaster, noting the role of the Jesuits in the revolutionary machinations, and in the years to come, the situation of the Jesuits in France became uneasy.[44] It is unclear if Bayle was aware of these critical Jesuit remarks as early as 1690, but what is certain is that by the second edition of the *Avis* in 1692, he saw in the 1688 revolution in Thailand a chance to untangle religious and political narratives of revolution and fundamentally alter French perceptions of Huguenots and the English Revolution.

In sum, Bayle's reflections on revolution assert three basic points. First, he rebuked implicitly the Catholic narrative about the Protestant propensity for revolutionary rupture while at the same time admonishing Protestant thinkers like Jurieu who prophesied revolutionary action as a sign of the Apocalypse. Bayle's *Avis* disconnected religion from politics and in the process reduced the image of the Glorious Revolution as well, noting that "the year 1689 ended, without … any great crises or *miraculous* revolutions."[45] This all incensed Jurieu, who in 1691 revealed Bayle as the author of the *Avis* and simultaneously denounced him as an enemy of the Calvinist faith and the Dutch Republic. Jurieu went so far as to insist that Bayle must have been in league with Louis XIV and his secret cabal meant to undermine the diaspora community.[46] Bayle did not let such slight go without vitriolic response. In general, Bayle's take on the English Revolution drew out, as Walter Rex has noted, "the conflict of loyalty haunting the *réfugiés*: could they somehow be loyal to the leaders of both their old and new fatherlands, even if those leaders were at war with each other, or should they take sides."[47]

Second, Bayle insisted that the example of the Siamese Revolution did not mean that Catholicism was an inherently violent faith either. For Bayle, the religious question is cursory in comparison to the question of established power. Bayle lamented the persecutions that the French faced in Thailand, but most crucially, he noted that the King's dethronement owed more to his adoption of new ideas in general than Catholic ideas specifically. Power politics were at play in Thailand, just as they were in England. Bayle resisted the urge to place blame, as other Huguenot polemicists may have done, for revolutionary violence at the feet of Catholicism. Instead, Bayle further lamented the hyperbolic claims of the Jesuits who portended the "extinction of the Christian religion in the Siamese kingdom," if not in the wider "Eastern" world, by pointing to the relations that Jesuits maintained in China and throughout Europe.[48]

Third, and building on the first two, Bayle disconnected religion altogether from revolutionary violence, imagining an areligious, essentially political phenomenon, which in turn precipitated the notion of the secular revolutionary script – sans scripture. Since revolutionary violence should be understood in areligious terms, according to Bayle, then the state should be understood in secular terms. Bayle emphasized the supremacy of temporal authority over all religious parties. In doing so, Bayle engaged in subterfuge against papal authority as well as the imagined *corpus christianum*, or the unity of church and state often referenced during the medieval period that Jurieu hoped to revive. Bayle was hardly the only one to make the case for the predominance of the secular state, and in many ways it was a natural response to the religious-coloured violence of the seventeenth century. Locke agreed with Bayle and in his *A Letter Concerning Toleration* noted:

> [T]here is absolutely no such thing under the Gospel as a Christian commonwealth. There are, indeed, many kingdoms and cities that have embraced the faith of Christ. But they have retained and preserved their ancient forms of government, with which the law of Christ hasn't at all meddled. Christ taught men how, by faith and good works, they may attain eternal life. But he instituted no commonwealth; he prescribed no new form of government peculiar to his followers; nor did he put the sword into any magistrate's hand with the commission to make use of it to force men to abandon their former religion and receive his.[49]

Locke, completely aware of the anti-Protestant policies of Louis XIV, took a chance to slight the French regime; whereas Bayle promoted secular state power in order to subvert any "Huguenot Pope" or authority, who had wrought more damage to sovereigns around Europe since the Reformation than the Catholic pontiff had.[50]

Revolutionary Intolerance, Enlightenment Toleration

Bayle's reflections on the English Revolution and the revolution in Siam underscore a shift in revolutionary rhetoric of the early modern period. But they also help us appreciate the sheer complexity of Baylean politics pertaining to the refugee community. Bayle denounced the Protestant particularism imagined by Catholics – who emphasized the revolutionary and anarchical spirit of Protestants. Catholics portended the end of the sacral absolutist regime in France, and in a way they imagined the "disenchantment of the world" that is often attributed to the later Enlightenment period.[51] To what extent did religious ideals prefigure political, economic, and social behaviours, like the impetus to revolt against established, hierarchical power, whether within the Church or the polity? For his Catholic, virulent contemporaries, the Reformed faith's focus on freedom of conscience necessarily bred anarchy, licentiousness, greed, clannishness, and republicanism. These Calvinist cultural connotations proved to be the fodder for Louis XIV's continued persecution of the French Calvinist population over the course of the seventeenth century and well into the eighteenth. For many Catholics, the Glorious Revolution of 1688 only proved what Catholics had been saying in their controversialist diatribes. Many Huguenot leaders in exile, like Jurieu, seemed to prove such formulas by linking the Huguenot cause to the Dutch Williamite ascendency in Britain. Yet in many ways, the Catholic anti-Protestant script imagined a future that Bayle found preferable – one in which religion's influence over politics and society dwindled, or even dissipated. Most French revolutionaries and their later historians largely imagined the origins of the French Revolution as free from religion.[52] The year 1789 saw the birth of the secular state, but this secular script of revolution began much earlier in the context of the *Controverse.*

Bayle juxtaposed revolutions in England and Siam and, in the process, began to craft new understandings of revolutionary change. The English

Revolution of 1688, the Siamese Revolution of 1688, and "revolutions" as political acts were significant to Bayle's philosophy and were inseparable from his refugee politics. Bayle's focus on religious toleration, skeptical thought, and early encyclopedist work are often the focus of Baylean scholarship. His thoughts on the English Revolution have been little studied. The religious character of political actions at the end of the seventeenth century appeared as a Gordian knot. The harder one pulled on one end of the conceptual Christian string to prove the righteous character of their respective group, the tighter the knot became. It was left to Bayle to cut the conceptual knot – imagining the Revocation of the Edict of Nantes and the Glorious Revolutions of 1688 as political problems to be understood free from scriptural consideration. By cutting the knot, Bayle hoped to free the Huguenot population from the constraints of the louisquatorzean state, the memory of the violence of the Wars of Religion, and the *Controverse*.

Bayle also figured into a genealogy of Huguenot intellectuals in the diaspora, whose refugee background in a Dutch Republic, intertwined with the seventeenth-century English revolutionary tradition, radicalized their thought. Such an argument has been made forcefully by Margaret Jacobs and rather haphazardly by Jonathan Israel.[53] Bayle insisted that Huguenots remain loyal to the French Regime and to the absolutist throne, a line upon which many of the leading French philosophes would later insist. Yet many Huguenots did not follow Bayle's lead; instead, French Huguenots like Jean Rousset de Missy found in the English Revolution and those early Calvinist leaders like Jurieu a spark that would lead them to rail against the French crown.[54] What many nineteenth-century historians often argued, and what Andrew Jainchill has recently restated, is that these Huguenots established a revolutionary, often republican, intellectual tradition that eroded the power of the French state.[55] A focus on Bayle's *Avis* reveals the fractures within the Huguenot diaspora on the place of Protestantism within the early revolutionary tradition. These fractures continued to characterize the Huguenot leadership, eroded over time, as generations of Huguenots sought assimilation into their homelands as opposed to return to France.

Caught in the thick of these Protestant-Catholic debates, in the precarious position of the Huguenot diaspora and facing a future further coloured by the Protestant Williamite Revolution of the English state, Bayle continued his spiritual journey, which had begun decades earlier in southern France. Many historians now explore the ways that Christianity and Christian theology acted as a "chrysalis of modernity," capable of carrying subversive ideas into the conservative echelons of European society, and laying the ground for revolutionary action.[56] If Bayle were to interject in this long historiography, he would undoubtedly tow the secular line, emphasizing how power politics determined revolutions, instead of religious particularism as was often the grist of seventeenth-century polemics. His rhetorical approach and skeptical philosophy were the by-product of a period of intense religious and political exchange, as well as persecutions in the Age of Louis XIV and the Revocation of the Edict of Nantes. His stance and these debates informed the development of revolutionary rhetoric from the Enlightenment forward.

Bayle's works represented and inspired Calvinist leaders to distance themselves from the prophecies of theologians like Jurieu or lay preachers in southern France who played a significant role in the Camisard Wars. In distancing Huguenots from revolutionary violence, Bayle set the stage for later Huguenots to insist against their supposedly unchecked freedom of conscience and individualism, in favour of emphasizing the collective. The writings and speeches of pastors like Antoine Court and Rabaut Saint-Étienne, which are explored in the next two chapters, follow Bayle's lead to a greater extent than Jurieu's, even if both Huguenot leaders held more staunchly to their religious doctrine and identity. Both emphasized the Huguenot population's connection to their own communities as well as to the kingdom. These communities united Huguenots. Sentiment, as it developed in the Protestant Enlightenment of the eighteenth century, would provide yet another pole for Huguenots to tether themselves to in order to resist the polemical pull of the Catholic Church's anti-Huguenot individualism.

4

Enlightenment Patriot: *Antoine Court*

From his refuge in Lausanne, Switzerland, Antoine Court "dissipated the untoward storm" of Huguenot persecution[1] and nearly "at the very time that Louis XIV was lying on his death-bed at Versailles ... conceived the idea of reviving the pastorate, and restoring the proscribed Protestant Church of France."[2] Court was often the target of historical paeans.[3] His efforts to rebuild the Church of the *Désert*, or the Calvinist community in France, appear even greater when considering that his parents were peasants in the Villeneuve-de-Berg in Languedoc, unlike Jurieu or Bayle, whose fathers were both Calvinist ministers. Court became a refugee in the late 1720s only when a hefty bounty was placed on his head. From his refuge in Switzerland, he worked to sustain and rebuild the Calvinist community in France and its connections with the wider Huguenot refuge.

Court cut his teeth in the clandestine meetings of Calvinists held in quarries, in rural barns, and in the natural temples of the forests, which provided refuge within France. Indeed, it was Court who organized underground Calvinist revivals in the south of France during the Bourbon Regency following Louis XIV's death in 1715. It was Court who pushed back against those within the Calvinist sect that had taken to prophesying and inciting violence in southern France. From 1702 to 1704, outright guerrilla war between Calvinists, Catholics, and the king's forces wreaked havoc on the countryside. The revolt finally ended in 1715 after years of sporadic conflict. The actions of the Camisard "rebels" appalled Court; he saw them as undermining his vision of a theologically and politically uniform, as well as moderate, French Protestant creed.[4] For Court, the Calvinist faith needed to be viewed as moderate and rational as opposed to fanatical and violent.

Court was merely one leader in a network ranging from Geneva to the United Provinces to Great Britain, Sweden, and Denmark, all of whom bore some responsibility and are owed some acknowledgment for reconstructing the Reformed Church in France and on France's frontiers.[5] This Protestant international – stretching from England through the Netherlands, along the Franco-German frontier, south through Switzerland, and then west into southern France – fostered an epistolary, ecclesiastical, and publishing network. This web of Huguenots in the diaspora and in France also fostered a European Protestant Enlightenment, which mobilized reason and eventually sentiment to promote religious toleration and end the sectarian conflict of the late seventeenth and early eighteenth centuries. If we take J.G.A. Pocock's definition of the Enlightenment as a "series of programs for reducing the power of either churches or congregations to disturb the peace of civil society by challenging its authority," then we must include individuals like Antoine Court who fought from France's frontiers for toleration and the reestablishment of the Church of the *Désert*.[6]

Court's Protestant Enlightenment was not disconnected from the broader French Enlightenment, and indeed, his use of patriotism coincided with increasing references to the *patrie* in eighteenth-century France. Court, like Jurieu and Bayle before him, attempted to navigate the complex identity politics at work in eighteenth-century France and the Huguenot diaspora within his apologetical writings. Court mobilized the refugee identity cemented by Brousson, Jurieu, and Bayle in the late seventeenth century, as well as the metaphorical *Désert*, when promoting religious toleration in his publications. He published for the literate bourgeois public sphere. He educated successive generations of Calvinist pastors to return to France under the cloak of darkness, including Rabaut Saint-Étienne, the subject of the following chapter. While he never won the sponsorship of the French state during his lifetime, many of the arguments he made for religious toleration would find their way into the 1787 Edict of Toleration and the early French Revolution's promotion of religious tolerance.[7]

Court's Protestant Enlightenment, which sought state support, also presented a vision of the state that was conducive to Huguenot inclusion, much like other religious Enlightenment thinkers had proposed in Berlin, Vienna, and London.[8] Michael Sauter has argued the French public sphere and the more anticlerical Enlightenment in France that it fostered was "the outlier" rather than the "archetype." He argues that the Prussian public sphere and the Enlightenment in Prussia as in other European countries fostered a model of state-led religious toleration, accomplished through piecemeal legislation rather than Voltairean calls to *écrasez l'infâme* ("crush the infamy," meaning the source of irrationality, namely religion) that were far more common in the French model.[9] By focusing on Court, it becomes clear that the French Enlightenment was neither a monolith nor hermetically sealed. Court penetrated the French Enlightenment, drew upon its discourse, and translated the hidden transcript of the Huguenot diaspora and *Désert* into arguments capable of fostering the reconstruction of the Calvinist Church of the *Désert* and courting tolerance in France.[10] The threat of persecution that Huguenots faced in France meant that they usually evaded any recognition of wrongdoing, in favour of laudatory overtures to the King's good graces. In order to establish religious toleration, Court believed that Huguenots needed to reconstruct their communities, which required the diagnosing of those ills that plagued their congregations, inflamed passions, and led to bloodshed, and then also necessitated the offering of a remedy. The cure, according to Court, was the reestablishment of Calvinist orthodoxy in France.

Court's use of patriotism in his writings on the Calvinist population was an extension of his pursuit to rebuild the French Calvinist community after the Revocation and to subdue those Calvinists prophesying and engaging in sectarian violence. In his pursuits, Court articulated what was an anti-individualist ideology of patriotism. This is surprising for those familiar with Protestant claims to freedom of conscience, which is often read as an expression of early modern individualism, or as a variant of emergent discourses of individual rights. As Charly Coleman argues, anti-individualist strains of Enlightenment actively countered claims of enlightened reason.[11] For Court, anti-individualism countered Catholic arguments of errant Protestant individualism, especially as they manifested in Calvinist republicanism (a cover-up for Calvinist anarchism) and business acumen (read as greed by Catholics). Anti-individualism also served as a basis for insisting that Calvinists could be a part of a larger community, like that of the French nation.

This chapter focuses on four of Court's most important works: *Apologie des protestans du royaume de France sur leurs assemblées religieuses* (1745), *Le patriote français et impartial* (1751), *Lettre d'un patriote sur la tolérance civile des protestans de France* (1756), and his three-volume *Histoire des troubles des Cévennes* (1760). The provenance of *Le lettre d'un patriote* is difficult to substantiate. It is possible that Court may have only had a hand in its creation, or no involvement at all. For certain, someone in the Huguenot diasporal leadership authored the piece and managed to parrot many of the critical points Court made in *Le patriote français et impartial.* Such is the hazard of working with anonymously published works by refugee and persecuted communities. Where possible, I have included citations to both texts for key arguments.[12] Each work reflects Court's adoption of refugee rhetoric in ways that witness the intellectual impact of Jurieu and Bayle on subsequent Calvinist leaders, and new arguments Court chose to promote. Like Bayle, Court believed direct confrontation with the French monarchy would only deepen the chasm between Catholic state and Calvinist Church. Unlike Bayle, Court chose not to emphasize the power of individual conscience that he recognized as the seed for most anti-Calvinist arguments made by Catholics. Instead he emphasized the power of the collective body of the Calvinist Church through which Calvinists could establish themselves, tame their communities' more violent impulses, fashion their fealty to the king anew, and promote the return of Huguenot refugees to France.

Fashioning Court: Rebuilding French Calvinism in the *Désert*

While Court's educational and organizational efforts to reconstruct the Calvinist community in the south of France have been the subject of several studies, fewer historians have analyzed his writings in light of the larger Enlightenment. Court emphasized a loyal, industrious, and peaceful image of Calvinists while de-emphasizing the republican, individualistic, and violent character of the Protestant population. In the process, he promoted a type of moderate Calvinism, which balanced the importance of revelation with reason. He played a significant role in the larger Protestant Enlightenment taking place during the *Désert* period.

In August 1715, a clandestine National Synod convened in an old quarry outside of Nîmes, where Court proposed a complete overhaul of Calvinist Church structure. He called for open-air services, the re-creation of consistories and synods (by which means the population might be effectively policed), and the replacement of inexperienced pastors, especially the lay leaders, known as *prédicants* who had guided communities in the absence of trained pastors with thoroughly educated ministers. For Court, the fate of the Huguenot Church depended on rebalancing the community divided between those faithful Calvinists practicing in private and those intoxicated with inspiration and driven to sectarian conflict. Court believed the best antidote to the latter was to embolden the former, who might also serve as a vehicle to bring those new converts (i.e., Calvinists recently converted to Catholicism) back into the Calvinist Church.

Court had firsthand experience preaching in these clandestine settings – both the good and the bad. As a young child, like so many Calvinist children after the Revocation, Court had been forced to attend a Jesuit school, but was teased by his fellow classmates for being the son of Huguenots. His mother, a resolute Calvinist by Court's accounts, allowed Court to attend clandestine meetings, where he was emboldened to become a pastor. It was in these meetings that he first encountered the "mystical inspiration" that he would spend much of his adulthood combatting. Court's mother and many female friends practiced prophecy. Like Jurieu's efforts in the Netherlands to assuage persecuted Huguenots, prophetesses sustained many Huguenot communities in the wake of the Revocation in southern France.[13] Despite this, it came out in Court's work that women preachers were particularly grating for him. In 1715, the members of the first synod explicitly aimed to "defend against women preaching in the future."[14] Access to books and recognized, educated ministers were needed to combat women's and lay people's would-be errant beliefs, but Court faced one significant problem.

The pursuit of legitimacy in a time of disciplinary dissolution consumed Court. How could he receive his ordination without an ecclesiastical structure in place to decide such matters? In order to combat the prophetism of his peers, he needed his authority to be recognized, and yet he had received no formal ordination. Court and two of his friends, Corteiz and Bonbonnoux, went to Geneva to ask Benedict Pictet if the members of the 1715 synod had the ability to administer sacraments. Pictet encouraged them to do so as their church was without a minister and needed to appoint one. Corteiz had been ordinated in Zurich and therefore took it upon himself to ordinate Court. Pastor Jacques Basnage urged Calvinists throughout southern France to avoid these large outdoor worship sessions.[15] In 1724, the Bourbon throne outlawed such secret meetings and placed a price on Court's head. Soon the men established synods in Dauphiné, Vivarais, and Languedoc again – at least until 1726, the year of the National Synod.

Court's efforts to legitimate himself through his contacts in Geneva proved fortuitous. When he needed to flee France in 1729, with a bounty on his head, the network of Calvinist pastors in Geneva aided his escape and ultimately helped him get established at the seminary in Lausanne. Geneva seemed like the obvious place for Court to secure refuge, but the "Protestant Rome"[16] was ever vigilant not to upset its French neighbours. While they were wary of explicitly supporting the Church of the Désert, the Vénérable Compagnie des Pasteurs formed an important part of Court's support network, as did the secret Genevan Committee for French Protestantism founded three years earlier in 1726.[17] Through Geneva, funds were collected for the seminary in Lausanne, which was situated just beyond France's frontiers and controlled by the government in Bern, who held greater power in the region and proved less wary of upsetting the French crown. Students at Court's school received theological training and came into contact with some of the most innovative religious thinkers of the time – Newton's friend Jean-Alphonse Turrettini and Antoine-Noë Polier de Bottens, later contributor to the *Encyclopédie*, to name a few. For the remainder of Court's life, he concentrated on the education of pastors, many of whom crossed the border to preach illegally to the remaining incognito Calvinists in France.[18]

From Lausanne, Court trained new generations of ministers, but he also built a position of authority from which he could speak to larger political concerns. Court corresponded with Huguenots positioned throughout the diaspora, and many of their letters revolved around the state of the Reformed in France and the Bourbon's continued persecution of the benighted population. Between 1718 and 1755, Court exchanged five thousand letters, many of them political in nature.[19] The early 1740s witnessed an increased preoccupation with the War of Austrian Succession (1744–48), which many Huguenots interpreted as a possible opening to sway the Bourbon monarchy into considering toleration measures. Most of Court's Calvinist confidants agreed with the Baylean rejection of armed resistance, but differed on the more public manifestations of their faith and how such public gatherings for worship would be interpreted as an extreme transgression against the French sacral state. Distilled to its core, the issue split Huguenots between those on the one side who encouraged private worship (as did Basnage) and the intentional effacement of the Protestants from the public sphere, and those on the other who insisted on public assemblies for the health of the Calvinist community and as a means to police dissenting Protestant positions that might flare into sectarian conflict.

In 1745, Court set to work on his *Apologie*.[20] The preceding year had been calm as royal troops had been busy fighting the War of Austrian Succession, but in 1745, many had returned to hunting down Calvinist assemblies, sending participants to the galleys and prisons. Court's apologia was controversial in Huguenot circles, and they actively debated the tone Court should take, the place of publication elsewhere in Europe, and even whether Court should conceal himself in anonymity

– a common tactic taken in the refuge.[21] For the pastor at Cassel, Rochemont's Calvinist tract would be viewed not as expression of religion, but as an explicit political act, because for some at court, the Protestants were seen "not as Christians of a different sect or opinion from the Papists, but as a political party that could threaten the State."[22] Yet in his position of authority amongst the refuge pastors, Court did not back down from the politics of religion, as noted in the first draft of the *Apologie* he had sent to the London minister Jacques Serces: "One ought to fear a zeal that believes that everything is permitted and that believes it is rendering service to God by doing harm to those which it believes are heretics. One should fear this in a commander, in an intendant, in a subdelegate, in a bishop, and in a simple village priest. It is a false zeal which creates fanaticism and revolt, or the so-called war of the Camisards, which has such terrible results."[23] What emerged in the final published version of Court's *Apologie* reflected a middle ground between Court's polemical predilections and those who wanted simple, humble descriptions of the Calvinist community as it continued to exist in southern France. Such a middle ground meant that Court could forcefully make the case for the reconstruction of the Calvinist Church in France, while not painting a target on the backs of those still under threat of persecution.

Court was not the only strident Calvinist defender of the *Désert* Church. Three years after the publication of Court's *Apologie*, Laurent Angliviel la Beaumelle published his *L'Asiatique tolerant* (1748), drawing inspiration from Montesquieu's *Lettres persanes* (1721) to use a fictional Asian kingdom as a cipher for discussing the natural inclinations of people toward religious toleration.[24] Beaumelle had joined the Reformed in 1744 and in 1745 moved to Geneva. Two years later, he left for Denmark, making valuable connections with Huguenot publishers in the Netherlands. He soon became a professor of French literature at the University of Copenhagen and even attended the Prussian court at the same time as Voltaire. Early modern orientalism was often employed to promote toleration, as Pierre Bayle did with the Siamese Revolution of 1688. Similarly, the Huguenot publisher Jean Frederic Bernard and Huguenot engraver Bernard Picart produced *Cérémonies et coutumes religieuses de tous les peoples du monde* from 1723 to 1737. Bernard's family had been expelled from France in the years following the Revocation. Born in Paris, Picart later moved to the Netherlands and converted. Their volume catalogued the history of world religions. The volumes covered the origins of Judaism, Catholicism, Amerindian, and East and South Asian religions, and religions in Asia and Africa, before discussing the historical developments within Islam and Protestantism. Their work "sowed the radical idea that religions could be compared on equal terms, and therefore that all religions were equally worthy of respect – and criticism."[25] Against the background of the more radical Huguenot publishers in the Netherlands, Court was emboldened to translate some of their arguments for toleration. Furthermore, his resolute goal to insist on the "Frenchness" and patriotism of the Church of the *Désert* led him to avoid orientalist rhetorical strategies.

Contextualizing Court within his larger epistolary, ecclesiastical, and Huguenot publishing community in the diaspora reveals an important insight into the hidden transcripts of the Huguenot diaspora and the *Désert* community. If Catholics and the state feared Protestants as a political party, it was certain the Huguenots were playing the political game as best they could, weighing the needs of safety and survival with those of toleration along the way. Court was an arbiter of this hidden script, and his careful attention to political positioning became even clearer in the fifteen years that followed with the publication of *Le patriote français et impartial* in 1751, *Lettre d'un patriote sur la tolérance civile des protestans de France* in 1756, and his three-volume *Histoire des troubles des Cévennes* in 1760. In each text, one can find subtle critiques behind the lines of the monarchy with the proper contextualization. One poignant example of this is the careful selection of an epigraph in *Lettre d'un patriote* which reads: "A large population is a king's glory." A quote from Proverbs 14, this epigraph encouraged the formal recognition of the Calvinist population for the glory of the monarchy. Yet the well-versed Christian would know this epigraph cuts the second half of the line out. The full proverb is: "A large population is a king's glory, *but without subjects a prince is ruined*."[26] The context of the script is key to understanding Court's subtle protests, just as understanding Court's life and position within the refuge community helps us to recognize the variant meanings his script was capable of carrying.

Contending with the Context of Catholic Polemics

In all of Court's writings, he remained vigilant of the common arguments used against Calvinists. Their republicanism as an expression of their preference for unbridled freedom of conscience in the realm of politics, their propensity for violence, and their greed unmasked by their business success would become hallmarks of the progressive Protestant trope of the post-revolutionary era; but in the *Désert*, these propositions continued to ring the death knell of the French Calvinist Church in France. At its core, Court realized the Catholic argument against freedom of conscience, which Bayle had so stridently promoted as a means to dispel the communal threat Calvinists might pose to the French king, was the Calvinist Church's greatest obstacle. It was also at the core of anti-Huguenot arguments concerning Reformed republicanism and economic greed. Court refuted Catholic arguments directly, by emphasizing the collective nature of Calvinism.

Court coupled his narrative of victimization with an emphasis on the economic benefits of an enlightened absolutist policy of religious toleration. In his *Le patriote français et impartial*, Court identifies commerce as the greatest "advantage to recalling the refugees tranquilly to their *patrie*" and the central reason why the monarchy should encourage "others to value their rich talents."[27] In the *Lettre d'un patriote*, for example, he argues that "[w]hat merits the most attention from the government, is not only the number of refugees, but what advantages have been lost to foreign lands"; and that "French refugees have advanced the manufacturing" of those countries that welcomed them.[28] The return of the Protestant diaspora to France promised economic benefits. First, the Protestant acumen for industry and commerce was well-known, and in no way was Court the first one to discuss it. Catholics had associated Protestants with finance in France since the seventeenth century. Barthélemy d'Herwarth, a famous seventeenth-century French Protestant in French economic history and eventually the *intendant des finances* under Louis XIV, ascended in the government despite his faith. Élie Benoît, a Protestant theologian, minister, and historian, noted that "public finance became the refuge of the Reformed, to whom other employment was refused."[29] According to the twentieth-century historian of

French Protestantism E.G. Léonard, Herwarth's professional story was the genesis of the myth that Protestant theology fostered a propensity for modern capitalism.[30] Court saw the implications of the Revocation in many aspects of French society. Not only did the Revocation stunt French "industry," but the army and the state also became less effective.[31] Court noted that the economy bounced back rather quickly following the Revocation, and this was due to some two million Calvinists who remained and filled the void left by their brethren – a strategic overestimation.[32] If the king promulgated an edict within the span of ten years, perhaps a million more prosperous Protestants would return to the kingdom. Such a hope continued to be a mainstay of the Protestant cause for the remainder of the century.

Court also believed the Protestant propensity for business was a survival technique more than an innate quality. If intolerance ceased, then the entire population could develop their industry. Tolerance begot prosperity, whereas intolerance led to economic hardship. Huguenots regularly presented English religious toleration as a model:

> The Catholic, the Protestant, the Jew, and the Quaker live there in a union, in perfect tranquility. Persecuted in other nations, they find in London an asylum against the inquisitors and against the bloody tribunals. Obliged to live there, their industry fills the need; persuaded that no one will trouble them in their tranquil possession of their acquisitions … the countryside is cultivated, their arts are rewarded, their commerce flourishes; and the nation is one of the most powerful in Europe.[33]

The inclusion of Catholics and Jews is important to note here because it underscored the benefits of toleration for all groups, not just the persecuted. To tolerate the Protestant and other "others" in France, then, had reciprocal benefits for the French Catholic population itself.

Court did not call for total equality before the law – he called for the end of the physical and institutional persecutions that Huguenots continued to face. Court urged the crown to grant to the Calvinists what it had already provided to French Jews and Lutherans: an edict allowing them to worship and to perform their own marriage ceremonies. If such a measure were issued, Court would have given up equal access to bureaucratic posts and honours for French Protestants. After the Revocation's promulgation, French Calvinists were largely concerned about their ability to worship their faith and to document the major life events of their followers. Marriages, in particular, were a key issue, as all property-ownership and inheritance transfers depended on recognized, official marriages.[34]

Arguably, one of the most lasting anti-Protestant tropes was their inherent republicanism, but Court eschewed Catholic claims of the "politics of the refugees," who owed more to their *patrie* than to any imagined political inclinations.[35] Court argued against the republican-Calvinist connection espoused by a wide variety of thinkers, including Jean Novi de Caveirac, ill-reputed Catholic author of a defense of both the Saint Bartholomew's Day Massacre and the Revocation, and one of Court's staunchest critics[36] – along with the philosophe Montesquieu as was noted in the last chapter.[37] Both authors of different ideological bents ended their debates in the same place. The Reformation's freedom of conscience had done more than just "disenchant" the world of Catholic piety. The Reformation had entered the realm of politics.[38] Just as Antoine Court defended the Calvinist population against charges of inherent republicanism, so, too, was it common to critique Montesquieu's notion of a natural affinity between Catholicism and monarchy. Was not the Pope the head of a spiritual republic? Were not bishops and priests truly republicans in this international republic? "The Christian community forms a kind of nation," he wrote. "The bishops are those whom Providence has destined to govern the nation. The Pope is the head of this spiritual republic. Their decrees are always respectable, but they are not seen as guided by faith. Is the hierarchy of the Catholic Church more like a republican government than it is a monarchy?"[39] And did not the Protestant population lack such a clearly defined hierarchical structure? The Protestant was a true "patriot" both in politics and in spirit because only the sovereign king rested atop Protestant hierarchical society: "Their [Calvinist] religion [believes] … in nothing contrary to royalism."[40]

Further, the Catholic claims that Protestants only prospered in republics throughout Europe was remarkably incorrect to Court, who argued that the Danish king, an iron-fisted despot, ruled over a large population of Protestants. The Prussian monarchy also benefited from its Protestant population. In areas where a republican government existed – as in Switzerland, where Court lived – the state had no positive or negative effect on the religion of their polity.[41] In terms of royal loyalty or Christian belief, republicanism had not affected the Calvinist population, nor did Protestants seem to have an innate desire for republics.

Just as the damaging evidence of the Wars of Religion proved to be the necessary fodder for the Revocation of the Edict of Nantes, so, too, did the Camisard revolt in southern France further legitimate the Revocation. This revolt "proved" for most Catholics that Protestant fanaticism fuelled their subversive actions. Court did not deny that Protestants had committed atrocious crimes against the state. His three-volume *Histoire des troubles des Cévennes* (1760) detailed many of the internecine conflicts, the "barbarous murder" of unbelievers, and even the misguided notions of the Calvinist Camisards – indeed, his entire portrayal of the intra-Christian conflict was remarkably objective.[42] Nevertheless, he argued fanaticism and subversion were not innate qualities to Calvinism; instead, these Cévenol peasants merely reacted to the repressive measures of the Catholic clergy. By 1685, most Calvinists would have passively accepted the Revocation, according to Court, but they quickly learned that peaceful resolution was no longer on the royal court's table. The Catholic desire to convert Protestants, to reunite the Christian faith, had "burdened consciences more and more," with the end result of making would-be Catholics into "libertines, impious men, atheists, and finally rebels."[43] For Court, Calvinism did not lead man to impiety and disbelief – the actions of religious violence disturbed consciences. These reactionary rebels defended themselves against their most immediate oppressor, the Catholic Church, not the crown. One generation of Camisard revolt was eventually replaced by a timorous population, in large part frightened from public worship, but loyal to the king. Protestants were not simply religious dissidents, or the enemy in a just Christian war; they were victims of Catholic aggression.

Court's efforts to educate the population and to make concessions to Louis XV set the tone for later advocates of Protestant civil rights. By deemphasizing the alterity of the Protestant population, Court envisioned a French *patrie* defined by its social utility rather than by claims to cosmological truths. To best mobilize the Calvinist community for the betterment of the French kingdom, the Calvinist Church would need to be reinstated to civil life and to the public sphere. For Court, this institutionalization of the Calvinist Church was key to stopping sectarian conflict. And while the politics of loyalty and political economy figured greatly into Court's writing, his focus on the community, on the *patrie*, and on the dual character of the patriot refugee underscored a shift in the Protestant Enlightenment, from one based in reason to one based in sentiment.

Court's Protestant Enlightenment and the Rise of Sentimentalism

Court's most important writings from this period were *Le patriote français et impartial* (1751) and *Lettre d'un patriote sur la tolérance civile des protestans de France* (1756). *Le patriote fran ais* was his first attempt at crafting a vision of French Calvinist patriotism, but the latter document is more developed. In it, Court regularly makes reference not only to the lost potential that Huguenot refugees represented, but also to the plight of the Protestant refugees, who "wished with all their hearts to return to France."[44] Court used "reason" to promote toleration, but in his turn toward a discourse on patriotism, he was also in the avant-garde of the Enlightenment's turn toward sentimentalism. Living in French-speaking Switzerland, Court would have had ample opportunity to encounter Protestant Enlightenment ideals. Court's Genevan contact Jean-Alphonse Turrettini had argued that Christian doctrines could not contradict reason and combat the tripart threat of Protestant fanatics, early Deists and materialists, and the old-fashioned orthodox dogmatists. Turrettini's disciple Jacob Vernet had published his *Théorie des sentimens agréables* in 1750, and in it he argued that God had created man to be governed by reason, as well as instinct and sentiment. Both approaches underscore Court's writings on patriotism.[45]

That reason and sentiment might combine in the works of Court on patriotism only made sense. As David Bell rightly observes, *patriotisme* entered the French lexicon in the middle of the eighteenth century, precisely as Court seized upon its usage. For Court, patriotism referred to "an emotional attachment to a place thought of as 'home,' and more specifically ... to a territorial entity whose rulers possess final coercive authority over the persons living within it; in this case, the kingdom."[46] In positioning Huguenot refugees as patriots, he did not abandon their suffering, but rather infused it into a broader discussion of belonging. Huguenot suffering evidenced their drive to belong to France.

In his *Lettre d'un patriote sur la tolérance civile des protestans de France*, Court commonly employed terms familiar to the enlightened individual: tolerance, nation, patriotism, and rights, to list a few. The choice of *patriote* in the title of Court's apology sought to displace distinctions like Catholic and Protestant. *L'esprit protestant* lost its place to "*cet esprit de patriotisme qui convient à tout véritable citoyen*" – this spirit of patriotism that comes to every true citizen.[47] "Patriot" is an identity, manageable, mouldable, and capable of coinciding with religious identity. Court realized this; he took the arguments for Calvinist loyalty to the king and recast them in terms other than sacral allegiance. Court did not lean on arguments emphasizing the bifurcation of Catholic allegiance between king and Pope, but rather put forth a new identity and claim to subservience to the Bourbon throne.

It is important to note that when Court used the terms *patriote* or *patrie*, he did not use them like later revolutionaries did, but like his sixteenth-century constitutionalist predecessors. The "nation" was not synonymous with the population as a whole. Nor did he use this term with the idea of a social contract or natural rights in mind. He was not claiming the right to change the ancient constitution of France, or to dramatically alter the hierarchical social order of the Ancien Regime. His patriot was less a holder of natural rights and more someone bestowed with the privilege of "positive rights."[48] Court called for the "restitution to Protestants of a part of their ancient privileges."[49] The protection of the law and the state designated subjecthood, and justification for these laws required some discussion of the past and past politics. The Protestant needed the law to be turned into a Frenchman, and to make the Protestant case, Court needed to contend with the set of associations that legitimized the Revocation.

A patriot maintained an emotional link to France, and this link transcended religious affiliation, according to Court. But the notion of a patriot under the French monarchy and written beyond France's borders needed more than just territorial sentimentality. It needed to be bound to the person of the king, the patriarchal father figure of the French, who only through folly brought on by subterfuge could have let such a disaster befall the Huguenots.

> Instead of sacrificing the good of the State to flattery, let us rather deplore the evils of which this disastrous Revocation edict was the cause; evils which cause grief in any true patriot; evils which would never have happened, if the truth of the facts had been able to cross the barriers which had been placed between it and the Throne; evils which would have made this great Prince shed tears, whose magnanimity is known to everyone; finally, evils of which he would surely have stopped, if he had been able to foresee the fatal consequences, and if he could have heard the cries of the unfortunate people who endured them.[50]

Of course, it is easy to read the first clause of the passage as an empty gesture, meant to disguise what follows as hollow praise for a king in pursuit of religious tolerance; but doing so in an unadulterated fashion risks losing sight of the bond between Protestant and royal personhood that underscored much of the discourse surrounding the Huguenot refugees and the subtlety of the hidden transcript taking place behind such Protestant efforts. An ignorant king was capable of redemption; an evil one was not. In his representation of Louis XIV, Court humanized the deceased king, hoping for an empathetic reciprocal exchange. Empathy for the revoker was the only path, then, toward royal empathy for the Huguenot refugee population. But it could also stand that if a king was capable of erring, so were the Huguenots of the age. As Court readily admitted the guilt of Calvinists in the Cévennes, he was positioning himself to request forgiveness for past crimes of his fellow Protestants. Mutual forgiveness required empathy and a modicum of sentiment for the plight of the other.

Words and expressions key to sentimental philosophies of the coming half-century fill Court's *Le patriote français et impartial* and *Lettre d'un patriote*. In particular, he made sure to justify his characterization of his patriotism in rational and sentimental terms, in case anyone was to question how he could call himself a patriot as a resident of Switzerland. Court prefaced his argument for the loss of the Huguenot community industry by reflecting on their "love for their country that deplores them so."[51] Frenchmen needed to "study the heart of man" who, when faced with violence and force, remained stalwart in both his faith and his patriotism.[52] Court insisted that a deep attachment to the fatherland was one way of mobilizing early sentimental language in order to imagine a refugee identity capable of swaying the French monarchy to promote religious toleration.

Many of the themes of the *Lettre d'un patriote* were present in Court's *Histoire des troubles des Cévennes*. The overarching purpose of the *Histoire des troubles des Cévennes* was to offer an apology for the role that Calvinists played in the violence that erupted in 1702, engulfed the Cévennes for roughly three years, and continued, however less fervently, for the next ten years. Court refused to turn his *histoire* into an absolute admission of guilt; instead, he seized the opportunity to claim that new Calvinist leadership had "*sauvèrent la France*" from the sectarian conflict that would have continued to fester for the foreseeable future.[53] Attributing the close of the war to Calvinist leadership further reinforced Court's argument that supporting the synodal and ecclesiastical structure of the Church of the *Désert* would calm fanatical outbreaks of violence. This argument also combatted the Catholic argument for force against the Calvinists and in pursuit of their conversion.

Foregrounding the pain and suffering of Huguenot bodies was paramount for Court in his *histoire*. It offered him a chance to humanize the Calvinist population (so often demonized by the Catholic Church) and to further imagine their refugee suffering. In his history of persecution and violence in the Cévennes, Court cites an anonymous letter detailing the "suffering" his coreligionists had faced since the Revocation. Describing the "horrors of the internecine and Civil War," the author of the letter demands that the reader – in this case, Court – "suspend for a moment your fury," and consider what has caused man's "hands to tremble in the innocent blood of your Brothers." Calvinists faced with the "last extreme of misery," without "further recourse," "see nothing better than death."[54]

In seizing the empathetic turn of the eighteenth century for the Huguenot toleration cause, Court made sure to reaffirm the principles of patriotism that he laid out in his *Lettre d'un patriot*: "[I]n order to illuminate the Civil War in the Kingdom, and to spare the blood of our compatriots, we have suffered patiently, in the hope that God would touch the hearts of our enemies who would recognize their injustices in persecuting" Calvinists.[55] Language of brotherhood and compatriots regularly appeared in Court's history of the Cévennes, showing that national identity transcended religious affiliation.

It is important to reiterate that for Court and most Calvinists, these displays of victimhood were necessarily prefaced with statements of the king's ignorance of the plight of Calvinists. Read against the grain of the Huguenot's hidden transcript, Court's writings can and should be read as a critique of the French Catholic's grip over governance – something that was of regular thematic use in the blatantly anticlerical writings of more mainstream French Enlightenment figures. At the same time as Antoine Court was writing his apologies, a new discourse of public opinion had begun to emerge and was often posited as an additional, if not alternative, source of authority to appeal to in times of political crisis.

Court's public writings were an effort to appeal to public opinion on behalf of the Huguenot population, but rarely does Court explicitly call attention to this alternative discursive source of power. At no point does Court explicitly call upon the court of public opinion to weigh on the Revocation or the Huguenot diaspora. And yet, phrases like "good opinions," "bad opinions," and "popular opinions" litter his writings. The very actions of writing first his *Apologie* and then later his *Lettre* and history of the Camisard Wars were appeals to a larger literate bourgeoisie and an increasingly political public sphere and opinion. Court reserved the use of the term *publique* for public worship. This may strike the student of the eighteenth century as odd, but given the precarious and persecuted fates of Calvinists remaining in France, Court could not risk challenging the king's authority so directly. The eighteenth century was rife with talk of public opinion. For Jürgen Habermas, public opinion represented an ideal model of democratic communication, whereas for the political thinker Alexis de Tocqueville, public opinion was the primary vehicle of dangerous politics, as evidenced by the role public opinion played during the French Revolution. For both Habermas and Tocqueville, "public opinion" represented a nebulous, unregulated court capable of appealing to uncodified cultural mores, which remained separate from the state even as it shaped the pronouncements of the state.[56] To appeal directly to public opinion, then, would have evidenced a Calvinist attempt to circumvent the sacral state, or at least Catholic polemicists would have read it as such. This is not to say that public opinion always stood as antithetical to government interests. In fact, as Keith Michael Baker has argued, public opinion regularly appeared in state records, especially those of the Parlement of Paris in the 1750s, right around the time that Court made his case for Huguenot toleration and reconstruction of the synodal community.[57]

Other religious communities dared to dabble in the public opinion politics, as Arlette Farge noted in her classic study on the popular underground Jansensist newspaper the *Nouvelles ecclésiastiques*. In encouraging the "participation of the lay people" as early as 1728, Jansenists, often libelled as Catholics masquerading as Calvinists, sought out an alternative space for religious debate and controversy, especially given the detrimental blow of the Bull of Unigenitus, which levelled Jansenist influence. In the *Nouvelles ecclésiastiques*, Farge notes the paradox that belied Jansenist calls for the public opinion. While the newspaper regularly spoke of those effaced by the press more generally, it also "ignored most of the scenes, which brought those ordinary people on stage." The "heart of the *Nouvelles* did not beat to the world's rhythm, or even that of the people but to that of the threatened Jansenist movement in its encounter with the people."[58] For Court, appealing to public opinion was not the same as calling for lay practitioners to join the Calvinist apologetical realm of the *Désert*. Doing so would only have endangered Huguenot position in the country further, and undoubtedly catalyzed the *dragonnades*. Court emphasized the collective in his appeals for public worship.

For Court, the appeal to the collectivity of the patriot in apologetic forms further underscored his decision to push for the reorganization of the Calvinist community in the *Désert* and the recognition of the Calvinists' communal needs. Only through their community could they hope to temper the more enthusiastic extremes of lay preachers and would-be prophets. In this aspect, Court differs from Bayle, who emphasized the individuality of the Calvinist population to neuter their collective action. Curiously, Court represented a strain of anti-individualism in the Enlightenment born out of refugeedom and the politics implicit in his apologetics, despite the normative assumptions about the individuality of Calvinist freedom of conscience. This is best explained by Court's desire to rebuild the Church of the *Désert* and the arguments that association – in both religious and patriotic communities – instills loyalty and decreases sectarian conflict.[59] For Court, patriotism built on the sentimental elements of early modern constructions of refugeedom, but it also pointed to the search for collective identities capable of carrying a collective voice.

***

Court, like many Huguenot refugees, contended with both the historical writing on Huguenot refugees and the politics of intolerance. In doing so he actively sought to rewrite the narrative that surrounded Calvinists in the *Désert* and the refuge, by positioning Calvinists in relation to the state, rather than separate from it. Insisting that Calvinist communities could organize for stability rather than sectarian conflict was paramount, and the patriot identity proved vital in this rewriting. A healthy congregational body would strengthen the national body, and thereby strengthen the body of the king.

Court was caught at the crossroads of the Huguenots' struggle for toleration. In his search for the reconstitution of the Huguenot synodal system, he had to choose between a silence and private worship on one side – which would spell the death of the French Calvinist Church and condemn the French to further outbreaks of sectarian conflict – and on the other, jeopardizing Calvinist safety by making the case for their toleration to both the state and the burgeoning public sphere of the eighteenth century. Court navigated the middle ground through these two positions. He also navigated the crossroads of reason and sentimentalism, finding in patriotism an avenue toward toleration. Reason allowed him to explain why Huguenots should be recognized as Frenchmen; sentiment helped to explain how Huguenots had never stopped being Frenchmen despite their faith and their flight into the refuge.

5

Protestant Philosopher: *Rabaut Saint-Étienne*

During his life, Jean Paul Rabaut, more commonly known by his *Désert* name Rabaut Saint-Étienne, wrote copiously about the plight of French Calvinists in France and displaced Huguenots abroad.[1] Born in Nîmes to Paul Rabaut, one of the most prominent *Désert* Calvinist pastors, Saint-Étienne left France for Lausanne to study under Antoine Court and his son Antoine Court de Gébelin, two defenders of the French Calvinist community and prolific writers. Saint-Étienne officially became a Calvinist pastor in 1764, returning to Nîmes shortly after. Inspired by the Calas Affair two years earlier in 1762 – the case, popularized by Voltaire, of a Calvinist father wrongly sentenced to death after his son's suicide – Saint-Étienne found himself thrust into the defense of the Calvinist community on national and international levels. His first book, *Le vieux Cévenol*, was a short fictional account of a despondent French Calvinist named Ambroise Borély.[2] In it, Saint-Étienne expressed a vision of enlightened religious liberty that embraced individual reason and universal sentiment. His status as a defender of the Calvinist minority all but guaranteed his place in the Estates General, and then later elevated him to the presidency of the Constituent Assembly.

Before the Revolution, Saint-Étienne played a part in a much larger Protestant Enlightenment, which is often neglected in the narrative of religious toleration and the French Enlightenment. Saint-Étienne experienced and witnessed firsthand religious persecution. Geoffrey Adams and other historians who trace the rise of religious toleration during the eighteenth century focus on the efforts of statesmen, lawyers, and philosophers, who expounded upon the ills of an intricately bound Catholic Church and state, and subsequently drafted laws, proclamations, and legislation in the hopes of instituting religious tolerance. In his *French Protestantism and the French Revolution*, Burdette Poland noted that after 1750, "the devising of such legislation had become a professional pastime for enlightened legists."[3] The goal of lawyers like Gilbert de Voisins, Malesherbes, Amelot, and the Baron de Breteuil was to rationally explain the benefits of an *état civil* for the benighted Calvinists. They emphasized that Louis XIV's *lettres mortes* existed in ink only, having largely been ignored in recent years throughout much of the kingdom. Saint-Étienne's fictional approach mirrored the legist efforts but adopted a sentimental tactic common in the late Enlightenment.

In the debate over religious toleration, few historians focus on Protestant efforts to recast their faith during the post-Revocation period.[4] A veritable "unnatural alliance," according to David Bien, emerged in which philosophers, lawyers, and statesmen defended the French Protestant population and elevated their status in the process, but this "alliance" remained one-sided.[5] Calvinists remained passive and largely grateful for their allies' philosophical and often litigious efforts, while the philosophes built their own pantheon in part on the cause of French Calvinism.[6] Montesquieu's wife Jeanne de Lartigue was a Calvinist who depended on the prominence of her husband to safeguard her fortune, but also likely influenced him to issue some of the earliest and most potent critiques of religious intolerance. In fact, Voltaire took on two very notable cause célèbres in the 1760s, defending the Calas and Sirven families.[7] And Rousseau, a man from a Protestant family and a Genevese, seemed the ideal candidate to defend Calvinist interests following the 1755 publication of *Discours sur l'origine et les fondements de l'inégalité parmi les hommes*.[8] While Rousseau's writings inspired many Calvinists, including Saint-Étienne and his turn to sentimentality, Rousseau proved to be a rather reluctant defender of French Calvinists.[9] This study on Saint-Étienne, like the recent work by David Garrioch, attempts to balance the historiographical scales.[10] Saint-Étienne played a part in a much larger Protestant international.[11] This link between the *Désert* community in southern France and the exiled Calvinist community in Lausanne and Geneva fostered a vibrant Protestant Enlightenment that persisted through the eighteenth century – a community that responded to the Deist and anti-religious impulses of the more "mainstream" Enlightenment by adopting a language of sentiment, predicated on the victimization of a French Calvinist population. In this sense, Saint-Étienne's Protestant Enlightenment also reflected broader shifts in Enlightenment thought owing greatly to another traveller through the Swiss Cantons, Jean-Jacques Rousseau.

This sentimental turn in the Protestant Enlightenment is absolutely essential to understanding the more extensive genealogy of refugees; this is one of the central arguments of this book. Saint-Étienne's old Cévenol is a refugee, comes into contact with other refugees, and by virtue of his age – a man victimized by Louis XIV and the Catholic Church and still alive well into the second half of the eighteenth century – embodies the persistence of the persecution that Calvinists longing for subjecthood in France continued to face. In her discussion of the invention of human rights during the Enlightenment and revolutionary era, Lynn Hunt never discusses Huguenots or refugees, but her analysis of "imagined empathy" as a central feature of the Enlightenment invention of human rights runs parallel to the innate sentimentalism that Saint-Étienne ultimately espouses in *Le vieux Cévenol*. As Hunt explains, "[a]ccounts of torture produced this imagined empathy through new views of pain. Novels generated it by inducing new sensation about the inner self. Each in their way reinforced the notion of community based on autonomous, empathetic individuals who could relate beyond their immediate families, religious affiliations, or even nations to greater universal values."[12] Huguenots had plenty of material to tap into this imagined empathy. Depictions of Jean Calas's body being broken appeared in many accounts of the Protestant patriarch's execution. And as this chapter shows, Saint-Étienne went to great lengths to capture Huguenot suffering in ways that reflected real experiences of Reformed.

As Saint-Étienne is the biographical nodal point for this chapter, I have chosen to mirror his life's work chronologically, starting with his earliest encounters with the Protestant Enlightenment. Only after the context of Saint-Étienne's Protestant Enlightenment is established can

Figure 5.1 In this image Jean Calas, seated, is surrounded by family members and those preparing to take him to his execution.

the sentimentalism of *Le vieux Cévenol*, one of his most significant pre-revolutionary writings on religious toleration, be examined. Finally, this chapter concludes with a discussion of his role in the drafting of the *Declaration of the Rights of Man and Citizen*, which further evidences the agency of a French Calvinist in France despite the illegality of his faith.[13]

Sources of Sentiment and Protestant Enlightenment

Historian of Enlightenment thought J.G.A. Pocock argues that any understanding of Enlightenment needs to consider the trauma inflicted on the European conscience by the Wars of Religion. If any single unifying factor existed to connect the many versions of "Enlightenment," it was that they all pursued "a series of programmes for strengthening civil sovereignty and putting an end to the Wars of Religion."[14] Saint-Étienne's vision of Enlightenment resulted from a similar position, though it emerged during a renewed climate of religious persecution thriving at the time of his birth in 1743. As his *Le vieux Cévenol* reminded its readers, the French Wars of Religion had not ceased. Henri IV's efforts only momentarily assuaged the power of theologians – "men cladded in white" – to wage "sacred war … against men in black." They banished peace from the terrestrial plane and spun falsehoods in the process to provide a "pretext for persecution."[15] Moreover, Saint-Étienne found the Revocation to be more egregious than the St Bartholomew's Day Massacre. The massacre lasted "one day and the courts countermanded them two days later; but the delirium of the Revocation lasted for several years."[16] Huguenots found 1685 to be the source of their nadir. Calvinist women found themselves imprisoned in the Tour de Constance, and men were sentenced to hard labour in the galleys. Only three years after Saint-Étienne's birth, the young pastor Mathieu Majal was burned alive on the esplanade in Montpellier. A much older, octogenarian pastor met a similar fate that same year in Grenoble. His body was removed from the scaffold only to be tossed into the Isère River. Saint-Étienne's own father, the well-known *Désert* Calvinist pastor Paul Rabaut, was wanted by the French magistrate who set a warrant for his arrest at six thousand livres.[17] While the Camisard Wars (1702–15) had ended, the Reformed faith remained simultaneously policed and persecuted.

It was this persecution in France that led Paul Rabaut to send Saint-Étienne from their family home in Nîmes to Lausanne for a "proper" Calvinist education. Under the direction of the best-known *Désert* pastor, Antoine Court, and his son Antoine Court de Gébelin, Saint-Étienne first encountered the arguments of the more mainstream Enlightenment. Saint-Étienne advanced in his studies, bearing "*fruits précoces*," as Court noted in a letter to Paul Rabaut.[18] Saint-Étienne developed a fascination with ancient Greece, from which his famed *Lettres a Mr. Bailly sur l'histoire primitive de la Grèce* resulted in 1787.[19] Saint-Étienne differed from Court in important ways. While Court sought to promote an image of Huguenots as essentially loyal, Saint-Étienne chose to focus on the victimization of the Huguenot body and community. Both pastors painted Calvinists in pacifist strokes, emphasizing the nonviolent character of Calvinists after the Camisard Wars at the beginning of the century; but Court's argument for Huguenots' patriotism did not go far enough for Saint-Étienne, who wanted to emphasize the pain, tribulation, and corresponding detriment to French society that had resulted from the persecution of Huguenot bodies.

Saint-Étienne's turn toward sentiment owed more to his later move to Geneva with his brothers, where he continued his theological, philosophical, and linguistic studies. There, Saint-Étienne undoubtedly met Jacob Vernet, a disciple of the Genevan theologian Jean-Alphonse Turrettini. Both men stressed the use of reason and the importance of moderation. Here, too, Saint-Étienne would have encountered the writings of German *Aufklärer* (Enlightenment philosopher) on one side, who sought a middle ground between reason and revelation. On the other side, Saint-Étienne would have been equally opposed to the sterility of the German Lutheran orthodoxy and the radical "enthusiasm" of the Pietists, whose evangelical fervour undoubtedly would have reminded him of the enthusiasts who fuelled the Camisard Wars in France at the beginning of the eighteenth century.[20] Vernet had promoted a work published in 1748 entitled *Théorie des sentimens agrébles*, which insisted that "proofs of sentiment" could effect change more effectively than could "useful arguments."[21] Such an argument was a jab at the overtly rationalistic arguments of thinkers like Pierre Bayle. In fact, what emerged in Geneva was what Rosenblatt has called "Enlightened Christian sentimentalism."[22] In part a reaction to the claims of D'Alembert that the pastors of Geneva had become Socinians, embracing reason at the expense of revelation, this turn to sentiment implicitly recognized the growing divisions predicated on a secular rationality. The year before Saint-Étienne published his *Le vieux Cévenol*, Gal-Pomaret had published one of the most widely purchased texts of the Protestant Enlightenment, *Chrétien par conviction et par sentiment, ou La Foi sans incertitude et la piété sans superstition (1778)*, which stressed the sentimental needs of believers to foster conviction.[23] A language of sensitive hearts made sense to Saint-Étienne for whom hardened hearts had historically led to the plight of the French Calvinist. Such sentimental language reified the pacifist character of Calvinists and added an additional layer of support for their toleration.

Because of financial hardship, Saint-Étienne returned to Nîmes to study under his father's supervision, delivering his first sermon in January 1763 while Voltaire issued his *Traité sur la tolérance* during the Calas Affair. Returning to Lausanne for a year, Saint-Étienne passed his exams, formally matriculating from the seminary in November 1764.[24] Over the next fifteen years, Saint-Étienne remained in the environs of Nîmes and developed his own sense of Protestant Enlightenment. He began to imagine how sentiment might be employed for the purposes of toleration in France, drawing inspiration from the cadre of philosophers and writers who cut their teeth in the wake of the Revocation of the Edict of Nantes. Those skeptical, critical, and "tolerationist" works of Pierre Bayle, Isaac de Beausobre, and Jean Le Clerc, as well as the historical writings of Élie Benoît, provided the historical realism Saint-Étienne needed to make his book relatable. Benoît's name, specifically, appears five times in the citations at the close of Saint-Étienne's *Le vieux Cévenol*. A French Protestant pastor and historian of the Edict of Nantes, Benoît provided much of the historical fodder Saint-Étienne used to substantiate his claims in his *Histoire de l'Edit de Nantes*, published in the decade following the Revocation. Many of the scenes of persecution, of the disinterment and mutilation of Calvinist corpses, and of the imprisonment of men and women found in *Le vieux Cévenol* are accompanied with a footnote to Benoît.[25] The shift marked by Benoît's work cannot be understated in the intellectual history of the period. While intended to reassure Louis XIV of the loyalty of the French Calvinist population and to establish their sect as the victims in an unholy holy war, the text did not attempt to make any theological arguments. Instead, Benoît's historiographical treatment of the Edict of Nantes established Calvinism as a "*culte*," a loyal religious community with the best interests of the kingdom at heart worthy of recognition and protection.[26] Saint-Étienne's own mentor in Lausanne, Antoine Court, had published a tract on the Camisard Wars, where he continued the legacy of Benoît by calling for Calvinist loyalty to the Bourbon crown and the end of Calvinist prophecies.[27] In addition to the writings of Benoît and Court, other writings from the Huguenot diaspora, such as Bayle's *Nouvelles de la République des Lettres* (1684–87) and Pierre Jurieu's *Lettres pastorales aux fidèles qui gémissent sous la capivité de Babylone* (1686–

89), informed the historical backdrop of Saint-Étienne's novel. Persecution histories rested on themes of pain and injustice, which laid the foundations for empathetic accounts.

From the late seventeenth-century boom of historical works on religion came the creation of "religions" and their comparative study.[28] At the core of this movement, to which Saint-Étienne's work is deeply indebted, was the idea that every religion shared certain principles. As Lynn Hunt, Margaret Jacob, and W.W. Mijnhardt show in *The Book that Changed Europe: Picart and Bernard's Religious Ceremonies of the World*, the comparative study of religions of the early Enlightenment moved away from the polemics of the so-called Age of Confessionalization, filled a desire to dispassionately and rationally outline the contours of many faiths alongside one another, and distilled what they perceived as the "natural," and even as the "essences" of universal faith. Picart and Bernard – men deeply embedded in the Huguenot diaspora – emerged out of the Republic of Letters largely influenced by the Huguenot diaspora and the early Protestant Enlightenment, which saw the rise of reason. Such a goal should be understood as an offshoot of the eschatological dream of universal conversion within the Christian tradition. Finding the single unifying factor of religious expression could translate into homogeneity, curtail the endless confessional division that ardent Catholics like Bossuet blamed on the early Reformers, and thus end internecine religious conflict. The coterie of "high Enlightenment" thinkers showed a similar tendency toward erudition. The same desire to catalogue and compare world religions manifested itself in the bastion of Enlightenment publishing, the *Encyclopedie*. In the 1765 version of the *Encyclopedie*, the entry for *religion* describes it in simple terms, as the common expression of honouring God.[29] This almost anthropological impulse toward the study of religion reduced faith to its "nature," a set of socially-constructed commonalities. Saint-Étienne similarly detailed a common religious element, the existence of which supported man's need for religion, specifically a form of public worship capable of fostering moral and sentimental growth.

Reducing religion to common impulses then freed the French Protestant Enlightenment of the Désert period to make non-religious political claims about the Protestant population. Saint-Étienne's instructor at the Lausanne seminary, Court, had already published works defending French Calvinists as "patriots" first, and Calvinists second. In his *Lettre d'un patriote sur la tolérance civile des protestans de France* (1756) Court used the word choice of *patriote* in the title to displace distinctions like Catholic and Protestant. *L'esprit protestant* lost its place to "*cet esprit de patriotisme qui convient à tout véritable citoyen*" – this spirit of patriotism that comes to every true citizen.[30] It is important to note that when Court used terms like *patrie* or *nation*, he used them like his sixteenth-century constitutionalist predecessors. The "nation" was not synonymous with the whole population. Nor did he use this term with the idea of a social contract or natural rights in mind. He was not claiming the right to change the ancient constitution of France, nor to dramatically alter the hierarchical social order of the *Ancien Regime.* His "nation" referred less to natural rights and more to "positive rights," or those outlined by French law.[31] Court called for the "restitution to Protestants of a part of their ancient privileges."[32] At the core of Court's plea was the victimization of the Calvinist patriot people and their alienation from their country, two themes taken up by Saint-Étienne in his pursuit of religious toleration.

Saint-Étienne found sources for his Protestant sentimentalism in the "bestsellers" of the Enlightenment. As Céline Borello has appropriately noted, Saint-Étienne was not merely a "partisan of philosophical thought," nor was his mind "soft wax" shaped by the simple imposition of enlightened ideas.[33] Montesquieu and Beccaria received explicit mention in *Le vieux Cévenol.* Others like Voltaire and Locke appear through clear and veiled references, often just alluded to in Saint-Étienne's text as philosophers or men of greater mental acumen. What is certain is that Saint-Étienne interpreted these philosophes in sentimental terms, noting how "readers of this history" with "especially strong nerves" and "endowed with a certain coarseness of soul ... may be able to note with pleasure that in the fine century of Louis XIV, the minds of men had a peculiar energy, and that they had not "been softened" (*été amolli*) by reading Montesquieu and the Marquis de Beccaria."[34] That choice of phrase did not correspond with the normative understanding of the "Age of Enlightenment" as an "Age of Reason." Instead, Saint-Étienne's rhetoric suggests a hardened conscience in desperate need of sentimentalism. In this sense, the more mainstream Enlightenment spawned a kind of empathetic revolution, one which was conducive to sentiment and religion.[35]

Jean-Jacques Rousseau, the "citizen of Geneva," inspired Saint-Étienne's turn to the sentimental novel in two primary ways. First, Rousseau calls for a kind of sentimental realism, or a sentimentalism that is both relatable and seemingly worse than the reader's experience. One without the other distances the reader from the plight to the point where sentiment is lost. In *Émile*, Rousseau describes his three maxims on compassion and the proper sentimental education. The first imagines compassion as a "part of human nature." The second insists on the personal and ultimately selfish nature of sentimentalism, or the need for one to fear a similar fate. And the third maxim deals specifically with empathy or the "feelings we attribute to the sufferers."[36] In his *Julie, ou la nouvelle Héloïse*, Rousseau explored sentiment in the form of an epistolary novel, which, as Robert Darnton notes, became one of the bestsellers of the eighteenth century and popularized the form of sentimental fiction.[37] Saint-Étienne became attuned to the power of sentimentalism, as well as the idea that passions drive action and change in a way that reason devolves into inaction.[38] This sentimental connection made between individuals then forms one of the social bases for the General Will for Rousseau – the glue that binds society together. While Rousseau may have popularized the idea of the General Will, it is necessary to recognize that the idea's invention lay in the theological discord between Protestant and Catholic in the seventeenth century – in the debates between the Jansenists Antoine Arnauld and Blaise Pascal on the one side and the Jesuit Nicolas Malebranche on the other – specifically within the context of the idea of God's divine will to save all men.[39] Such debates were taken up by early Protestant Enlightenment philosophers like Bayle, whose writings influenced Genevan Calvinists in the *Désert* to a great extent, Saint-Étienne included. Rousseau then was part of a much larger religious dialogue, which he pulled into the social and political sphere.[40]

The late Protestant Enlightenment in France was best defined by sentimentalism, and other Protestants in France used this rhetoric to their advantage, as well. The Genevan-born finance minister to Louis

XVI, Jacques Necker, incorporated the language of Christian sentimentalism in two apologetic works, rarely interrogated by historians. In his 1788 *De l'importance des opinions religieuses*, as Rosenblatt has correctly noted, Necker adopts a view of justice, which forefronts sentiment rather than cold reason. "The timorous sentiment of a judge's conscience" or his "sensible clairvoyance" combined with the natural sensibilities produced just rulings.[41] Necker's apologetics also speak openly about religious morality as a basis for sentiment, towing a very similar line between Christian sentimentalism and the need for public worship and religious education.[42]

Saint-Étienne found his vision of Protestant Enlightenment more conducive with the sentimental side of the Enlightenment, or the "Enlightenment of Sympathy" explored by Michael Frazer. This sentimental Enlightenment had cosmopolitan roots linking the Protestant Enlightenment of Rotterdam to Geneva to southern France and Paris. Saint-Étienne took the "Age of Reason" in a religious sense by placing greater emphasis on feeling, as well as moral and political reflection.[43] In the wake of the Revocation of the Edict of Nantes, he chose to probe the King's and the public opinion's moral and Christian conscience through a gruesome, albeit fictional account of one refugee – Amboise Borély – whose struggles reflected Calvinist experiences.

Memory, Sentimentality, and Emotion as Basis for Religious Toleration

In 1779, Saint-Étienne published the first edition of his sentimental novel. Saint-Étienne's goal was to give a firsthand account of the man's life – forging a sentimental bond between Borély and the reader – and to mimic the escape memoirs produced at the turn of the century.[44] His *Le vieux Cévenol* was a fictional, masquerading as nonfictional, account of a man whose birth to Protestant parents came at the most inopportune time. Throughout the text, Saint-Étienne refers to Huguenots as "refugees," and in each instance, he coupled their persecution – the pain of their bodies, personal, familial, and communal – with the lost opportunity they represented for French society. "Prodigious networks of refugees" established colonies in the Indies, and thousands of "fugitives" spread their disdain for the French king, according to Saint-Étienne.[45]

Early in his childhood, Borély witnessed his father killed on suspicion of having attended a clandestine meeting. Ruthless dragoons ransacked his home. Despite these events, Borély's mother found a way to support her children and to continue raising them as Calvinists. At fifteen, he planned for his future employment, only to be turned away from the legal profession, expressly forbidden by the king's ordinances from holding the positions of judge, solicitor, advocate, or notary – or physician, apothecary, or even horse-riding instructor. The military remained open to Protestants, but advancement was impossible, and it seemed likely that if he stood at the beck and call of Louis XIV, he would inevitably have to run down his fellow Protestants. He found trade to be his only professional refuge. A once-close family friend, Claude Hypocris, then informed on the Calvinist family and took advantage of an edict which placed in his hands the wealth and property of any captured Calvinist.

The mother became further impoverished; Borély's sisters were carried off to convents; Catholics tricked the youngest brother, only seven years old, into converting for treats; and a recently deceased Protestant's corpse was dragged through the streets, subjected to calumny and insolent mockery, before being flung into a sewer. Borély resolved to flee the country for Switzerland but was arrested and turned over to galley ship authorities, who then sent him to America on a rickety ship incapable of making the transatlantic voyage. His French captors abandoned the ship at sea, and Borély, who clung to its floating remains, chanced upon a passing English vessel. He arrived in London, naturalized, and took up his trade. Soon he became wealthy enough to entertain the thought of returning to his homeland, only to find that one of his sisters was in possession of the family's property. Borély returned, incognito, to a petty sister who misunderstood his intentions. Borély left his former home and sister, ready to return to London, only to meet and fall in love with a Roman Catholic girl by the name of Sophie Robinel. They consecrated their nuptials in front of a Protestant minister. Their romance soon led to the birth of child, after which the wife died. Later, a bill arrived informing Borély that he must turn over all his late wife's possessions to her mother and father. Borély defended the rights of his son only to be informed that the boy, under Louis XIV and Louis XV, was considered to be a bastard and thus was not owed any of the family's property. Borély's lawyers took a stand, evoked the laws of nature, and failed. The judges refused to justify their actions – choosing to enforce part of the law, but not the other. They spoke of a type of de facto toleration of the Protestant, but despite their vague assurances, Borély fled the country once again. Once safe back in England, he renounced any future desires to return to France, his place of birth where man's most sacred, most natural rights were proscribed, yet his mind never left his homeland. In his final moments, and included in the last sentence of the story, were the names "Henri IV," the protector of the Huguenots, and "Louis XVI," a king capable of recapturing the good legacy of Henri IV.[46]

The imaginary Huguenot protagonist, Borély was simultaneously a man of the past and of the present. His story disrupts a linear temporality of the eighteenth century, bringing 1685 to the present. This literary strategy allowed Saint-Étienne to make this *histoire* a political and moral tale for his times. A son of one of the most prominent French Calvinists of the *Désert* period, Saint-Étienne realized his contemporary battle for Calvinist rights hinged on memory. The latter part of his title – "*Anecdotes de la vie d'Ambroise Borély, mort à Londres âgé de 103 ans, sept mois, et quatre jours*"[47] – served to simultaneously emphasize and de-emphasize the time between the Revocation and the present. Nearly a century had passed since the Revocation, but only a single man had recently died. In metaphorical terms, Borély stood for the displaced Huguenot population – a group persecuted in the past and suffering from the traumatic event in the present.

Originally titled *Triomphe de l'Intolérance*, published in London in 1779, and written under the nom de plume W. Jesterman, Saint-Étienne's fictional account of the tribulations of one French Calvinist in the wake of the Revocation of the Edict of Nantes became a relatively quick success, warranting reprintings in 1784 and 1788, and several more following the Bourbon Restoration in the nineteenth century. From the second edition onward, Saint-Étienne opted for a less ostentatious title – *Le vieux Cévenol*. The original title would have signalled to censors the seditious, even combative character of the text, which ran contrary to Saint-

Étienne's goal of showing the loyalty of French Calvinists to France and the French crown. Saint-Étienne did not choose the original title.

As many historians of print culture have shown, authorship could hardly belong solely to a single voice. From the literary muse to editors and publishers, the identity of the "author" oftentimes became muddled with multiple voices.[48] In Saint-Étienne's case, the very title of the first edition of his work was crafted by another: the editor and Swiss pastor, Vernes. An aspiring philosopher himself, but ultimately a novice to the eighteenth-century book trade, Saint-Étienne looked to his mentor and friend, Étienne Chiron, who recommended Vernes. Well-known for his literary talents, Vernes took remarkable and "strange liberty" with the text.[49] He added a new title to its front page, giving it a layer of audacity that Saint-Étienne's humble literary style could not match; nor could Saint-Étienne stomach the defeatist tone of Vernes's title. Vernes also added three additional salacious chapters, purportedly to court sales, that detailed the love and marriage of Borély to Sophie Robinel in such great detail that it made the text seem almost foreign to Saint-Étienne.[50] Many of these more amorous moments were kept for later editions, but by the 1788 edition, Saint-Étienne rectified those moments where Vernes's additions compromised the historical reality of the *Désert*.

In many ways, the change in title reflected Saint-Étienne's aim to reinvigorate the memory of the Revocation and depict French Calvinists as Frenchmen first. *Cévenol* had largely become synonymous with *Reformed*, as the Cévennes was both the refuge of the Reformed and the site of the Camisard Wars (1702–15). His desire to cast Calvinists as Frenchmen precluded other options for the title like *le vieux Huguenot*, *calviniste*, or *réformé*. The "triumph of intolerance" would have signaled to the censors a subversive work, and most certainly would have warranted further attention. This same reason would have precluded a title like *le vieux Huguenot*. The inclusion of the term *Huguenot* would have harkened back to the Revocation of the Edict of Nantes, religious intolerance/tolerance, and subversive politics. In general, the term *Huguenot* had fallen from favour in linguistic terms in France. First, if one believed the "fiction of a Catholic France" or the complete disappearance of the French Calvinist community – as Louis XIV asserted – then the term no longer applied to those French Calvinists still in the hexagon. If the term was used, it most likely referenced those who sought refuge beyond France's borders, becoming *fugitifs* and *étrangers*. At only one point in Saint-Étienne's text does he use the word *Huguenot*. Describing the inability of French Calvinists to sell their property legally without being taken advantage of by a Catholic, Borély's *advocat* laments: "A Huguenot, honest man is less happy at this point than a villain who has the good fortune to be Catholic."[51] *Le vieux Cévenol* reflected Saint-Étienne's desire to emphasize the history of loyal Calvinists in the kingdom, while emphasizing their locality (i.e., Cévennes), rather than their sect.

Saint-Étienne's use of sentiment functioned on two planes – one anthropological and the other rhetorical. He identified sentiment as a universal and natural human quality. Sentiment, more than any other quality, lay at the core of human existence. Man was born with a "sentimental slate," not a blank one. Saint-Étienne referred to this universal principle as sentiment. Moral lessons brought out the social component of that innate sentiment, known as sensibility.[52] For Saint-Étienne, religion remained the most important fount of moral lessons, and the Reformed faith was more capable of crafting sensibility than any other religion. "Sympathy for the sufferings of others is a sentiment to be found deep down in every heart," Saint-Étienne argued; "personal interest and prejudice may often stifle it, but there come moments when it will develop, when it will burst forth with greater force for having been repressed."[53] The Revocation had been reasoned into existence and guided by greed.

How could one prove the Revocation of the Edict of Nantes was an immoral and ill-intended piece of legislation through a discussion of sentiment? During a conversation between Borély, members of the Church of the *Désert*, and two *étrangers*, Saint-Étienne revealed his understanding of the "General Will":

> [Rousseau] held that laws should be framed according to the opinions of the majority of the people, and that the object of legislation should be to reform prevailing customs when they were vicious, to tolerate them when they were harmless, or to encourage them when they contributed to the moral good and prosperity of

> the community. It was his opinion that observers should note with the greatest care the general spirit of a people, which exhibits greater varieties than either climate or habits.[54]

Like Rousseau, Saint-Étienne envisioned a legal system that reflected the "general spirit of the people," rather than one that tried to manipulate or control it. Popular sovereignty relied on the sentimental inclinations of the people. That is, the law should enhance man's sentimental morality, not hinder it through its "vicious" customs. While this quote explicitly refers to "secular" law, Saint-Étienne equated it to religious law, as well. We see an overlap between the juridical and the theological.

Saint-Étienne understood public worship as integral to the General Will. Here, he differed from the more radical Enlightenment, which sought to eliminate religion's influence in the public sphere. He also differed from many lawyers and statesmen who promoted what Jeffrey Merrick and others have referred to as the "privatization of religion" by insisting on the public good that public worship could provide when tolerated.[55] Saint-Étienne wrote, "Observe, it is not domestic worship that we see established all over the earth, but public worship. All people have had temples or religious rendezvous in which worship has taken a certain form."[56] Prejudice, avarice, and tradition threatened the simple "universal instinct" behind worship, according to Saint-Étienne. "A law hidden deeply in their nature" draws all of humankind to worship – the human artifice of tradition added practices to the natural principle of public worship.[57] Calvinists, with their religious regeneration, had only sought to return to the purest forms of religious practice – an idea only furthered by the very real return to the wilderness experienced by many *Désert* Calvinists, who reinvigorated communal worship in rural, "natural" settings.[58]

For all his discussion of sentiment, natural religion, and morality, Saint-Étienne managed to cover legal ground similar to that covered by his contemporaries, especially in the context of the family. For example, Malesherbes detailed the plight of Protestant children recognized as bastards, stripped of family lands and ancestral wealth after the Revocation of the Edict of Nantes.[59] The resulting problem was the impoverishment of the nation and the dislocation of families from the land, which became unproductive. Saint-Étienne illustrated the issue of bastardry through the central character – an angry father (Ambroise Borély) who, already in the throes of depression after losing his Catholic wife (Sophie Robinel), chose to relocate with his child back to London at the end of the story, rather than sentence his son to an "illegitimate" life. As Meghan Roberts has rightfully noted, the Enlightenment was an age of sentiment in which "domestic narratives were infused with new importance. Loving ties were the foundation of natural virtue, sociability, patriotism, and social utility."[60] Borély's connection to his wife and child pulled on the heartstrings of those readers who empathized with the family unit and the bonds between husband and wife or father and son.

The right to life also resonated with Saint-Étienne with the importance of the "body." Saint-Étienne described in excoriating detail the oftentimes vulgar and brutal treatment of Protestant bodies. As Antoine de Baecque effectively argues, bodies in prerevolutionary France were often metaphorically interpreted in three ways: as anthropomorphic symbol of the political system, as mode of discursive persuasion, and as spectacle.[61] In the story, Borély catches the sight of a disinterred Calvinist body, mutilated in an almost festival setting. He actively recognized this as a religious and political spectacle, and as an oft-used warning to the "so-called Reformed" to abandon their heresy.[62] In addition, the extreme violence perpetrated on the Huguenot body served empathetic purposes or offered cause for personal reflection. During a dragoon raid, Borély recounts, "from nursing mothers they took their infants, leaving them to be distressed by the accumulation of milk in their breasts."[63] Sentiment with the Huguenot mother comes both from the loss of a child and the lost opportunity to provide for one's child. Just before Borély's mother dies early in the story, she begs her son, "[P]reserve my bones from persecution by burying me in some solitary place."[64] Historical evidence in the notes at the end of each chapter further cemented the idea that such atrocities were relatively recent and deserved attention. Calvinist bodies remained threatened under the Revocation. In short, the body acted as a site of sentimentality, capable of carrying with it political and moral connotations. The mutilation of this individual Calvinist body mirrored the plight of the broken familial body and the tortured body politic. Happiness (*bonheur*) became the sentimental cure to the ailments of the persecuted Calvinist body and the body politic.

Saint-Étienne relied on a new language of emotion in the eighteenth century to plead his case for religious toleration. In particular, his use of happiness reveals much about his fictional text's mission. Happiness existed on two planes for Saint-Étienne. For the Jesuits, he noted their "zeal for the eternal happiness for the soul."[65] This pursuit of the eschatological happiness acted as cause and warrant for forced conversions. To counteract the use of this caustic and casuistic definition of *happiness* as a modus operandi for conversion campaigns, in Saint-Étienne's opinion, it was necessary to locate happiness in this world. Like many philosophers of the eighteenth century, Saint-Étienne referred to happiness as an obtainable treasure, something worthy of pursuit, a product of one's actions, and something to be savoured.[66]

Saint-Étienne's definition of *happiness* reflected the legal status of Calvinists in the kingdom. Happiness derived from the state. It was bestowed upon the populace through the law. In *Le vieux Cévenol*, one judge repudiates the Revocation and the laws that followed, which ran afoul of the "eternal laws of nature." Once the law reflected the law of nature, this judge notes, he would finally be happy to contribute to the happiness of the state and his *patrie*. Only by aligning the laws of the nation with morality could a "happy revolution" occur in France. The moral, "happy" revolution Borély speaks of would make the French more "likable, tolerant, sociable, and polite." In short, happiness stood in direct opposition to fanaticism and persecution.[67]

Borély's happiness hardly seems to be based on material gain, but rather on his propensity for work. He finds his "happiness and liberty" in England, where the climate of religious tolerance encouraged his "happy industry."[68] Rather than view this emphasis on "industry" as a result of the ascetic Calvinism, as Max Weber would likely have insisted, Saint-Étienne explained the Calvinist penchant for industry in socio-economic terms.[69] Borély is excluded from nearly every job that someone of upward mobility would pursue in the eighteenth century. Legal restraints preclude Borély from pursuing a career in law, medicine, or education. Borély cannot become a notary or hold any kind of public position. The only avenue left open is business.

> The way of commerce is still open to you ... Protestants saved the business of France. The principal merchants of Bordeaux, Lyons and Marseilles, the most famous bankers of Paris, are Protestants. Protestants are carrying on the finest silk manufactories of Languedoc. These useful and oppressed subjects applied themselves to industry all over the kingdom, whilst their brothers who took refuge in England contributed to carry to perfection their art in the land of their exile, so that the foreign productions soon became the object of our emulation and envy.[70]

Saint-Étienne's association between wealth and Calvinism was not new in the eighteenth century. Apologists and defenders of the Huguenots in France had long attempted to overcome the king's religious intolerance by appealing to his financial senses.[71]

Saint-Étienne's plea for religious toleration, then, relied on sentiment, both religious and secular, owing both to the Protestant and mainstream Enlightenment he took part in. Sentiment remained universal and best shaped by the Protestant faith, a religion at once regenerated to the "Ancient Church" and conducive with modern "progressive," egalitarian ideals. Calvinists in southern France were Cévenols first and Calvinists second, but being Calvinist could make them better Cévenols and then better Frenchmen. Saint-Étienne accorded his theological education an important position in his writings. The Protestant Enlightenment in France insisted on the necessity of public worship and its natural role in the formation of sentiment. Public worship was a universal and natural condition of man.

Freedom of Religion in Revolutionary France?

On the precipice of the French Revolution, Saint-Étienne continued to insist that public worship and freedom of conscience remained inalienable natural rights. He spent most of the 1780s in Paris, moving in enlightened circles, working with Lafayette and Malesherbes to gain Louis XVI's ear and to ensure that the most important needs of the Calvinist population were represented in any legislation that advanced their cause. The result of this effort was the Edict of Toleration in 1787. The document itself lamented the violent means perpetrated in pursuit of conversion – those false, coerced conversions – and the "dangerous contradictions between the rights of nature and the dispositions of the law."[72] Yet Louis XVI and Saint-Étienne maintained different conceptions of the "rights of nature." The first article of the Edict dashed Saint-Étienne's hopes for a religiously tolerant France. "The Catholic, Apostolic and Roman religion," the Edict reads, "will continue to enjoy alone, in our kingdom, the right to public worship."[73] As Saint-Étienne maintained that public worship remained instinctual, natural, and necessary for developing man's sentiment, the inclusion of such an article denied the most important natural right to Calvinists. In Saint-Étienne's address to the National Assembly two years later in 1789, he attacked the limited tolerance institutionalized by the Edict of Toleration. He insisted that the freedom of religious opinion remained an "inviolable sanctuary," and that "to constrain it is an injustice, to attack it is a sacrilege."[74]

Saint-Étienne continued to view the pursuit of religious coexistence and the Revolution through a lens of sentiment. During his plea to the members of the National Assembly, he noted that in order to wake his audience to the horrors faced by French Calvinists, he was forced to "incite your [members of the Assembly] humanity by sentiment, *after* having tried to convince it through reason."[75] The turn to Terror of later years, by which he, too, would be consumed, was a violation of the "revolution in sentiments, manners, and moral opinion," to borrow a phrase from the conservative Edmund Burke's *Reflections on the Revolution in France* – a revolution that Saint-Étienne had sought to advance through *Le vieux Cévenol*.[76] Saint-Étienne concluded his speech in front of the Assembly by reverting back to arguments laden with sentiment, "humanity," and emotion.

Probably sensing that the Assembly would not champion freedom of religion, Saint-Étienne made one last push for the freedom to public worship. Such a principle was expressly restricted in the Edict of Toleration. As he argued in *Le vieux Cévenol*, the cultivation of sentiment occurred in the most natural of religious, communal settings. He insisted that "every *culte* is necessarily a *culte* of many. The *culte* of one solitary person is merely of adoration or of prayer … [the *culte*] then consists in the reunion of many." The nature of religious community needed to fall under the umbrella of freedom of religious belief, because the idea of "common worship" is a religious opinion, and therefore falls under the "justness of the expression."[77] Public worship based on natural law and bolstered by an empathetic defense of Calvinists remained a hallmark of Saint-Étienne's argument. Article 10 of the *Declaration of the Rights of Man and Citizen* (1789) states: "No one should be disturbed for his opinions, even in religion, provided that their manifestation does not trouble public order as established by law." The Constitution of 1791 would finally address Saint-Étienne's call for public worship, and in that same year, the Parisian Protestant community would relocate into the former Catholic Church, Saint-Louis-du-Louvre.[78] Other Calvinist churches soon began appearing across the country.

The cautious royalism that Saint-Étienne had cultivated proved his undoing. Sat amongst the Girondists, he rallied against the creation of the Republic and opposed the trial of Louis XVI. His political opponents took aim at Saint-Étienne and drove him into hiding. His anti-republicanism would likely have confounded earlier critics of Calvinists who maintained their natural affinity with republicanism. He was arrested during the purge of the Girondists and guillotined on 5 December 1793.

***

Saint-Étienne was an exemplar of the growing Protestant Enlightenment in France. From his pastoral position, he navigated a broad field of several Enlightenment discourses. His efforts led the way to freedom of religion, and his corpus revealed a form of Protestant Enlightenment persisting on France's periphery, a cosmopolitan creation indebted to the Huguenot diaspora in general, as well as to the particular community in Lausanne and Geneva. Saint-Étienne struck a balance between the theological calls to moderation on the Protestant Enlightenment on the one side and the more mainstream French Enlightenment hostile to religious privilege on the other. He did this by turning to Genevan-inspired Rousseauian sentiment, a concept fostered amongst Protestant circles in Geneva, which offered him an alternate route to follow for religious toleration and the natural right of public worship. The Protestant Enlightenment of Saint-Étienne and its carrier – the sentimental novel *Le vieux Cévenol* – atoned for the sins of those Calvinists who had fanned the Wars of Religion, while carrying a form of apologetics that rendered Calvinism compatible with an empathetic, tolerant, polite, and enlightened society.

Saint-Étienne's text further embraced the refugee identity, just as Jurieu, Bayle and Court had done before him, but his definition hinged on a clear articulation of natural empathy, universal to all human beings and prefiguring reason, which could be moulded for ill-intended aims. Intrinsic and innate empathy proved the most important evidence for Saint-Étienne as he promoted religious toleration and, during the Revolution, religious liberty; but today this imagined empathy continues to undergird refugee media representation and the work of nongovernmental organizations (NGOs) and organizations lobbying for refugee rights. Broken Huguenot bodies and stranded outcasts forced across France's frontiers bear a remarkable resemblance to images of Syrian families fleeing for their lives in the twentieth century. If an early incarnation of human rights discourse was born during the Enlightenment, then it was owed, in part, to the Huguenot population who shaped the rhetoric of the Enlightenment – from its periphery through their broken bodies, but also oftentimes directly by influencing its most prolific philosophes, and in Saint-Étienne's case, by lobbying for the community's interests with his own words.

Conclusion

Deputies to the National Assembly made French Calvinists full citizens on Christmas Eve 1789. Revolutionaries congratulated themselves for ending over one hundred years of Calvinist illegality launched by Louis XIV's Revocation of the Edict of Nantes, which led to the flight of over two hundred thousand individuals from the kingdom to Switzerland, the Netherlands, England, and then across Europe and the Atlantic World.

Nearly a year later, in 1790, French revolutionaries turned to debating how best to court Huguenot refugees, and specifically their descendants, back to France. Granting them French citizenship was the first step, and some form of reparations upon repatriation followed. On 9 December 1790, prominent Montagnard Bertrand Barère argued that their reparative justice decree gave the status of French citizenship to immigrant children even if their parents refused to accept such a status for themselves. Barère insisted, "I have come to pronounce their true name – French … No, they have never ceased to be, and your committee proposes to you an article as equally virtuous as political, which will assure those descendants of religious fugitives, the right to the honour of being French citizens."[1] Received by resounding applause, this motion symbolized the revolutionary desire to break with the sectarian past and speak to the international community. Soon after, Huguenots born abroad received citizenship, and the revolutionaries created a pathway to the return of Huguenot property for those Huguenots who returned with the proper documentation (and provided their ancestral lands were held in the *royal domaine*).[2] Barère supported the Committee of Public Safety, promoted the Cult of the Supreme Being, and later became an opponent of Maximilien Robespierre, leading up to the Thermidorian Reaction. The question I want to explore in this conclusion is: Why did the revolutionaries not adopt refugee rhetoric for Huguenots?

The word *refugee* does not appear in Barère's speech nor any of the other speeches around this legislation found in the *Archives Parlementaires*. This does not mean, though, that a refugee rhetoric did not pervade revolutionary discourse. It is just that the word "refugee" had been disconnected from the Huguenot cause, as I have shown throughout this book. Huguenots had insisted on their French character over the course of the eighteenth century, following the line of reasoning that Pierre Bayle promoted. Huguenots like Antoine Court and Rabaut Saint-Étienne insisted on depicting Huguenots as suffering Frenchmen, whose religious identity could comfortably meld with a tolerant French state.

A text-mining search of the Stanford-hosted digital *Archives Parlementaires* reveals an interesting linguistic imbalance. *Réfugié*, or some iteration of it, appears twice as frequently (at around 1,400 occurrences) as *fugitive* and its iterations (at 754); and both appear more frequently than does *religionnaires fugitifs* (religious fugitives, at 133), which is the most common way revolutionaries referred to Huguenots.[3] *Réfugié* is never used to refer to the Huguenot population explicitly, and instead is used to refer to places of refuge, or individuals, like princes, displaced. Collocation searches for iterations of *fugitive* reveal revolutionary concerns over religious fugitives of both Catholic (counterrevolutionary) and Huguenot stripes. The two words that appear most frequently in conjunction with *fugitives* are *biens* and *religionnaires* (see figure 6.2). Often these two terms appear alongside each other and *fugitive*, as Barère and others were concerned with the return of properties to Huguenots, so that they might re-establish themselves and their businesses quickly.

Barère was not alone in his verbiage when it came to the Huguenots, whether internally displaced or in the diaspora. Barère, like other revolutionaries, recognized that their revolution had displaced many and

Figure 6.1 *Top* A word cloud showing the one hundred terms most frequently collocated with *réfugié(s)* in the *Archives Parlementaire* between 1789 and 1793. The collocation search which produced this word cloud ran with a 90 per cent match, allowing for other common variants of the word.

Figure 6.2 *Bottom* A word cloud showing the one hundred terms most frequently collocated with *fugitif(s)* and *fugitive(s)* in the *Archives Parlementaire* between 1789 and 1793.

that they needed to atone for past dispossession. The eighteenth century was an "age of refugees," as much as it was an Age of Revolutions.[4] To define the former was to define the latter, and for Barère, the Huguenot refugees stood as exemplars by which the revolutionaries could stamp the French citizenry – not in terms of confessionalization, which had driven the Wars of Religion, but in terms of nationalism. J.G.A. Pocock defined the Enlightenment, as much as any singular Enlightenment could be said to exist, as "a series of programmes for strengthening civil sovereignty and putting an end to the Wars of Religion."[5] Such a definition applies to the revolutionaries who promoted their new order with a new citizenry – determined not by confession, but by "Frenchness." As David Bell has rightly noted, the Wars of Religion remained "perhaps the most basic political reference point during the last two centuries of the Old Regime."[6]

Barère's statement, then, helps to plumb the depths of the Revolution's politics of religion, but also helps us to understand the ways that revolutionaries acted within their international context. Such a historiography has been dominated by studies of *émigrés* who fled the early revolution following the dismantling of feudalism and the early attacks on the Catholic Church's fiscality. The revolutionaries largely held the *émigrés* as a source of fear and enmity (at least until Napoleon Bonaparte offered amnesty to them in 1802),[7] defining themselves against the French *émigrés* who represented a "convenient aristocratic and clerical scapegoat for all revolutionary ills."[8] These aristocrats often used the same language used to define the Huguenots as a means to emphasize their victimization at the hands of the revolutionaries, just as the Huguenots had faced in the louisquatorzean Ancien Regime.[9] Huguenot refugees gave the revolutionaries a chance to define themselves directly and right the wrongs of the Old Regime.

Lands were at the forefront of the revolutionary mindset, especially given the grain shortages and famine that the French had experienced in the years leading up to the French Revolution. This concern for French lands, for the return of workers to the lands, and for the promotion of religious toleration was embedded in the *cahiers de doléances* (lists of grievances submitted by each estate) received by members of the Estates General in 1789. The *cahier* from the small Poitou village of Vouvant described the following situation:

> The edict of 1685, by revoking the edict of Nantes, depopulated several of our provinces, and principally that of Poitou, by forcing the Protestants to leave the kingdom; hence many of our fields are uncultivated; those which would occupy seven or eight men to cultivate them have only two to three. Agriculture, this first wealth of the State, is neglected. The edict of November 1787, by granting a civil status to non-Catholic subjects, is not sufficient to recall the French fugitives to the bosom of their fatherland. One could perhaps procure this advantage for the nation by giving a suitable extension to this edict; Above all, it would be very interesting to return to the families the property seized from these religious fugitives, and consequently to abolish the administration.[10]

This might be particularly striking to read, given the fact that Vouvant was also in the area of the Vendée, famous for its counterrevolutionary insurrectionism only a couple of years later.

The concern over properties and their return is also present in the *cahiers* from regions with a much heavier Calvinist presence. In their *cahier* to the Estates General from Aix-en-Provence, they argued that "the goods of religious fugitives" needed to be returned to their "legitimate heirs."[11] Another from the Languedocian town of Castres called for the "abrogation" of all penal laws made against Protestants and for "seized goods [to] be returned to the religious fugitives."[12] These calls for the returning of Huguenot properties are numerous and most often appear in the *cahiers* from towns and regions with a significant Calvinist population.

The choice of the word *fugitive* might strike us as curious, and this curiosity might be driven further when one reads the entry for *fugitive* in Diderot's *Encyclopédie*:

> FUGITIVE, (Gramm.) fleeing, escaping; it is taken adjectivally in this phrase, fugitive circumstances; substantively therein, a fugitive. It is said today of any man who has moved away from his

> homeland, where he was not in safety, for any reason whatsoever; it used to be said of a slave who ran away. If the fugitives brought him back, his master was authorized by law, either to have him branded with a hot iron, or to lock him up in the public prison, or to condemn him to the mill, or to cut off the muscles of his legs, or even take his life. See Slave. If a slave was sold, and he was liable to flee, it seems from a place in Horace, that one was obliged to warn of it.[13]

Most historians argue the nation and nationalism emerged over the course of the eighteenth century, but few recognize the role that international refugees played in shaping the discourse around the nation. Huguenots were at the forefront of constructing a French national identity – one capable of absorbing them from their diaspora, but which also needs to be understood in its colonial context.

Bertrand Barère's choice of the term *fugitive* was intentional and ultimately dependent on a much longer semantic and conceptual history, shaped and reshaped by Huguenots themselves. His choice also reflects the colonial crisis faced by the revolutionaries as well. In the Estates General, Gouy d'Arsy and others requested that France's colonies, but specifically Saint-Domingue in the Caribbean, have representatives of equal standing in the proceedings. Bertrand Barère, who was there for the motion, wrote about Gouy's "noble and energetic manner" in his newspaper, *Le Point du jour*. "The colony of Saint-Domingue, French in origin, French by choice, French in its administration and by the tribute with which it enriches the treasure of the mother country, deserves to be admitted to explain its important interests," explained Barère, while not entirely agreeing with the reasoning behind Gouy's concerns. Barère argued that a new designation needed to be adopted in order for Saint-Domingue to hold representatives, specifically, the title of "colony" needed to be replaced by "province." This shift was important and needed to "reconcile the rights of humanity with the calculations of politics, in order to improve in our American provinces, the condition of so many unfortunates condemned to slavery and debilitating labour in a burning climate."[14] The conceptual latticing of the Huguenot situation and the colonies then coalesced for Barère within the context of colonial slavery, even if slavery was rarely discussed and recorded in the *Archives Parlementaires.*

How do we conclude such a sketch of refugee and fugitive discourse? *Refugee* and *fugitive* share an etymological origin in the Latin word "fugere" or "to flee." The reason for fleeing seems to not matter much, but the relationship to the place that one flees from does seem to offer some distinction between the two concepts. While *refugee*, in the Huguenot sense, denoted the refuge to which they fled, *fugitive* implies a requirement to their original place, which is vested with authority over them. A slave owner maintained legal claim to their fugitive slaves. The French nation maintained a patriotic claim over its fugitive Huguenots. The extent to which Barère's use of the word *fugitive* in the case of the Huguenots reflected his feelings about abolitionism is likely minimal; instead, we should see this word as accomplishing two discursive goals. First, the word *fugitive* replaced the word *refugee*, and thus distanced the new French regime from the religious politics of the Huguenots themselves. Second, it reified the authority of the French state to define the French citizenry, capable of distinguishing itself from the would-be sacral absolutist Old Regime, so that it might extend that definition beyond France's borders.

On this view, an exploration of the two terms from the Revocation to the Revolution in France shows that the evolution of the term *refugee* was not simple, but rather was bound up in the development of natural rights (and even human rights discourses),[15] the shifting sacred and secular sands,[16] and the emergence of nationalism and its expression in revolutionary politics,[17] as well as an evolution of the ways a nation-state and kingdom regarded displaced people, both across their borders and internally displaced. The prevalence of the word *refugee* likely became preferable as the "refugee problem" intensified in scale and scope with twentieth-century wars, which displaced millions. International bodies then preferred a term that did not invest authority in the state, as *fugitive* did, and the temporal distance between the Revocation and twentieth-century global warfare likely diminished the religious exceptionalism originally invested in the term to the point that its utterance would not have inflamed religious tensions, as it would have during the French Revolution of 1789.

***

The United Nations High Commission on Refugees estimated in 2019 that more than 79.5 million people worldwide had been displaced, including 6.6 million Syrians, 3.7 million Venezuelans, 2.7 million people from Afghanistan, 2.2 million from South Sudan, and 1.1 million from Myanmar. An additional 45.7 million had undergone some form of internal displacement as well.[18] Numbers impress. They give us a sense of the gravity of the suffering, but humans need images to empathize with those facing persecution. The media landscape of the twenty-first century does this remarkably well. Images of refugees make it onto the nightly news; can be found splashed across the front-pages of newspapers, disseminated through social media platforms, and even communicated directly from refugee camps through cell phone apps. Our technological world has ways to communicate and foster the recognition of suffering in ways that those in the eighteenth century, who regularly imagined the future in utopian terms, could not fathom. The origins of that imagined empathy emerged during the Enlightenment era, which owed its force, at least in part, to the French Huguenots trying to survive their own persecution. In ending this book with the French Revolution's efforts to court Huguenot refugees I am not trying to advance a narrative of closure or even one of success. The history of the Huguenot's invention of the refugee discourse evidences the ways that refugees have and can advocate for their own interests, form alliances, and build international networks to provide refuge, and how in the end they can abandon those images to foster inclusion.

In Hannah Arendt's 1943 essay "We Refugees," she describes the pressure that Jewish refugees faced in exile. Arendt bemoaned the experiences of those Jews, like herself, in exile. "Those few refugees who insist upon telling the truth, even to the point of 'indecency,' get in exchange for their unpopularity one priceless advantage: history is no longer a closed book to them and politics is no longer the privilege of the gentiles." Huguenots a couple of hundred years before the Holocaust understood that naming their suffering and claiming the mantle of the refugee people could empower them. "Refugees driven from country to country represent the vanguard of their peoples – if they keep their identity," Arendt argued.[19] Huguenot refugees created communities abroad for successive waves of Huguenots, but they also remained active supporters of those Huguenots in the *Désert*. Huguenots turned themselves into Frenchmen, only after experimenting with an international identity, based in Christian symbolism. Huguenot apologetic writers also shaped a lasting link between Calvinism and protocapitalism, which would last for many generations. Arguments about their refugee experience and identity shaped the Enlightenment discourse around individual rights, the emphathetic connections among humankind, and how those rights were coded into citizenship during the French Revolution.

Notes

PREFACE

1 Howell, "Rousseau and the Huguenots."
2 Hobsbawm and Ranger, *The Invention of Tradition.*

INTRODUCTION

1 Voltaire, *Le Siècle de Louis XIV*, chapter 36.
2 Office of the United Nations High Commissioner for Refugees (UNHCR), *Convention and Protocol Relating to the Status of Refugees.*
3 Arendt, *The Origins of Totalitarianism*, 289.
4 Historians have increasingly been calling for a trans-historical perspective within refugee and forced migration studies, which tends to lean heavily on the twentieth century. See Marfleet, "Refugees and History," 137. Early modern refugee studies have seen a renaissance in recent years. See Terpstra, *Religious Refugees*, 2–3; Lachenicht, "Refugees and Refugee Protection"; Ther, *The Outsiders*; and Teller, *Rescue the Surviving Souls.*
5 "Réfugiés," in Diderot and d'Alembert, *Encyclopédie*, 13:907.
6 Utt and Strayer, *The Bellicose Dove*, 134.
7 Kwass, *Contraband*, 205.
8 The Babylonian Captivity refers to the forced internment of Jews in Babylonia following the conquest of the kingdom of Judah, first in 597

BCE by the Babylonian King Jehoiachin and again in 586 BCE by King Nebuchadnezzar. In 538 BCE, Cyrus the Great gave the Jewish refugees permission to return to Palestine.

9 See Alphonse Coquerel, *Jean Calas et sa famille*; Allier, *Voltaire et Calas*; Maugham, *The Case of Jean Calas*; Coutet, *Jean Calas, roué vif et innocent*; Bien, *The Calas Affair*; and Nixon, *Voltaire and the Calas Case*. On the Sirven case, see Voltaire, *Avis au public sur les parricides*. For an analysis of the Sirven case, see Galland, *L'Affaire Sirven*; Cebe, *L'Affaire Sirven*; Gargett, "Voltaire and the Sirven Case"; and Inchauspe, *L'intellectuel fourvoye*.

10 Migration, borderland, and frontier historians, especially of imperialism have debated the methodological implications for how a scholar defines *frontier spaces*. See, for example, Kristof, "The Nature of Frontiers and Boundaries"; Duroselle, "*Les frontiers: Vision historique*"; Baud and Van Schendel, "Toward a Comparative History of Borderlands"; and Hämäläinen and Truett, "On Borderlands." Lucien Febvre's analysis of the etymological history of the word *frontière* is interesting insofar as the word's medieval usage denoted less a liminal space and more the façade of a church or the front lines of a military formation. These two interpretations had fallen out of favour by the Revocation and the eighteenth century. Febvre, "*Frontière*: The Word and the Concept."

11 Adelman and Aron, "From Borderlands to Borders," 815–16.

12 Terpstra, *Religious Refugees in the Early Modern World*, 2–3. "Forced migrations" may seem an ill-suited phrase for the Huguenot case since Louis XIV forbade Huguenots from leaving, but for those who wanted to guard their faith and had the means to flee France, flight felt forced.

13 Maya Jasanoff argues that the age of revolutions of the late eighteenth century was an "age of refugees," but she fails to explore the religious contours of this refugee era that pre-dated the political revolutions. See Jasanoff, "Revolutionary Exiles: The American Loyalist and French Émigré Diaspora," 38.

14 Terpstra, *Religious Refugees in the Early Modern World*, 3; Stanwood, *The Global Refuge*.

15 See Bell, *The First Total War*; Nelson, "Making Men: Enlightenment Ideas of Racial Engineering"; Tricoire, *Enlightened Colonialism*; and Pichichero, *The Military Enlightenment*.

16 Adorno and Horkheimer, *Dialectic of Enlightenment.*

17 Malesherbes was arguably one of the most prodigious Huguenot defenders. For his earlier writings on Protestant rights, see Malesherbes, "Mémoire sur les affaires de religion"; Malesherbes, "Mémoire sur le mariage des Protestants"; Malesherbes, *Mémoire sur le mariage des protestans, en 1785*; and Malesherbes, *Seconde mémoire sur le mariage des Protestans*. Lafayette, a close collaborator of Malesherbes, informed George Washington of the plight of the French Calvinists in a letter written in 1785. Lafayette decried the "intolerable despotism," which rested on the capricious whims of the royalty and governing officials, that plagued French Protestants: "Their marriages are not legal, their wills are not protected by law, and their children are to be bastards, their parsons to be hanged." See "Les promoteurs de l'édit de 1787 qui a restitué l'état civil aux protestants de France.".

18 Schwab, "Un encyclopédiste Huguenot," 46. John Lough and others have made the case for Vivans's authorship of "Falbala" and "Fontagne." See Schwab, Rex, and Lough, *Inventory of Diderot's Encyclopédie*, 529.

19 Zurbuchen, "Jaucourt, Republicanism, and Toleration," in Laursen, *New Essays*, 155–70.

20 Becker, *The Heavenly City of the Eighteenth-Century Philosophers*; Gillespie, *The Theological Origins of Modernity*; and Gauchet, *The Disenchantment of the World*. In recent years, historians have begun to speak of a Religious Enlightenment, various religious enlightenments, or the continuing importance of religious dissent. See Sorkin, *The Religion Enlightenment*; Pocock, *Barbarism and Religion* (6 vols); Haakonssen, *Enlightenment and Religion*; Sheehan, "Enlightenment, Religion, and the Enigma of Secularization"; Van Kley, "Christianity as Casualty and Chrysalis of Modernity."

21 Woodbridge, "An 'Unnatural Alliance' for Religious Toleration," 508; Bien, *The Calas Affair*; Adams, "Myths and Misconceptions"; Adams, *The Huguenots and French Opinion, 1685–1787*; Garrioch, *The Huguenots of Paris and the Coming of Religious Freedom, 1685–1789*; Graham, *Voltaire and Protestantism*.

22 On the Protestant Enlightenment, see Pocock, *Barbarism and Religion*, 1:92; Bradley and Van Kley, *Religion and Politics in Enlightenment Europe*, 15.

23 Rosenblatt, "The Christian Enlightenment," 295.

24 Cassirer, *The Philosophy of the Enlightenment*; Gay, *The Enlightenment: An Interpretation*. On national Enlightenments, see Porter and Teich, *The Enlightenment in National Context*. Pocock introduced the idea of lower-case enlightenments as a means to undercut unifying and therefore obscurantist definitions of a monolithic Enlightenment. It was common to accept the Enlightenment as an Age of Reason, following Immanuel Kant's own attempt at defining the movement in his famous essay "Was ist Aufklärung?" Postmodernists who viewed the enlightenment through the lens of power preferred words akin to *program* or *project* to emphasize the power struggle between self-defined new age thinking and old, antiquated world views. On the Enlightenment as project of modernity, see Lyotard, *The Postmodern Condition*; Foucault, "What Is Enlightenment?"; Baker and Reill, *What's Left of Enlightenment?*; Adorno and Horkheimer, *Dialectic of Enlightenment*.

25 Sorkin, *The Religion Enlightenment*. Dan Edelstein took a novel approach in defining the Enlightenment in narratological terms, as the by-product of the battle of the Ancients versus the Moderns. See Edelstein, *The Enlightenment*. And more recently, Jeffrey Burson describes a "culture of enlightening," composed of a discursive field capable of crossing myriad enlightenment movements, but ultimately providing a shared language. See Burson, "Entangling the 'Century of Lights' to Disentangle the Enlightenment."

26 Taylor, *Modern Social Imaginaries*; Taylor, *A Secular Age*.

27 Burson, *The Culture of Enlightening*. See especially Van Kley, *The Religious Origins of the French Revolution*; Werner and Zimmermann, "Beyond Comparison."

28 See in particular Dodge, *The Political Theory of the Huguenots of the Dispersion*.

29 Perry, *From Theology to History*, 7.

30 Beik, *Absolutism and Society in Seventeenth-Century France*; Root, *Peasants and King in Burgundy*; Blaufarb, *The Politics of Fiscal Privilege in Provence*.

31 Pocock, "Conservative Enlightenment and Democratic Revolutions," 84.

32 Van der Linden, *Experiencing Exile*, 2.

33 The Huguenot historiography is vast. Here are a few key English read-

ings: Butler, *The Huguenots in America*; Cottret, *Huguenots in England*; Benedict, *The Huguenot Population of France*; Mentzer and Van Ruymbeke, *A Companion to the Huguenots.* On business networks, see Cullen, "The Huguenots from the Perspective of the Merchant Networks of Western Europe." On family networks, see Lougee, *Facing the Revocation.*

34 Van Ruymbeke and Sparks, *Memory and Identity*; Stanwood, *The Global Refuge.*

35 Coleman, *The Virtues of Abandon.*

36 Stepan and Taylor, *Boundaries of Toleration.*

37 Hunt, *Inventing Human Rights*, 32. Lynn Hunt does not, however, explore the religious origins of human rights discourse.

38 Frazer, *The Enlightenment of Sympathy.*

39 Intellectual historians have called for a renewed "trans-historical" intellectual history approach, combining the rigorous contextualization of the so-called Cambridge School with genealogical approaches to the history of ideas and concepts as diverse as happiness, genius, civil war, and democracy. See McMahon, *Happiness: A History;* McMahon, *Divine Fury*; Armitage, *Civil Wars*; Rosenfeld, *Democracy and Truth.*

40 Chimni, "The Birth of a 'Discipline,'" 16.

41 Gatrell, "Refugees – What's Wrong with History?" 170, 178. See also Gatrell, *The Making of the Modern Refugee.*

42 Soguk, *States and Strangers.*

43 Marfleet, "Refugees and History," 138.

44 Haddad, *The Refugee in International Society*, 63.

45 Caestecker, "Refugees in the European Historiography: Beyond the Administrative Category."

46 Fuentes, *Dispossessed Lives.*

47 Montesquieu, "Lettre CXVIII," in *Lettres Persanes*, vol. 3, letter CXVIII.

48 See Banks, "Jeanne de Lartigue, Madame de Montesquieu."

49 Sorel, *Montesquieu.*

50 Perceval, *Montesquieu et la vigne*, 99.

51 Fuentes, *Dispossessed Lives*, 7.

52 Choudhury, *The Wanton Jesuit and the Wayward Saint*, 43–5.

53 Here I am drawing from Saba Mahmood, who argues that would-be conservative religious spaces offered women ways to advocate for themselves and effect change. As Mahmood articulated in the context of

Islamic revivalism in Egypt in the 1990s, women in nominally understood religious restrictive spaces developed modes of activism for both political and social change. Mahmood, *Politics of Piety*, 4.

54 Scott, *Domination and the Arts of Resistance*, 27, 57.

55 For a fascinating example of female Huguenot authorship, see Lougee, "'The Pains I Took to Save My/His Family,'" 1–64.

56 Famously, Jaucourt had authored a multivolume work on anatomy, but, afraid of publishing it in France, he had it sent to the Netherlands for publication. The ship that carried the work sank, and it was lost at sea. No additional copy existed.

57 Habermas, *The Structural Transformation of the Public Sphere*; Baker, *Inventing the French Revolution*, 167–72; Farge, *Subversive Words*.

58 Weber, *The Protestant Ethic and the Spirit of Capitalism*.

CHAPTER ONE

1 "Revocation of the Edict of Nantes (October 22, 1685)," 2:288–9.

2 Louis XIV, *Mémoires pour l'instruction du Dauphin*, 80.

3 For a list of the abjurations, see Douen, *La Révocation de l'Édit de Nantes*, 438–88.

4 Fontaine, *Memoirs of a Huguenot Family*. I have chosen to use the Francophone version of his name. He was also known as Jacques de la Fontaine, but was said have dropped the indication of ancient nobility (i.e., de la) for reasons of humility.

5 Michelet, *Histoire de France jusqu'au XVIe siècle*, 13:111.

6 Sahlins, "Fictions of a Catholic France."

7 These edicts are reproduced in Bergeal, *Protestantisme et tolérance en France au XVIIIe siècle*.

8 Isambert, "Recueil general des anciennes lois françaises," 2:180–3.

9 On the interplay and dependency between the realm of reality and the symbolic realm, see Toews, "Intellectual History after the Linguistic Turn"; Baker, *Inventing the French Revolution* 1–11; Scott, "The Evidence of Experience."

10 Mours, *Essai sommaire de géographie du protestantisme réformé français au XVIIe siècle*; Krumenacker, "Une perception protestante de l'espace au XVIIIe siècle?" 146–7.

11 Joutard, *Les camisards.*

12 Greengrass, *The French Reformation*, 46. Poland refers to it as a "semi-circle." Poland, *French Protestantism and the French Revolution*, 9.

13 Mandrou, *Introduction to Early Modern France, 1500–1640*, 81–2.

14 Chartier, Compère, and Julia, *L'Education en France du XVIe au XVIIIe siècles*, 17, 23–6.

15 Greengrass, *The French Reformation*, 46.

16 In the commune of Puylaurens, just west of Toulouse, the average number of *abjurations* jumped from fifteen to forty-two in 1685. This trend of former Protestants baptizing their newborns in the Catholic Church mirrored this increase. Only with the death of Louis XIV and Antoine Court's efforts in the region did these numbers return to their pre-Revocation rates. See Frêche, "Contre-Réforme et dragonnades (1610–1789)," 368–9, 377; McManners, *Church and Society in Eighteenth-Century France*, 2:565; Mours, *Essai sommaire de géographie du Protestantisme réformé française au XVIIe siècle.*

17 Benedict, *The Huguenot Population of France*, 7–10.

18 The best summary of these estimates is Lods, *Traité de l'administration des cultes protestants*, 549–55. See also Annex I in Poland, *French Protestantism and the French Revolution*, 283–6.

19 Condorcet, "Réflexions d'un citoyen catholique," v, 447; Condorcet, *Le roi doit modifier les loix portées contre les Protestans*, 14, 31, 68, 92, 100. Saint-Étienne and others used the 3,000,000 figure when they found it convenient as well. See Saint-Étienne, "Instructions aux pasteurs du Languedoc au sujet de l'édit de tolérance."

20 *BSHPF* 35 (1886): 471–3. No author indicated.

21 Poland, *French Protestantism and the French Revolution*, 286.

22 Stanwood, "Between Eden and Empire." See also Stanwood, *The Global Refuge.*

23 See Probasco, "Catherine de Medici and Huguenot Colonization, 1560–1567."

24 See Hulton, *The Work of Jacques Le Moyne de Morgues.*

25 Stanwood, "Between Eden and Empire."

26 Van Ruymbeke, "Minority Survival," 11–13.

27 Van Ruymbeke, "Minority Survival."

28 Boucher, *France and the American Tropics to 1700*, 212.

29 Lafleur and Abénon, "The Protestants and the Colonization of the French West Indies," 285–309. See also Lafleur, *Les protestants aux Antilles françaises du Vent sous l'ancien régime.*

30 Law, "Jean Barbot as a Source for the Slave Coast of West Africa."

31 Hair, Jones, and Law, *Barbot on Guinea.*

32 Denis, "The Cape Huguenots and Their Legacy in Apartheid South Africa."

33 Weber, *The Protestant Ethic and the Spirit of Capitalism*, 16–26.

34 I will not venture to list every author that contributed to this debate, but it is sufficient to say that most criticisms can fall into two categories: 1. Forms of capitalism thrived in Catholic Europe prior to the Protestant Reformation; 2. The driving force behind the development of capitalism was rationality rather than asceticism. See Tawney, *Religion and the Rise of Capitalism*; Trevor-Roper, *Religion, the Reformation and Social Change*; Viner, *Religious Thought and Economic Society*; Chaicraft and Harrington, *The Protestant Ethic Debate*; and Jacob and Kadane, "Missing, Now Found in the Eighteenth Century."

35 Wood, *Benjamin Constant: A Biography*, 1.

36 Not all aristocratic families converted. Some, like those in Burgundy, remained true to their religious confession despite royal pressure. See Ligou, *Le Protestantisme français en France de 1598 à 1715*, 193–203; Romane-Musculus, "L'Église réformé de Pouzauges de l'Édit de Nantes à sa Révocation."

37 Lougee, *Facing the Revocation*, 3.

38 Ligou, "Le Protestantisme français dans la seconde moitié du XVIIIe siècle," 10; Amand, "La bourgeoisie protestante."

39 Poland, *French Protestantism and the French Revolution*, 17.

40 *Mémoire au sujet des religionnaires du Bas Languedoc et des Cévennes, présenté à la cour par l'abbé de Saint-Maximin, docteur de Sorbonne, prévôt et grand vicaire d'Alais*, quoted in Poland, *French Protestantism and the French Revolution*, 17.

41 Vauban, *Mémoire pour le rappel des Huguenots*, 14.

42 Hands and Scouldoudi, *French Protestants Relieved through the Threadneedle Street Church*, 192.

43 Court, *Lettre d'un patriote*, 12; Court, *Le patriote français et impartial*, I, 379.

44 Caveirac, *Apologie de Louis XIV et de son conseil,* 72ff; Read, "L'Opinion du duc de Bourgogne," 347.

45 Scoville, *The Persecution of Huguenots.* For the most thorough critique of Scoville's monograph, see Grassby, Review of t*he Persecution of Huguenots.*

46 Scoville, *The Persecution of Huguenots,* 118–30.

47 Ibid., 434–47.

48 For more details, see Lüthy, *La banque protestante en France.*

49 Émile G. Léonard made this case forcefully in 1955. See Léonard, *Le Protestant français,* esp. chapter 4.

50 Nicolet, *L'Idee republicaine en France.* See also Robbins, *The Eighteenth-Century Commonwealthsman*; Pocock, *The Machiavellian Moment*; Higonnet, *Sister Republics*; Baker, "A Classical Republican in Eighteenth-Century Bordeaux: Guillaume-Joseph Saige"; Wright, *A Classical Republican in Eighteenth-Century France*; Gojosso, *Le concept de la république en France.*

51 Herman, "The Huguenot Republic and Antirepublicanism in Seventeenth-Century France," 251.

52 Beik, *Absolutism and Society in Seventeenth-Century France.*

53 Maimbourg, *Histoire du Calvinisme,* 2, 51.

54 Koenigsberger, "Republicanism, Monarchism, and Liberty," 71–2.

55 Galland, "Les pasteurs français Amyraut, Bochart etc."

CHAPTER TWO

1 "Lettre de Monsieur Arnauld, docteur de Sorbonne, à Monseigneur l'Évêque de Malaga."

2 Robin Gwynn argues that in the 1680s the word *réfugiés* became widely used in the British Isles, and Huguenots fled France across the channel; yet the word also became more widely used in French-language writings in France and throughout the diaspora. See Gwynn, *Huguenot Heritage,* 1.

3 The best work on Pierre Jurieu remains Dodge, *The Political Theory of the Huguenots of the Dispersion.* See also Knetsch, *Pierre Jurieu: Theoloog en politikus der refuge*; Howells, *Pierre Jurieu: Antinomial Radical*; Knetsch, "Pierre Jurieu and the Glorious Revolution According to His '*Lettres pastorales.*'"

4 For a thorough examination of the debates between Bayle and Jurieu, see Van der Lugt, *Bayle, Jurieu, and the* Dictionnaire Historique et Critique.

5 Jurieu, *L'esprit de Mr Arnaud.*

6 Bayle, *Avis important aux réfugiez.* In this chapter, I am placing Bayle with the other exiled Protestants. This choice favours an understanding of the Calvinist sect as a sociological category more than an expression of a true religious community. Bayle's relationship with religion changed frequently over the course of his life. He was a rather ambiguous Calvinist.

7 Laursen, "Introduction," in Laursen, *New Essays*, 2.

8 See Labrousse, "Reading Bayle in Paris."

9 Hazard, *The Crisis of the European Mind*, xiii.

10 Jurieu, *Lettres pastorales.*

11 Jurieu, *Traité de la puissance de l'Eglise.*

12 Jurieu, *La politique du clerge de France.*

13 Galland, *Les Pasteurs français Amyraut, Bochart etc.*, 54; Merlat, *Traité pouvoir sur les absolus des souverains.* Merlat's text, according to Dodge, had been written closer to the beginning of the decade and only printed in 1685. Dodge, *The Political Theory of the Huguenots of the Dispersion*, 7.

14 Bossuet described Jurieu as such in *Oeuvres completes*, 1447. See Claude's rebuke of the Jansenists Antoine Arnauld and Pierre Nicole. Claude died in the Netherlands two years after the Revocation. Claude, *Réponse au livre de M. Arnaud*; Claude, *La Défense de la reformation contre le livre intitule Préjugez légitimes contre les Calvinistes.* The Jansenist Nicole had published the *Préjuges légitimes contre les Calvinistes* two years earlier to great controversy.

15 Benoît, *Histoire de l'Édit de Nantes*, V, 730.

16 Jue, *Heaven Upon Earth*, 239.

17 Jurieu, *Accomplissement des prophéties*; Jurieu, *The Accomplishment of the Scripture Prophecies*, 26.

19 Stanwood, *The Global Refuge*, 11.

19 Bracken, "Pierre Jurieu: The Politics of Prophecy," 92.

20 Popkin, *The Third Force in Seventeenth-Century Thought.*

21 Jurieu, *Lettres pastorales*, 2:325. Acher published three volumes of Jurieu's letters between 1686 and 1689.

22 Jurieu, *Lettres pastorales,* 1:112. The Babylonian captivity lasted 1,260 days, and the Roman Empire had fallen 1,260 years before Jurieu's time of writing. Jurieu argued that this signaled the coming destruction of the Roman Empire. See Jurieu, *Lettres pastorales,* 3:269, 505.
23 Ibid., 3:253.
24 Ibid., 3:242.
25 Ibid., 3:506. Jurieu's better-known prophecies can be found in Jurieu, *Accomplissement des prophéties.*
26 Certainly untenable, Jurieu's argument assumed belief in the truth of Calvinist doctrine. See Jurieu, *La Politique du clergé*; Lennon, *Reading Bayle,* 81–106; Van der Lugt, *Bayle, Jurieu, and the* Dictionnaire Historique et Critique, 71.
27 Gregory, *Salvation at Stake,* 55.
28 Stanwood, *The Global Refuge,* 11–12.
29 Perry, *From Theology to History,* 5.
30 Jurieu, "Lettre XIX," in *Lettres pastorales,* 3:451.
31 Jurieu, "Lettre XXI," in *Lettres pastorales,* 3:510. Jurieu maintains this theme in his sixteenth letter as well. Jurieu, "Lettre XVI," in *Lettres pastorales,* 2:378.
32 Van der Linden, "A Tearful Diaspora."
33 Rosenwein, *Emotional Communities in the Early Middle Ages.*
34 Jurieu, "Lettre XXI," in *Lettres pastorales,* 3:510.
35 Jurieu, "Lettre XVII," in *Lettres pastorales,* 1:406.
36 Douen, "Claude Brousson, séjour en Hollande, 1694–5," 62.
37 Utt and Strayer, *The Bellicose Dove,* 94.
38 Brousson, *La Manne mystique du Désert,* 236; Utt and Strayer, *The Bellicose Dove,* 20, 45, 56, 98, 134, 269.
39 De Tocqueville, *L'Ancien régime et la Révolution,* 40.
40 Jurieu, *Accomplissement des prophéties,* 18.
41 Jurieu, *The Accomplishment of the Scripture Prophecies,* 8–10.
42 Ibid., 10–11.
43 Ibid., 13–14.
44 See Hochstrasser, "The Claims of Conscience," 24.
45 Varillas, *Histoire des révolutions arrivées dans l'Europe en matière de religion,* vol. 1. Not all Huguenot supporters of James II maintained such religious inflammatory positions as Jurieu. Some Protestant ministers,

like Jean de la Brune, reflected on the political improvements of the post-1688 revolutionary English world and only subtly dabbled with the pro-Protestant elements of the revolution. *Histoire de la révolution d'Irlande*, attributed to the Calvinist minister of the diaspora La Brune, traced the history of the English Revolution in Ireland and its positive effects for Protestants "where the majority of the nation is Catholic." La Brune, *Histoire de la révolution d'Irlande*, 47.

46 Howells, *Pierre Jurieu: Antinomial Radical*, 59.

47 Jurieu, *The Accomplishment of the Scripture Prophecies*, 279.

48 Ibid., 85–6, 94, and 244–5.

49 Ibid., 251.

50 Ibid., 220–1.

51 Gillespie, *The Theological Origins of Modernity*; Gregory, *The Unintended Reformation*. Gregory does not discuss how the concept of revolution was shaped by theological interpretation.

52 Kors, *Atheism in France, 1650–1729*, 288.

CHAPTER THREE

1 On Bayle as Orthodox Calvinist, see Labrousse, *Pierre Bayle*, 2:440; as "Catholic-Calvinist," see Lennon, *Reading Bayle*, 44. On Jurieu's charge against Bayle as a Socinian, see Hazard, *The Crisis of the European Mind*, 104; and Tinsley, "Sozzini's Ghost." Enlightenment philosophers often imagined Bayle to be their intellectual ancestor; on Bayle as early Deist, see Labrousse, "Reading Bayle in Paris." On Bayle as indifferent to theology altogether, see Kamen, *The Rise of Toleration*, 239. On Bayle as a crypto-atheist hostile to theological, dogmatic thought – this is generally Jonathan Israel's position – see Israel, *Enlightenment Contested*.

2 Bost, *Pierre Bayle*, 40–52.

3 Cassirer, *The Philosophy of the Enlightenment*, 167.

4 Popkin, *The History of Skepticism*, 300.

5 Jurieu, *Des droits des deux souverains*, 4; Rees, "Kant, Bayle, and Indifferentism"; Popkin, *The History of Skepticism*, 300.

6 Generally, there are two schools of thought when it comes to Bayle's religion: the contextualists, or "Revisionists," and a smaller Italian school

of "counter-Revisionists." Élisabeth Labrousse led the pack in insisting that Bayle be read in his own context, free from the contortions forced upon him by the later Enlightenment period. This meant emphasizing his seventeenth-century intellectual tradition, one guided by Calvinist theology and his own particular brand of fideism. This leads us to imagine Bayle as a skeptical philosopher with Christian roots – a radically different image than the rampant atheist philosopher that counter-Revisionists posit. For the Revisionists, see Dibon, *Pierre Bayle: Le philosophe de Rotterdam*; Labrousse, *Pierre Bayle*; Rex, *Essays on Pierre Bayle and Religious Controversy*; Brush, *Montaigne and Bayle*; Popkin, *The History of Skepticism*; and Bost, *Pierre Bayle*. For the counter-Revisionist stance on Bayle, see Brogi, *Teologiea senza verità*; Mori, *Bayle Philosophe*; and Paganini, "Towards a 'Critical' Bayle." With his insistence on the intellectual dominance of Spinoza and radical atheism, it makes sense to put Jonathan Israel in the counter-Revisionist camp as well. See Israel, *Radical Enlightenment*, especially chapter 18.

7 Bastide, "Bayle est-il l'auteur de l'*Avis aux Réfugiés*?"; O'Cathasaigh, "Bayle and the Authorship of the *Avis aux réfugiés*."

8 Bayle, *Avis important aux réfugiez.*

9 My reading of Bayle tends to lean toward the dialogic interpretations of Thomas M. Lennon, who avoids the Revisionist and counter-Revisionist positions by adopting a "polyphonic" approach to reading Bayle. Rather than read Bayle's works, authored anonymously or under his name, as facsimiles of his political views, I read them as a form of intellectual exploration, a way of balancing arguments and finding possible solutions to the Huguenot refugee problem. This is the case for his arguments concerning the relationship between revolutionary and religious sentiment. See Lennon, *Reading Bayle*. On early French orientalism and Enlightenment thought, see Harvey, *The French Enlightenment and Its Others*. Other Huguenots began to explore east Asian history as a means to offer a critique of European culture, too, around the time of the Revocation. See La Brune, *La Morale de Confucius.*

10 Baker and Edelstein, *Scripting Revolution*. It is worth mentioning that religion is scarcely discussed in this volume, appearing only a few times outside of footnotes. Such a lacunae only further evidences the assumed

secularity of their revolutionary script – a secularity that has its own genealogy and deserves a more complicated discussion than is possible here.

11 Ibid., 2.

12 Tocqueville, *The Old Regime and the French Revolution*, 24–5.

13 Becker, *The Heavenly City of the Eighteenth-Century Philosophers*, 155; Van Kley, *The Religious Origins of the French Revolution*. Van Kley focuses on the role that Jansenist controversy played in the disenchantment of the sacral absolutist state.

14 Louis XIV established the Gallican Church with the Gallican Articles in 1682.

15 See Denis, "The Cape Huguenots and Their Legacy in Apartheid South Africa."

16 Benedict, *The Huguenot Population of France*, 7–10.

17 Perry, *From Theology to History*, 5.

18 Alan Charles Kors makes a similar argument concerning atheism. Rather than imagining prototypical atheists as progenitors of atheistic thought, Kors contends that Catholic polemicists (men of faith and learning) invented atheist straw men in order to undercut those same arguments and deter their parishioners away from heresy at a time when atheistic heresy was not a real threat to the intellectual or social Catholic community. See Kors, *Atheism in France, 1650–1729*.

19 Jurieu, *La Politique du clergé de France*.

20 Maimbourg, *Histoire du calvinisme*. The Huguenot lawyer Jean Rou was the first to respond to Maimbourg. See Rou, *Remarques sur l'Histoire du calvinisme de M. Maimbourg*.

21 Bayle, *Critique générale de l'Histoire du calvinisme de M. Maimbourg*.

22 Jurieu, *Histoire du calvinisme et celle du papisme mises en parallèle*.

23 Bost, *Pierre Bayle*, 308.

24 On the millenarian tradition within the Huguenot diaspora see Laborie, *Enlightening Enthusiasm*, 23.

25 Bost, *Pierre Bayle*, 310.

26 Van der Lugt, *Bayle, Jurieu, and the* Dictionnaire Historique et Critique, 73.

27 Larroques, *Nouvelles accusations contre M. Varillas*, 5.

28 Voltaire, "Des mensonges imprimés," in *Œuvres complètes de Voltaire*, 31b: 352. In a note on Varillas, Voltaire sarcastically noted that "not everyone has the gift of invention."

29 Antoine Varillas, *Histoire des révolutions arrivées dans l'Europe en matière de religion*, 1:6, 89.

30 McMahon, *Enemies of the Enlightenment.*

31 This religious "anthropology" coincided with the rise of the idea of "religion" and "religions" as explored in works like Harrison, *"Religion" and the Religions in the English Enlightenment*; and, more applicable for its focus on the Huguenot community, Hunt, Jacob, and Mijnhardt, *The Book that Changed Europe.*

32 Bayle, *Avis important aux réfugiez.*

33 This has normally been interpreted as "Carus Larebonius, avocat au Parlement de Paris." Carus Larebonius was Bayle's pseudonym in his 1692 *Janua Coelorum Reserata.* See Dodge, *The Political Theory of the Huguenots of the Dispersion*, 94–5.

34 Anonymous, *Réponse d'un nouveau converti à la lettre d'un réfugié* (Paris, 1689), quoted in Dodge, *The Political Theory of the Huguenots of the Dispersion*, 42.

35 Van der Lugt, *Bayle, Jurieu, and the* Dictionnaire Historique et Critique, 118.

36 Bayle, *Avis important aux réfugiez*, 8–9.

37 Ibid.

38 Ibid., 11.

39 Van der Lugt, *Bayle, Jurieu, and the* Dictionaire Historique et Critique, 155.

40 English works on the Thai Revolution of 1688 are few. For the French influence in the region see Hutchinson, "The Retirement of the French Garrison from Bangkok in the Year 1688," 159–99; and Hutchinson, *1688 Revolution in Siam: The Memoir of Father de Bèze.* See also Pombejra, "Seventeenth-Century Ayutthaya: A Shift to Isolation?" 250–72.

41 See "Lettre 830: Pierre Bayle à Claude Nicaise."

42 See d'Orléans, *Histoire de M. Constance.* D'Orléans also wrote two other books, which used the language of "revolution" in their titles: *Histoire des révolutions d'Angleterre* (1689) and *Histoire des Révolutions d'Espagne* (published posthumously in 1734).

43 Tachard, *Voyage de Siam*.

44 See Hutchinson, *1688 Revolution in Siam*, xi–xv.

45 Bayle, *Avis important aux réfugiez*, 7–8 (italics in original).

46 See Jurieu, "Avis important au public," 7.

47 Rex, *Essays on Pierre Bayle and Religious Controversy*, 227.

48 Bayle, *Avis important aux réfugiez*, 318–21.

49 Locke, *A Letter Concerning Toleration*, 73.

50 Dodge, *The Political Theory of the Huguenots of the Dispersion*, 99.

51 In particular see Gauchet, *The Disenchantment of the World*.

52 The obvious caveat to this statement is Van Kley, *The Religious Origins of the French Revolution*. Marxist histories of the French Revolution especially ignored the religious origins of the French Revolution or propagated the image of the eighteenth century, when the religious began to fade from public view and thus political importance – or so their arguments go. See especially Vovelle, *Piété baroque et déchristianisation*.

53 See Jacobs, *The Radical Enlightenment*, iv. For Jonathan Israel's thesis see Israel, *Radical Enlightenment*.

54 For work on Jean Rousset de Missy, see Jacobs, *The Radical Enlightenment*.

55 Jainchill, "1685 and the French Revolution." On the nineteenth-century tradition, see Quinet, *La Révolution*; and Michelet, *Histoire de France, nouvelle édition revue et augmentée*. See also Banks, "The Protestant Origins of the French Revolution."

56 See Van Kley, "Christianity as Casualty and Chrysalis of Modernity."

CHAPTER FOUR

1 Charles Coquerel, *Histoire des églises du désert chez les Protestants de France*, 1:293.

2 Smiles, *The Huguenots in France after the Revocation of the Edict of Nantes*, 205–6. Court is regularly referred to as the "restorer" of the French Calvinist Church, which takes on two meanings. First, it refers to his work to rebuild the Church in the wake of the Revocation; second, Court promoted a return to scripture within the Calvinist fold in Southern France that he hoped would displace the prophetic strains of

the Church and lead to a spiritual regeneration of the community. See Joutard, *La Révocation de l'édit de Nantes ou Les faiblesses d'un État*, 282.

3 See in particular Hugues, *Antoine Court*; and Borrel, *Biographie d'Antoine Court*.

4 Camisards were Huguenots in the Cévennes region and in the Vaunage in southern France who fought back against the king's forces after the Revocation of the Edict of Nantes. Their turn toward violence was often predicated, if not fuelled, by the prophetic claims of their leaders.

5 Duley-Haour, "Antoine Court and Refugee Political Thought"; Duley-Haour, "Correspondances Pastorales"; Duley-Haour, "Désert et Refuge."

6 Pocock, "Conservative Enlightenment and Democratic Revolutions," 84; Pocock, *Barbarism and Religion*, 1:7.

7 Sorkin, *The Religious Enlightenment*, 11.

8 Sorkin, *The Religious Enlightenment*.

9 Sauter, *Visions of the Enlightenment*, 21.

10 Duley-Haour's work reconstructing the epistolary matrix in which Court found himself represents an important methodological intervention in revealing this hidden transcript. Duley-Haour, "Antoine Court and Refugee Political Thought."

11 Coleman, *The Virtues of Abandon*.

12 Court, *Apologie des protestans du royaume de France*; Court, *Le patriote français et impartial*; Court, *Lettre d'un patriote*; Court, *Histoire des troubles des Cévennes*. Otto H. Selles argues that Antoine Court did not actually write the *Lettre d'un patriote*. He makes this argument drawing from stylistic differences between the two documents as well an odd cross reference in the later *Histoire des troubles des Cévennes*, which cites *Le patriote français et impartial*, but not the more recent *Lettre d'un patriot*. Selles does not make a convincing argument for an alternative author of the piece, and given the vagaries of anonymous Huguenot publishing during the period, we run the risk of falsely identifying authorship of such documents during the *Désert* period. See Selles's preface in Court, *Le patriote français et impartial*, CXXXIX, CXL.

13 Goldwyn, "Strange Language and Practices of Disorder." See also Rolland, *Dictionnaire des Camisards*; and Bost, *Les Martyrs D'aigues-Mortes*.

14 Hugues, *Les synods du Désert*, 1:2.

15 See Basnage, *Instruction et lettre pastorale aux réformés de France*. This

work was reprinted during the War of Austrian Succession in the hopes of subduing possible Protestant protest. Its reprinting caused Antoine Court and Armand de la Chapelle, a minister of a Walloon church at the Hague, to reply and to reiterate the importance of a public presence for the spiritual well-being of the populace. See Court, *Réponse à la lettre sur les assemblées*; and de la Chapelle, *La nécessité du culte public.*

16 Yardeni, *Le Refuge protestant*, 24.

17 Duley-Haour, "Antoine Court and Refugee Political Thought," 135.

18 Hugues, *Antoine Court.*

19 Duley-Haour, "Antoine Court and Refugee Political Thought," 131.

20 Court's *Apologie des protestans du royaume de France sur leurs assemblées religieuses* was published in Vevey, a small town outside of Geneva, but the title page indicated that it was published in the "Désert."

21 Matytsin, "Fictional Letters or Real Accusations?"

22 Rochemont, "Lettre de Rochemont à Court du 30 octobre 1745," quoted in Duley-Haour, "Antoine Court and Refugee Political Thought," 145.

23 Court, "Mémoire," 82.

24 Beaumelle, *L'Asiatique tolérant.*

25 Hunt, Jacob, and Mijnhardt, *The Book that Changed Europe*, 1.

26 Court, *Lettre d'un patriote*, title page (italics mine).

27 Court, *Le patriote français et impartial*, 73.

28 Court, *Lettre d'un patriote*, 16–17, 19, 36.

29 Élie Benoît, *Histoire de l'Édit de Nantes*, as quoted in Léonard, *Le protestant français*, 52.

30 Léonard, *Le protestant français.* Léonard's *Le protestant français* built on a growing literature debating the ethnographic nature of French Protestants. Their morality could not possibly cooperate with "l'esprit gaulois." Léonard challenged the notion that Protestants were "others" residing within a Catholic France. Half history and half sociology, Léonard's monograph pointed out that differences in geography, class background, and internal theological squabbling left French Calvinists as diverse as their Catholic neighbours. This historical ethnic diversity undermined Max Weber's Protestant ethic argument.

31 Court, *Le patriote français et impartial*, 70; Court, *Lettre d'un patriote*, 25–36.

32 Court, *Le patriote français et impartial,* 25; Court, *Lettre d'un patriote,* 12, 98.

33 Court, *Lettre d'un patriote,* 40.

34 Court, *Le patriote français et impartial,* 66–7; Court, *Lettre d'un patriote,* 28.

35 Court, *Le patriote français et impartial,* 12; Court, *Lettre d'un patriote,* 36. On the anti-Protestant, Catholic discourse of Huguenot republicanism, see Herman, "The Huguenot Republic and Antirepublicanism," 249–69; and Nicolet, *L'idée républicaine en France*, especially chapter 1.

36 Caveirac, *Paradoxes intéressans sur la cause et les effets de la révocation de l'Edit de Nantes.* See also Montégut, *La voix du vrai patriote catholique.*

37 Court had already launched an attack, in *Le patriote français et impartial,* against Montesquieu and Voltaire, the latter of whom had employed a similar republican-Huguenot connection in his *Le Siècle de Louis XIV*. But these criticisms of the philosophes were not as severe as in his *Lettre d'un patriote.*

38 See Gauchet, *The Disenchantment of the World*, xiii. Gauchet uses "disenchantment" to signal the growing distance between the celestial and terrestrial sphere. This differs from Max Weber's use of the word in terms of the growing importance of reason. For Weber's theory of "disenchantment" see Weber, "Science as Vocation," 13.

39 Court, *Lettre d'un patriote,* 70–1.

40 Court, *Le patriot français et impartial,* 25; Court, *Lettre d'un patriote,* 72.

41 Court, *Le patriote français et impartial,* 25; Court, *Lettre d'un patriote,* 59.

42 Court, *Histoire des troubles des Cévennes,* 2:142.

43 Ibid., 2:439.

44 Court, *Lettre d'un patriote,* 34.

45 On the sentimental turn of the Protestant Enlightenment and the place of Turrettini and Vernet, see Rosenblatt, "The Christian Enlightenment." Court is absent from Rosenblatt's work.

46 Bell, *The Cult of the Nation,* 20.

47 Court, *Lettre d'un patriote,* 47.

48 Bell, *The Cult of the Nation,* 25.

49 Court, *Le patriote français et impartial,* 17.

50 Court, *Lettre d'un patriote,* 86.

51 Court, *Le patriot français et impartial*, 28, 74; Court, *Lettre d'un patriote*, 13–4.

52 Court, *Lettre d'un patriote*, 52.

53 Court, *Histoire des troubles des Cévennes*, 3:401.

54 Ibid., 2:73.

55 Ibid., 1:278.

56 Habermas, *The Structural Transformation of the Public Sphere*; Tocqueville, *Democracy in America*, 296. See also Chisick, "Public Opinion and Political Culture in France," 48–77. For more on critiques of the bourgeois public sphere and public opinion, see Stieber, *Post-Independence Writing*, 10–16.

57 Baker, *Inventing the French Revolution*, 167–72.

58 Farge, *Subversive Words*, 40.

59 Court's collectivity and apparent anti-individualism in the face of French state repression further complicates Charly Coleman's argument for a theological assault on the individualistic impulses of the French Enlightenment. See Coleman, *The Virtues of Abandon*.

CHAPTER FIVE

1 The *Désert* period refers to the era between 1685 and 1787, when the French state outlawed Calvinism. To conceal their own identity and protect their families, many Calvinists adopted *Désert* names.

2 Saint-Étienne, *Triomphe de l'intolérance, ou Anecdotes de la vie d'Ambroise Borély, mort à Londres, âge 103 ans*. Other editions came out in 1784, 1788, 1820, 1821, 1826, 1846, and 1886. Unless otherwise noted, I will be referencing the 1788 version of the text. See Saint-Étienne, *Le vieux Cévenol, ou Anecdotes de la vie d'Ambroise Borély, mort à Londres agé de 103 ans*. Differences do exist between each text. Narrative arch and general argument do not change, but chapter organization does change from version to version. While arguments can be made about the organizational choices made from edition to edition, the goal of this chapter is to make the case for a larger Protestant Enlightenment and Saint-Étienne's role in it.

3 Poland, *French Protestantism and the French Revolution*, 75.

4 See Bien, *The Calas Affair*; Adams, *The Huguenots and French Opinion*; Bell, *Lawyers and Citizens.*

5 Bien, *The Calas Affair*, 25.

6 Ibid.; Woodbridge, "An 'Unnatural Alliance' for Religious Toleration" 508.

7 See Voltaire, *Traité sur la tolérance*; and Voltaire, *Avis au public sur les parricides.*

8 Jean-Jacques Rousseau, *Discours sur l'origine et les fondements de l'inégalité parmi les hommes* (Amsterdam, 1755).

9 In a letter to Paul Rabaut, Saint-Étienne's father, Rousseau sympathized with the Calvinist cause, but said his own poverty restricted his ability to assist in any substantive way. See Baird, *The Huguenots and the Revocation of the Edict of Nantes,* 2:517.

10 Garrioch, *The Huguenots of Paris.*

11 On the Protestant Enlightenment, see Pocock, *Barbarism and Religion*, 5:92; and Bradley and Van Kley, *Religion and Politics in Enlightenment Europe,* 15.

12 Hunt, *Inventing Human Rights*, 32.

13 For general overviews of Saint-Étienne's life, see Lods, *Essai sur la vie de Rabaut de Saint-Étienne*; and Dupont, *Rabaut Saint-Étienne, 1743–1793.*

14 Pocock, "Conservative Enlightenment and Democratic Revolutions," 84.

15 Saint-Étienne, *Le vieux Cévenol*, 112.

16 Ibid., 11.

17 Gaidan, "Paul Rabaut et sa famille," 27.

18 Dardier, *Paul Rabaut. Ses lettres a Antoine Court, 1739–1755*, 2: 121.

19 Saint-Étienne, *Lettres a Monsieur Bailly sur l'histoire primitive de la Grece.*

20 See Rosenblatt, "The Christian Enlightenment," 285.

21 Pouilly, *Théorie des sentimens*, vi, 3.

22 Rosenblatt, "The Christian Enlightenment," 295.

23 Gal-Pomaret, *Le chretien par conviction et par sentiment.* According to the French Book Trade in Enlightenment Europe database, 780 copies of Gal-Pomaret's book were printed in Neufchâtel, Switzerland – 775 of which were sold in southern France. Burrows and Curran, *The French Book Trade in Enlightenment Europe Database, 1769–1794*, browse title: *Chrétien (le) par conviction et par sentiment.*

24 Lasserre, *Le Séminaire de Lausanne,* 298. See also Dupont, *Rabaut Saint-Étienne, 1743–1793,* 11–72.

25 His name is sometimes spelled Elie Benoist. For Benoît's history of the Edict of Nantes and its Revocation, see Benoît, *Histoire de l'Edit de Nantes.* See also Bost, "Elie Benoist et l'historiographie de l'édit de Nantes," 267–79.

26 The most thorough examination of this historiography is Perry, *From Theology to History.*

27 Court, *Histoire des troubles des Cevennes.*

28 The invention of "religion" and "religions" is traced to the religious controversies of the seventeenth and eighteenth centuries in England as well as in France. See Harrison, *"Religion" and the Religions in the English Enlightenment.*

29 "Religion," in Diderot and d'Alembert, *Encyclopédie,* 14:83–8. It also recognizes that "religion" even into the second half of the eighteenth century could refer to the "so-called Reformed religion" or French Calvinism.

30 Court, *Lettre d'un patriote,* 47. See also Court, *Histoire des troubles des Cévennes.*

31 Bell, *The Cult of the Nation,* 25.

32 Court, *Lettre d'un patriote,* 25.

33 Borello, *Du Désert au Royaume,* 53; Chartier, *The Cultural Origins of the French Revolution,* 19.

34 Saint-Étienne, *Le vieux Cévenol,* 87 (italics mine).

35 Hunt, *Inventing Human Rights.*

36 Rousseau, *Emile,* 221–3.

37 See Rousseau, *Julie, ou la nouvelle Héloïse,* in *Oeuvres complète;* Darnton, *The Great Cat Massacre,* 248.

38 Louis Dupré makes a similar argument on the connection between emotion, compassion, sentimentalism, and political action in Dupré, *The Enlightenment and the Intellectual Foundations of Modern Culture,* 53–67.

39 On the "General Will," see Riley, *The General Will before Rousseau;* and Farr and Williams, *The General Will: The Evolution of a Concept.*

40 See Riley, *The General Will before Rousseau,* esp. ch 1.

41 Necker, *De l'importance des opinions religieuses*, 92–3; Rosenblatt, "The Christian Enlightenment," 283–301.

42 Necker, *De l'importance des opinions religieuses*, 326.

43 Frazer, *The Enlightenment of Sympathy*.

44 Lougee, "'The Pains I Took to Save My/His Family,'" 1–64.

45 Saint-Étienne, *Le vieux Cévenol*, 12, 32, 58, 70, 73, 82, 99. *Fugitive* and *rèfugee* were often used synonymously in the eighteenth century. Both owe their linguistic ancestry to *fugere*, meaning "to flee" in Latin.

46 Saint-Étienne, *Le vieux Cévenol*, 115.

47 See the 1784 version. The 1788 version lacks the same precision, detailing Borély's age to the year and not to the month.

48 For the role of editors, see Iliffe, "Author-mongering: The 'Editor' between Producer and Consumer," 166–92; Sher, *The Enlightenment and the Book*.

49 On the textual changes from edition to edition, see Borello, *Du Désert au Royaume*, 9–19.

50 Aulard, *La Révolution française*, 13:191.

51 Saint-Étienne, *Le vieux Cévenol*, 53.

52 See Hunt, *Inventing Human Rights*, 111.

53 Saint-Étienne, *Le vieux Cévenol*, 86.

54 Ibid., 102.

55 See Merrick, *The Desacralization of the French Monarchy*, 95–6; Van Kley, *The Religious Origins of the French Revolution*, 164.

56 Saint-Étienne, *Le vieux Cévenol*, 102.

57 Ibid.

58 See Krumenacker, "Une perception protestante de l'espace au XVIIIe siècle?" 146–7.

59 Malesherbes, *Mémoire sur le mariage des protestans, en 1785;* Malesherbes, *Seconde mémoire sur le mariage des Protestans*.

60 Roberts, *Sentimental Savants: Philosophical Families in Enlightenment France*, 4.

61 Baecque, *The Body Politic*, 12.

62 Saint-Étienne, *Le vieux Cévenol*, 46.

63 Ibid., 10.

64 Ibid., 56.

65 Ibid., 21.
66 Ibid., 66, 83.
67 Saint-Étienne, *Le vieux Cévenol* (1784 edition), 95.
68 Ibid., 108.
69 Weber, *The Protestant Ethic and the Spirit of Capitalism*. This is not to say that individuals did not connect Protestantism to modern capitalism vis-à-vis their religious tenets in the eighteenth century. See Jacob and Kadane, "Missing, Now Found in the Eighteenth Century."
70 Saint-Étienne, *Le vieux Cévenol* (1784 edition), 32.
71 Scoville, *The Persecution of Huguenots*. For the most thorough critique of Scoville's monograph see Grassby, Review of *The Persecution of Huguenots*. See also Yardeni, "Naissance et lessor d'un mythe," 191–206.
72 "Edict of Toleration, 1787," 40–3.
73 Ibid.
74 *Archives Parlementaires*, vol. 8, 478.
75 Ibid., 480 (italics mine).
76 Burke, *Reflections on the Revolution in France*, 119.
77 Ibid.
78 "Premier Exercise public du culte réformé à Paris en 1791," 512.

CONCLUSION

1 Barère, *Le Moniteur universel*. Barère's speech was printed on 11 December 1790.
2 Barère and the other supporters of reparative justice for the Huguenots eventually won out, but the extent to which they were successful is unclear and doubtful. How many Huguenots returned to France because of this policy? No complete study of its effects exists, nor does this study pretend to be complete. Anecdotal evidence hardly fills in for the absence of "hard numbers." The methodology used in Philip Benedict's work on the Huguenot population leading up to the Revocation is a good standard. See Benedict, *The Huguenot Population of France*, 1–164. But we do know from personal accounts that the policy attracted an important cadre of Huguenots including the politician and author Benjamin Constant, the sculptor James Pradier, the writer Paul-Jérémie Bitaubé, the diplomat Charles Guillaume Théremin, and many more

into the nineteenth century. Estelle Aebersold has identified 226 people that took advantage of the 1790 declaration – most were individuals of some wealth who returned at the end of the nineteenth and beginning of the twentieth centuries in response to further measures of the state to call back Huguenots. Very few communities ever returned en masse – as the revolutionaries had hoped for. See Aebersold, *Les rémigrés du refuge huguenot*; and Aebersold, "Résultats d'une enquête sur les rémigrés du Refuge huguenot," 45–8.

3 This text mining calculation also allows for a 90 per cent match rate.

4 Maya Jasanoff argues that the age of revolutions of the late eighteenth century was an "age of refugees," but she fails to explore the religious contours of this refugee era that pre-dated the political revolutions. See Jasanoff, "Revolutionary Exiles," 38.

5 Pocock, "Conservative Enlightenment and Democratic Revolutions," 84.

6 Bell, *The Cult of the Nation*, 30.

7 Carpenter, *Refugees of the French Revolution.*

8 Reboul and Philip, *French Emigrants in Revolutionised Europe*, 9.

9 Ibid., 10.

10 *Archives Parlementaires*, 1:427.

11 *Archives Parlementaires*, 1:696.

12 *Archives Parlementaires*, 1:570.

13 "Fugitif," in Diderot and d'Alembert, *Encyclopédie*, 7:360.

14 Barère, *Le Point du jour.*

15 There is much discussion of the emergence of rights discourse in the historiography of the French Enlightenment and revolutionary period. See Hunt, *Inventing Human Rights*; Edelstein, *On the Spirit of Natural Rights.*

16 Taylor, *Modern Social Imaginaries*; Taylor, *A Secular Age.*

17 Bell, *The Cult of the Nation.*

18 Office of the United Nations High Commissioner for Refugees (UNHCR), "Global Trends."

19 Arendt, "We Refugees," 274.

Bibliography

PRIMARY SOURCES

Archives Parlementaires. 1789–1793. Accessed 25 November 2023. https://sul-philologic.stanford.edu/philologic/archparl/.

Barère, Bertrand. *Le Moniteur universel.* Paris, 1790.

– *Le Point du jour*, no. 3 (21 June 1789).

Basnage, Jacques. *Instruction et lettre pastorale aux réformés de France.* Rotterdam, 1719.

Bayle, Pierre. *Avis important aux réfugiez sur leur prochaine retour en France.* 1690.

– *Critique générale de l'Histoire du calvinisme de M. Maimbourg.* Amsterdam, 1682.

Beaumelle, Laurent Angliviel de la. *L'Asiatique tolérant, traité à l'usage de Zéokinizul, roi des Kofirans, surnommé le Chéri, ouvrage traduit de l'arabe du voyageur Bekrinoll, par M. de *****. Amsterdam, 1748.

Benoît, Élie. *Histoire de l'Édit de Nantes contenant les choses les plus remarquables qui se sont passées en France avant & après sa publication, à l'occasion de la diversité des religions, et principalement les contraventions, inexécutions, chicanes, artifices, violences, & autres injustices, que les reformez se plaignent d'y avoir souffertes, jusques à l'édit de révocation, en octobre 1685; avec ce qui a suivi ce nouvel édit jusques à présent.* Delft, 1695.

Bossuet, Jacques-Bénigne. *Oeuvres completes, évèque de Meaux, classées, pour la première fois, selon l'order logique et analogique.* VIII. Paris, 1856.

Brousson, Claude. *La Manne mystique du Désert, ou Sermons prononcez en France dans les Déserts & dans les Cavernes Durant les ténêbres de la nui & l'affliction les années 1689, 1690, 1691, 1692, & 1693*. 3 vols. Amsterdam, 1695.

Brune, Jean de la. *Histoire de la révolution d'Irlande, arrive sous Guillaume III*. Amsterdam, 1691.

– *La Morale de Confucius, Philosophe de la Chine*. Amsterdam, 1688.

Burke, Edmund. *Reflections on the Revolution in France*. London, 1790.

Caveirac, Novi de. *Apologie de Louis XIV et de son conseil, sur la révocation de l'Édit de Nantes, etc.* N.p., 1758.

– *Paradoxes intéressans sur la cause et les effets de la révocation de l'Edit de Nantes, la dépopulation & répopulation du royaume, l'intolérance civile & rigoureuse d'un gouvernement. Pour servir de réponse à la Lettre d'un patriote sur la tolérance civile des protestans de France. Avec une dissertation sur la journée de la S. Barthelemi*. Paris, 1758.

Chapelle, Armand de la. *La nécessité du culte public*. The Hague, 1746.

Claude, Jean. *La Défense de la reformation contre le livre intitule Préjugez légitimes contre les Calvinistes*. Paris, 1673.

– *Réponse au livre de M. Arnaud*. Rouen, 1670.

Condorcet, Nicolas de Caritat, marquis de. *Le roi doit modifier les loix portées contre les Protestans*. London, 1784.

– "Réflexions d'un citoyen catholique, sur les lois de France, rélatives aux protestants." In *Œuvres de Condorcet*, edited by Arthur Condorcet O'Connor and François Arago. Paris, 1847.

Court, Antoine. *Apologie des protestans du royaume de France sur leurs assemblées religieuses*. Le Vevey, 1745.

– *Histoire des troubles des Cévennes; ou, De la guerre des Camisars, sous le regne de Louis le Grant; tirée de manuscrits secrets et autentiques et des observations faites sur les lieux mêmes*. 3 vols. Villefranche, 1760.

– *Le patriote français et impartial où réponse à la lettre de M. l'évêque d'Agen à M. le contrôleur général contre la tolérance des huguenots, en date du premier may 1751*. Villefranche, 1751.

– *Lettre d'un patriote sur la tolérance civile des protestans de France et sur les avantages qui en resulteroient pour le royaume*. N.p., 1756.

– *Réponse à la lettre sur les assemblées*. Geneva, 1745.

Diderot, Denis, and Jean le Rond d'Alembert, eds. *Encyclopédie, ou dictionnaire raisonné des sciences, des arts et des métiers, etc.* University of Chicago:

ARTFL Encyclopédie Project (Autumn 2022 Edition), edited by Robert Morrissey and Glenn Roe. Accessed 25 November 2023. http://encyclopedie.uchicago.edu/.

d'Orléans, Pierre-Joseph. *Histoire de M. Constance, premier ministre du roi de Siam, et de la dernière révolution de cet état.* Paris, 1690.

"Edict of Toleration, 1787." *The French Revolution and Human Rights: A Brief Documentary History*, 40–3.

Fontaine, James B. *Memoirs of a Huguenot Family.* Translated by Ann Maury. New York: George P. Putnam, 1853.

Gal-Pomaret, Jean. *Le chretien par conviction et par sentiment: ou la foi sans incertitude et la pitie sans superstition.* Neufchâtel: De l'imprimerie de la Societe typographique, 1778.

Isambert, François-André. "Recueil general des anciennes lois françaises." In James Harvey Robinson, *Readings in European History*, 2:180–3. Boston: Ginn, 1906.

Jurieu, Pierre. *Accomplissement des prophéties, ou la Déliverance prochaine de l'Eglise.* Rotterdam: Abraham Acher, 1686.

– *The Accomplishment of the Scripture Prophecies: Or the Approaching Deliverance of the Church.* London, 1687.

– "Avis important au public." In *Examen d'un libelle contre la Religion contre l'État et contre la révolution d'Angleterre, intitulé "Avis important aux réfugiez sur leur prochain retour en France."* The Hague, 1691.

– *Des droits des deux souverains en matière de religion, la conscience et le prince, contre un livre intitulé: Commentaire philosophique.* Rotterdam, 1687.

– *Histoire du calvinisme et celle du papisme mises en parallèle mises en parallèle … contre un libelle inititulé l'Histoire du Calvinisme par M. Maimbourg.* Rotterdam, 1683.

– *L'esprit de Mr Arnaud: tire de sa conduite, & des ecrits de luy & de ses disciples, particulierement de l'Apologie pour les catholiques.* Deventer, 1684.

– *La politique du clerge de France, ou, Entretiens curieux de deux catholiques romains, l'un Parisien & l'autre Provincial, sur les moyens dont on se sert aujourd'huy, pour destruire la religion protestante dans ce royaume.* Cologne, 1681.

– *Lettres pastorales adressées aux fidéles de France qui gemissent sous la captivité de Babylon.* 3 vols. Rotterdam, 1686–89.

– *Traité de la puissance de l'Eglise dans lequel on découvre la source de cette puissance … Divisé en diverses lettres écrites à M …. D. à l'occasion de ses ecrits contre la jurisdiction ecclesiastique.* Quevilly, 1677.

Larroques, Daniel. *Nouvelles accusations contre M. Varillas.* Rotterdam, 1686.

"Lettre 830: Pierre Bayle à Claude Nicaise." Lettres 720–901. *Correspondance de Pierre Bayle.* Jean Monnet University. Accessed 27 November 2023. https://bayle-correspondance.univ-st-etienne.fr/?Lettre-830-Pierre-Bayle-a-Claude&lang=fr.

"Lettre de Monsieur Arnauld, docteur de Sorbonne, à Monseigneur l'Évêque de Malaga." In *Oeuvres de Messire Antoine Arnauld*, 32:503–5. Paris, 1780.

Locke, John. *A Letter Concerning Toleration.* Edited by Kerry Walters. Broadview Press, 2013.

Louis XIV. *Mémoires pour l'instruction du Dauphin.* Edited by Pierre Goubert. Paris, 1992.

Maimbourg, Louis. *Histoire du Calvinisme.* Paris, 1682.

Malesherbes, Chrétien Guillaume de Lamoignon de. "Mémoire sur les affaires de religion (1776)." MS. H. 1639. Archives nationale.

– "Mémoire sur le mariage des Protestants (1779)." Fonds Français, MS. 10625. Bibliothèque nationale de France.

– *Mémoire sur le mariage des protestans, en 1785.* N.p., 1785.

– *Seconde mémoire sur le mariage des Protestans.* N.p., 1786.

Merlat, Elie. *Traité pouvoir sur les absolus des souverains, pour server d'instruction, de consolation, et d'apologie aux Églises Réformées de France qui sont affligées.* Cologne, 1685.

Montégut, Antoine-François Bouniol de. *La voix du vrai patriote catholique, opposée à celle des faux patriotes tolérants.* N.p., 1758.

Montesquieu. *Lettres Persanes.* Vol. 3. London, 1935.

Necker, Jacques. *De l'importance des opinions religieuses.* London, 1788.

Nicole, Pierre. *Préjuges légitimes contre les Calvinistes.* Paris, 1671.

Office of the United Nations High Commissioner for Refugees (UNHCR). *Convention and Protocol Relating to the Status of Refugees.* Geneva: United Nations High Commissioner for Refugees, 1951.

– "Global Trends." Accessed 25 November 2023. https://www.unhcr.org/flagship-reports/globaltrends/globaltrends2019/#:~:text=Forcibly%20Displaced%20People%20by%20Country%20of%20Origin&text=By%20the%20end%20of%202019,record%20according%20to%20available%20data.

Pouilly, Louis-Jean Levesque de. *Théorie des sentimens.* London: Jacques Brakstone, 1750.

"Premier Exercise public du culte réformé à Paris en 1791." Bulletin de la Société de l'histoire du protestantisme français [hereafter *BSHPF*] 36 (1886): 512.

"Revocation of the Edict of Nantes (October 22, 1685)." Translated by Dhirvat na Pombejra. In James Harvey Robinson, *Readings in European History*, 2:288–9. Boston: Ginn, 1906.

Rou, Jean. *Remarques sur l'Histoire du calvinisme de M. Maimbourg.* The Hague, 1682.

Rousseau, Jean-Jacques. *Discours sur l'origine et les fondements de l'inégalité parmi les hommes.* Amsterdam, 1755.

– *Emile, or on Education*. Mineola, NY: Dover, 2013.

– *Julie, ou la nouvelle Héloïse*, in *Oeuvres complète*, Paris, 1961.

Saint-Étienne, Rabaut. "Instructions aux pasteurs du Languedoc au sujet de l'édit de tolérance." *BSHPF* 36 (1887): 548–51.

– *Lettres a Monsieur Bailly sur l'histoire primitive de la Grece.* Paris, 1787.

– *Le vieux Cévenol, ou Anecdotes de la vie d'Ambroise Borély, mort à Londres agé de 103 ans.* London, 1788.

– *Triomphe de l'intolérance, ou Anecdotes de la vie d'Ambroise Borély, mort à Londres, âge 103 ans.* London, 1779.

Tachard, Guy. *Voyage de Siam, des pères jesuites, envoyez par le roy aux Indes & à la Chine: avec leurs observations astronomiques, et leurs remarques de physique, de géographie, d'hydrographie, & d'histoire.* Paris, 1686.

Varillas, Antoine. *Histoire des révolutions arrivées dans l'Europe en matière de religion.* 6 vols. Paris, 1686.

Vauban, Sébastien Le Pestre de. *Mémoire pour le rappel des Huguenots.* Carrières-sous-Poissy: La Cause, 1998.

Voltaire. *Avis au public sur les parricides imputés aux Calas et aux Sirven.* Geneva, 1766.

– "Des mensonges imprimés." In *Œuvres complètes de Voltaire.* Oxford: Voltaire Foundation, 1968.

– *Le Siècle de Louis XIV.* Paris, 1733. https://artflsrv03.uchicago.edu/philologic4/toutvoltaire/navigate/185/table-of-contents/.

– *Traité sur la tolérance.* 1763.

SECONDARY SOURCES

Adams, Geoffrey. *The Huguenots and French Opinion, 1685–1787: The Enlightenment Debate on Toleration.* Waterloo: Wilfrid Laurier University Press, 1991.

– "Myths and Misconceptions: The Philosophe View of the Huguenots in the Age of Louis XV." *Historical Reflections/Réflexions Historiques* 1, no. 1 (June 1974): 59–80.

Adelman, Jeremy, and Stephen Aron. "From Borderlands to Borders: Empires, Nation-States, and the Peoples in Between in North American History." *American Historical Review* 4, no. 3 (June 1999): 815–16.

Adorno, Theodor W., and Max Horkheimer. *Dialectic of Enlightenment.* Translated by John Cumming. New York: Verso, 1997.

Aebersold, Estelle. *Les rémigrés du refuge huguenot. Le retour des descendants des religionnaires fugitifs en France depuis la loi du 9 décembre 1790 jusqu'au Code de la Nationalité du 19 octobre 1945* [mémoire de maîtrise ss. dir. Eckart Birnstiel]. Toulouse: Université de Toulouse II – Le Mirail, 2005.

– "Résultats d'une enquête sur les rémigrés du Refuge huguenot." *Diasporas. Histoire et Sociétés* 8 (2006): 45–8.

Allier, Raoul. *Voltaire et Calas.* Paris, 1898.

Amand, Laura Maslow. "La bourgeoisie protestante. La Révolution et le mouvement de Déchristianisation à La Rochelle." *Revue d'histoire moderne et contemporaine* 31 (1986): 489–92.

Arendt, Hannah. "We Refugees." In *The Jewish Writings*, edited by Jerome Kohn and Ron H. Feldman, 264–74. New York: Schocken Books, 2007.

– *The Origins of Totalitarianism.* New York: Harcourt, 1973.

Aulard, Alphonse. *La Révolution française.* Paris, 1887.

Baecque, Antoine de. *The Body Politic: Corporeal Metaphor in Revolutionary France, 1770–1800.* Stanford: Stanford University Press, 1993.

Baird, Henry Martyn. *The Huguenots and the Revocation of the Edict of Nantes.* New York: Charles Scribner's Sons, 1895.

Baker, Keith Michael. *Inventing the French Revolution: Essays on French Political Culture in the Eighteenth Century.* Cambridge: Cambridge University Press, 1990.

Baker, Keith Michael, and Dan Edelstein, eds. *Scripting Revolution: A Histori-*

cal Approach to the Comparative Study of Revolutions. Stanford: Stanford University Press, 2015.

Baker, Keith Michael, and Peter Hanns Reill, eds. *What's Left of Enlightenment?: A Postmodern Question.* Stanford: Stanford University Press, 2002.

Banks, Bryan A. "Jeanne de Lartigue, Madame de Montesquieu: Calvinist Refugee and Wife of an Enlightenment Philosopher." In *The Wives of Western Philosophy: Gender Politics in Intellectual Labor*, edited by Jennifer Forestal and Menaka Philips, 88–106. New York: Routledge, 2021.

– "The Protestant Origins of the French Revolution: Contextualizing Edgar Quinet in the Historiography of the Revolution, 1789–1865." *Proceedings of the Western Society for French History* 42 (2014): 65–74.

Bastide, Charles. "Bayle est-il l'auteur de l'*Avis aux Réfugiés*?" BSHPF 56 (1907): 544–58.

Baud, Michael, and Willem Van Schendel. "Toward a Comparative History of Borderlands." *Journal of World History* 8, no. 2 (Fall 1997): 211–42.

Becker, Carl L. *The Heavenly City of the Eighteenth-Century Philosophers.* New Haven: Yale University Press, 2003.

Beik, William. *Absolutism and Society in Seventeenth-Century France: State Power and Provincial Authority in Languedoc.* Cambridge: Cambridge University Press, 1985.

Bell, David A. *The Cult of the Nation in France: Inventing Nationalism, 1680–1800.* Cambridge: Harvard University Press, 2003.

– *The First Total War: Napoleon's Europe and the Birth of Warfare as We Know It.* New York: Houghton Mifflin Harcourt, 2007.

– *Lawyers and Citizens: Making of a Political Elite in Old Regime France.* New York: Oxford University Press, 1994.

– "Questioning the Global Turn: The Case of the French Revolution." *French Historical Studies* 37, no. 1 (2014): 1–24.

Benedict, Philip. *The Huguenot Population of France, 1600–1685: The Demographic Fate and Customs of a Religious Minority.* Transactions of the American Philosophical Society 81, no. 5. Philadelphia: American Philosophical Society, 1991.

Bergeal, Catherine. *Protestantisme et tolérance en France au XVIIIe siècle: De la Révocation à la Révolution, 1685–1789.* Carrières-sous-Poissy, 1988.

Bien, David. *The Calas Affair.* Princeton: Princeton University Press, 1960.

Blanc, Louis. *Histoire de la Révolution français.* Paris, 1847.

Blaufarb, Rafe. *The Politics of Fiscal Privilege in Provence, 1530s–1830s.* Washington, DC: Catholic University of America Press, 2012.

Borrel, Abraham. *Biographie d'Antoine Court auteur de la restauration du protestantisme en France après la Révocation de l'Edit de Nantes, ou Episode de l'histoire des églises du désert cévenol de 1713 à 1760.* Toulouse, 1863.

Borello, Céline. *Du Désert au Royaume: Parole publique et écriture protestante (1765–1788): Édition critique du* Vieux Cévenol *et de sermons de Rabaut Saint-Étienne.* Paris: Champion, 2013.

Bost, Charles. *Les Martyrs D'aigues-Mortes: Prisonniers et Prisonnières protestantes enfermés dans les Tours d'Aigues-Mortes, et particulièrement dans la tour de Constance.* Paris: 1922.

Bost, Hubert. "Elie Benoist et l'historiographie de l'édit de Nantes." In *Ces Messieurs de la R.P.R. Histoire et écritures de huguenots, XVIIe-XVIIIe siècles*, 267–79. Paris: Champion, 2001.

– *Pierre Bayle.* Paris: Fayard, 2006.

Boucher, Philip P. *France and the American Tropics to 1700: Tropics of Discontent?* Baltimore, MD: John Hopkins University Press, 2008.

Bracken, Harry McFarland. "Pierre Jurieu: The Politics of Prophecy." In *Millenarianism and Messianism in Early Modern European Culture: Continental Millenarians: Protestants, Catholics, Heretics*, edited by John Christian Laursen and Richard H. Popkin, 85–94. Dordrecht, The Netherlands: Kluwer Academic Publishers, 2001.

Bradley, James E., and Dale Van Kley. *Religion and Politics in Enlightenment Europe.* Notre Dame, IN: University of Notre Dame Press, 2001.

Brogi, Stefano. *Teologiea senza verità: Bayle contro i "rationaux."* Milan: Franco Angeli, 1998.

Brown, Stewart J., and Timothy Tackett. *The Cambridge History of Christianity: Volume VII: Enlightenment, Reawakening, and Revolution, 1660–1815.* Cambridge: Cambridge University Press, 2006.

Brush, Craig Balcombe. *Montaigne and Bayle: Variations on the Theme of Skepticism.* The Hague: Martinus Nijhoff, 1966.

Burrows, Simon, and Mark Curran. *The French Book Trade in Enlightenment Europe Database, 1769–1794.* Accessed 15 November 2023. http://fbtee.uws.edu.au/stn/interface/.

Burson, Jeffrey. *The Culture of Enlightening: Abbé Claude Yvon and the En-*

tangled Emergence of the Enlightenment. Notre Dame, IN: Notre Dame University Press, 2019.
– "Entangling the 'Century of Lights' to Disentangle the Enlightenment." In *Belief and Politics in Enlightenment France: Essays in Honor of Dale K. Van Kley*, edited by Mita Choudhury and Daniel J. Watkins, 25–54. Oxford University Studies in the Enlightenment. Liverpool: Liverpool University Press, 2019.
Butler, Jon. *The Huguenots in America: A Refugee People in New World Society.* Cambridge: Harvard University Press, 1983.
Caestecker, Frank. "Refugees in the European Historiography: Beyond the Administrative Category." Paper presented at the conference Historiographies sans frontières. Les migrations internationales saisies par les histoires nationales (XIXe– XXe siècles), Paris, 4 October 2011 [podcast]. Quoted in Elie, "Histories of Refugee and Forced Migration Studies," 30.
Carpenter, Kirsty. *Refugees of the French Revolution: Émigrés in London, 1789–1802*. New York: Routledge, 1999.
Cassirer, Erns. *The Philosophy of the Enlightenment*. Translated by Fritz C.A. Koelln and James P. Pettegrove. Princeton, NJ: Princeton University Press, 1951.
Cebe, Olivier. *L'Affaire Sirven: les sursauts de l'intolerance en Languedoc*. Brassac: Éditions de Poliphile, 1987.
Chaicraft, David J., and Austin Harrington, eds. *The Protestant Ethic Debate: Max Weber's Replies to His Critics, 1907–1910*. Liverpool: Liverpool University Press, 2002.
Chartier, Roger. *The Cultural Origins of the French Revolution*. Translated by Lydia G. Cochrane. Durham, NC: Duke University Press, 1991.
Chartier, Roger, Marie-Madeleine Compère, and Dominique Julia. *L'Education en France du XVIe au XVIIIe siècles*. Paris: Sedes, 1976.
Chimni, B.S. "The Birth of a 'Discipline': From Refugee to Forced Migration Studies," *Journal of Refugee Studies* 22, no. 1 (2009): 11–29.
Chisick, Harvey. "Public Opinion and Political Culture in France during the Second Half of the Eighteenth Century." *English Historical Review* no. 470 (February 2002): 48–77.
Choudhury, Mita. *The Wanton Jesuit and the Wayward Saint: A Tale of Sex, Religion, and Politics in Eighteenth-Century France*. University Park, PA: Pennsylvania State University Press, 2015.

Coleman, Charly. *The Virtues of Abandon: An Anti-Individualist History of the French Revolution.* Stanford: Stanford University Press, 2014.

Coquerel, Alphonse. *Jean Calas et sa famille.* Paris, 1858.

Coquerel, Charles. *Histoire des églises du désert chez les Protestants de France depuis la fin du règne de Louis XIV jusqu'à la Révolution Française.* 2 vols. Paris, 1841.

Cottret, Bernard. *Huguenots in England: Immigration and Settlement, c. 1550–1700,* trans. by Peregrine and Adriana Stevenson. Cambridge: Cambridge University Press, 1991.

Coutet, Alex. *Jean Calas, roué vif et innocent.* Toulouse, 1933.

Cullen, L.M. "The Huguenots from the Perspective of the Merchant Networks of Western Europe (1680–1790): The Example of the Brandy Trade." In *The Huguenots and Ireland: Anatomy of an Emigration*, edited by C.E.J. Caldicott, Hugh Gough, and J.-P Pittion, 129–50. Dublin: The Glendale Press, 1987.

Dardier, Charles. *Paul Rabaut. Ses lettres a Antoine Court, 1739–1755.* Vol. 2. Paris, 1884.

Darnton, Robert. *The Great Cat Massacre.* New York: Basic Books, 1984.

Denis, Philippe. "The Cape Huguenots and Their Legacy in Apartheid South Africa." In Van Ruymbeke and Sparks, eds, *Memory and Identity*, 285–309.

Dibon, Paul, ed. *Pierre Bayle: Le philosophe de Rotterdam; études et documents.* Amsterdam: Elsevier, 1959.

Dodge, Guy Howard. *The Political Theory of the Huguenots of the Dispersion, with Special Reference to the Thought and Influence of Pierre Jurieu.* New York: Octagon Books, 1972.

Douen, Orentin. "Claude Brousson, séjour en Hollande, 1694–5." BSHPF 27 (1878): 62.

– *La Révocation de l'Édit de Nantes.* Vol. 3. Paris: Librarie Fischbacher, 1894.

Duley-Haour, Pauline. "Antoine Court and Refugee Political Thought (1719–1752)." In Laursen, *New Essays,* 131–54.

– "Correspondances Pastorales (XVIe-Xxe Siècles)." BSHPF 159, no. 1 (2013): 143–58.

– "Désert et Refuge: Sociohistoire d'une internationale huguenote, un réseau européen de soutien aux 'Églises sous la croix' (1715–1752)." *Études Théologiques et religieuses* 90, no. 4 (2015): 613–19.

Dupont, André. *Rabaut Saint-Étienne, 1743–1793: Un protestant défenseur de la liberté religieuse.* Introduction by Jean Baubérot. Paris: Labor et Fides, 1989.

Dupré, Louis. *The Enlightenment and the Intellectual Foundations of Modern Culture.* New Haven: Yale University Press, 2004.

Duroselle, Jean-Baptiste. "Les frontiers: Vision historique," *Relations internationals* 63 (Fall 1990): 229–42.

Edelstein, Dan. *The Enlightenment: A Genealogy.* Chicago: University of Chicago Press, 2010.

– *On the Spirit of Natural Rights* (Chicago: University of Chicago Press, 2021).

Elie, Jérôme. "Histories of Refugee and Forced Migration Studies." In *The Oxford Handbook of Refugee and Forced Migration Studies*, edited by Elena Fiddian-Qasmiyeh, Gil Loescher, Katy Long, and Nando Sigona, 23–35. Oxford: Oxford University Press, 2014.

Farr, James and David Lay Williams, eds. *The General Will: The Evolution of a Concept.* New York: Cambridge University Press, 2014.

Farge, Arlette. *Subversive Words: Public Opinion in Eighteenth-Century France,* trans. by Rosemary Morris. University Park, PA: Pennsylvania State University Press, 1994.

Febvre, Lucien. "*Frontière*: The Word and the Concept" (1928). In *A New Kind of History: From the Writings of Lucien Febvre*, edited by Peter Burke, 208–18. London: Routledge and Kegan Paul, 1973.

Foucault, Michel. "What Is Enlightenment?" *The Foucault Reader.* Edited by Paul Rabinow. New York, 1984: 32–51.

Frazer, Michael L. *The Enlightenment of Sympathy: Justice and the Moral Sentiments in the Eighteenth Century and Today.* Oxford: Oxford University Press, 2010.

Frêche, Georges. "Contre-Réforme et dragonnades (1610–1789): Pour une orientation statistique de l'histoire du Protestantisme." *BSHPF* 119 (1973): 362–83.

Fuentes, Marisa J., *Dispossessed Lives: Enslaved Women, Violence, and the Archive.* Philadelphia: University of Pennsylvania Press, 2016.

Gaidan, Claude-Annie. "Paul Rabaut et sa famille." In *Les Rabaut du Désert à la Révolution.* Montpellier: Presses du Languedoc, 1988.

Galland, A. "Les pasteurs français Amyraut, Bochart etc. et la royauté de droit divin de l'Edit de Nantes à la Révocation, 1629–1685." *BSHPF* 77, no. 3 (July–September 1928): 225–41.

Galland, Elie. *L'Affaire Sirven. Etude historique d'apres les documents originaux. Avec une lettre I. Emile Faguet.* Paris: Soc. francaise d'imprimerie, 1911.

Gargett, Graham. *Voltaire and Protestantism* (Oxford: Oxford University Studies in the Enlightenment, 1980).

– "Voltaire and the Sirven case: propaganda in a good cause?" in *Proceedings of the Huguenot Society of Great Britain and Ireland* 26, no. 4 (1996): 431–442.

Garrioch, David. *The Huguenots of Paris and the Coming of Religious Freedom, 1685–1789*. Cambridge University Press, Cambridge, 2014.

Gatrell, Peter. *The Making of the Modern Refugee.* Oxford: Oxford University Press, 2014.

—-, "Refugees – What's Wrong with History?" *Journal of Refugee Studies* 30, no. 2 (2016): 17–189.

Gauchet, Marcel. *The Disenchantment of the World: A Political History of Religion.* trans. by Oscar Burge. Princeton: Princeton University Press, 1997.

Gay, Peter. *The Enlightenment: An Interpretation.* 2 vols. New York: W.W. Norton, 1966–1969.

Gillespie, Michael Allen. *The Theological Origins of Modernity.* Chicago: University of Chicago Press, 2010.

Gojosso, Eric. *Le concept de la république en France (XVIe-XVIIIe siècle).* Marseilles: Presses Universitaires d'Aix-Marseille, 1998.

Goldwyn, Henriette. "Strange Language and Practices of Disorder: The Prophetic Crisis in France following the Revocation of the Edict of Nantes in 1685." In *Women Telling Nations*, edited by Amelia Sanz, Francesca Scott, and Suzan van Dijk, 103–18. Brill: 2014.

Greengrass, Mark. *The French Reformation.* New York: Basil Blackwell, 1987.

Gregory, Brad. *Salvation at Stake: Christian Martyrdom in Early Modern Europe*. Cambridge: Harvard University Press, 1999.

– *The Unintended Reformation: How a Religious Revolution Secularized Society.* Cambridge: Belknap Press, 2012.

Gwynn, Robin. *Huguenot Heritage: The History and Contribution of the Huguenots in Britain.* 2nd ed. Brighton: Sussex University Press, 2001.

Haakonssen, Knud, ed., *Enlightenment and Religion: Rational Dissent in Eighteenth-Century Britain*. Cambridge: Cambridge University Press, 2006.

Habermas, Jurgen. *The Structural Transformation of the Public Sphere: An Inquiry into a Category of Bourgeois Society*. Cambridge: Polity, 2015.

Haddad, Emma. *The Refugee in International Society: Between Sovereigns.* Cambridge: Cambridge University Press, 2008.

Hair, P.E.H., Adam Jones, and Robin Law, eds. *Barbot on Guinea: The Writings of Jean Barbot on West Africa, 1678–1712.* 2 vols. London: Hakluyt Society, 1992.

Hämäläinen, Pekka, and Samuel Truett, "On Borderlands." *The Journal of American History* 98, no. 2 (September 2011): 338–61.

Hands, A.P., and Irene Scouldoudi. *French Protestants relieved through the Threadneedle Street Church, London, 1681–1687.* London: Huguenot Society of London, 1971.

Harrison, Peter. *"Religion" and the Religions in the English Enlightenment.* Cambridge: Cambridge University Press, 1990.

Harvey, David Allen. *The French Enlightenment and its Others: The Mandarin, the Savage, and the Invention of the Human Sciences.* New York: Palgrave, 2012.

Hause, Steven C. "French Protestants, Laicization, and the Separation of the Churches and the State, 1802–1905." In *Religious Differences in France: Past and Present*, edited by Kathleen P. Long, 141–60. Kirksville: Truman State University, 2006.

Hazard, Paul. *The Crisis of the European Mind, 1680–1715.* New York: New York Review of Books, 2013.

Herman, Arthur. "The Huguenot Republic and Antirepublicanism in Seventeenth-Century France." *Journal of the History of Ideas* 53, no. 2 (April–June 1992); 249–69.

Higonnet, Patrice. *Sister Republics: The Origins of French and American Republicanism.* Cambridge: Harvard University Press, 1988.

Hobsbawm, Eric, and Terence Ranger, eds. *The Invention of Tradition.* Cambridge: Cambridge University Press, 1983.

Hochstrasser, T.J. "The Claims of Conscience: Natural Law Theory, Obligation, and Resistance in the Huguenot Diaspora." In Laursen, *New Essays*, 15–51.

Howell, Robin. "Rousseau and the Huguenots." *Huguenot Society Journal* 30, no. 1 (2013): 21–33.

Howells, R.J. *Pierre Jurieu: Antinomial Radical.* Durham: University of Durham Press, 1983.

Hugues, Edmond. *Antoine Court: Histoire de la restauration du protestantisme en France au XVIIIe. siècle d'après des documents inédits.* 2 vols. Paris: 1872.

– *Les synods du Désert. Actes et régulements des synods nationaux et provinciaux tenus au desert de France de l'an 1715 à la an 1793.* 3 vols. Paris: Fischbacher, 1885.

Hulton, Paul, ed. *The Work of Jacques Le Moyne de Morgues. A Huguenot Artist in France, Florida and England.* London: British Museum Press, 1977.

Hunt, Lynn. *Inventing Human Rights: A History.* New York: W.W. Norton, 2007.

Hunt, Lynn, Suzanne Desan, and William Max Nelson, eds. *The French Revolution in Global Perspective.* Ithaca, NY: Cornell University Press, 2013.

Hunt, Lynn, Margaret Jacob, and Wijnand W. Mijnhardt. *The Book that Changed Europe: Picart and Bernard's Religious Ceremonies of the World.* Cambridge: Harvard University Press, 2010.

Hutchinson, E.W. *1688 Revolution in Siam: The Memoir of Father de Bèze.* Hong Kong: Hong Kong University Press, 1968.

– "The Retirement of the French Garrison from Bangkok in the Year 1688." *Selected Articles from the Siam Society Journal* 8 (Bangkok, 1959): 159–99.

Iliffe, Robert. "Author-Mongering: The 'Editor' between Producer and Consumer." In *The Consumption of Culture, 1600–1800: Image, Object, Text,* edited by Ann Bermingham and John Brewer, 166–92. New York: Routledge, 1995.

Inchauspe, Dominique. *L'intellectuel fourvoye: Voltaire et l'affaire Sirven, 1762–1778.* Paris: Albin Michel, 2004.

Israel, Jonathan. *Enlightenment Contested: Philosophy, Modernity, and the Emancipation of Man, 1670–1752.* Oxford: Oxford University Press, 2006.

– *Radical Enlightenment: Philosophy and the Making of Modernity, 1650–1750.* Oxford: Oxford University Press, 2002.

Jacob Margaret C., and Matthew Kadane, "Missing, Now Found in the Eighteenth Century: Weber's Protestant Capitalist." *American Historical Review* 108, no. 1 (February 2003): 20–49.

Jacobs, Margaret C. *The Radical Enlightenment: Pantheists, Freemasons, and Republicans.* 2nd ed. Lafayette, LA: Cornerstone Books, 2006.

Jainchill, Andrew. "1685 and the French Revolution." In Hunt, Desan, and Nelson, *The French Revolution in Global Perspective*, 57–70.

Jasanoff, Maya. "Revolutionary Exiles: The American Loyalist and French Émigré Diaspora." In *The Age of Revolutions in Global Context*, edited by David Armitage and Sanjay Subrahmanyam, 37–58. New York: Palgrave MacMillan, 2009.

Joutard, Philippe. *Les camisards*. Paris: Gallimard, 1994.

– *La Révocation de l'édit de Nantes ou Les faiblesses d'un État*. Paris: Gallimard, 2018.

Jue, Jeffrey K. *Heaven Upon Earth: Joseph Mede (1586–1638) and the Legacy of Millenarianism*. Dordrecht: Springer, 2006.

Kamen, Henry. *The Rise of Toleration.* New York: McGraw-Hill, 1967.

Knetsch, Frederik Reinier Jacob. *Pierre Jurieu: Theoloog en politikus der refuge.* Kampen: J.H. Kok, 1967.

– "Pierre Jurieu and the Glorious Revolution According to His '*Lettres pastorales*.'" In *Church, Change, and Revolution: Transactions of the Fourth Anglo-Dutch Church History Colloquium, Exeter, 30 August–3 September 1988*, edited by Johannes van den Berg, 145–64. Leiden: Brill, 1991.

Koenigsberger, Helmut Georg. "Republicanism, Monarchism, and Liberty." *Royal and Republican Sovereignty in Early Modern Europe*, edited by Robert Oresko, G.C. Gibbs, and Hamish M. Scott, 43–74. Cambridge: Cambridge University Press, 1997.

Kors, Alan Charles. *Atheism in France, 1650–1729*. Princeton: Princeton University Press, 1990.

Kristof, Ladis K.D. "The Nature of Frontiers and Boundaries." *Annals of the Association of American Geographers* 49 (1959): 269–82.

Krumenacker, Yves. "Une perception protestante de l'espace au XVIIIe siècle?" In *Évolution et représentation du paysage de 1750 à nos jours*, 139–55. Montbrison: Ville de Montbrison, 1997.

Kwass, Michael. *Contraband: Louis Mandrin and the Making of the Global Underground.* Cambridge: Harvard University Press, 2014.

Laborie, Lionel. *Enlightening Enthusiasm: Prophecy and Religious Experience in Early Eighteenth-Century England.* Manchester: Manchester University Press, 2015.

Labrousse, Élisabeth. "Reading Bayle in Paris." In *Anticipations of the Enlightenment in England, France, and Germany*, edited by Alan Charles Kors and Paul J. Korshin, 7–16. Philadelphia: University of Pennsylvania Press, 1987.

– *Pierre Bayle*. 2 vols. The Hague: Martinus Nijhoff, 1963–4.

– *Pierre Bayle:* Vol. 2: *Heterodoxie et rigorisme*. The Hague: Martinus Nijhoff, 1964.

Lachenicht, Suzanne. "Refugees and Refugee Protection in the Early Modern Period." *Journal of Refugee Studies* 30, no. 2 (2017): 261–81.

Lafleur, Gérard. *Les protestants aux Antilles françaises du Vent sous l'ancien régime*. Basse-Terre, Guadeloupe: Société d'Histoire de la Guadeloupe, 1988.

Lafleur, Gérard, and Lucien-René Abénon. "The Protestants and the Colonization of the French West Indies." In Van Ruymbeke and Sparks, *Memory and Identity*, 267–84.

Lasserre, Claude. *Le Séminaire de Lausanne (1726-1812): Instrument de la restauration du protestantisme français*. Lausanne: Bibliothèque historique vaudoise, 1997.

Laursen, John Christian, ed. *New Essays on the Political Thought of the Huguenots of the* Refuge. New York: Brill, 1995.

Laursen, John Christian, and Richard H. Popkin, eds. *Millenarianism and Messianism in Early Modern European Culture: Continental Millenarians: Protestants, Catholics, Heretics*. Dordrecht, Netherlands: Kluwer Academic Publishers, 2001.

Law, Robin. "Jean Barbot as a Source for the Slave Coast of West Africa." *History of Africa* vol. 9 (1982): 155–73.

Lennon, Thomas. *Reading Bayle*. Toronto: University of Toronto Press, 1999.

Léonard, Émile G. *Le Protestant français*. Paris: Presses Universitaires de France, 1953.

"Les promoteurs de l'édit de 1787 qui a restitué l'état civil aux protestants de France: Corréspondance de Lafayette, Paul Rabaut, Rabaut-Saint-Étienne, de Poitevin (1785–1788)," BSHPF 3 (1855): 330–44.

Ligou, Daniel. "Le Protestantisme français dans la seconde moitié du XVIIIe siècle." *Information historique* 25 (1963): 8–14.

– *Le Protestantisme français en France de 1598 à 1715*. Paris: Sedes, 1968.

Lods, Armand. *Essai sur la vie de Rabaut de Saint-Étienne, pasteur à Nîmes, membre de l'Assemblée constituante et de la Convention nationale (1743–1793).* Paris, 1893.

– *Traité de l'administration des cultes protestants.* Paris, 1896.

Lougee, Caroline Chappell. *Facing the Revocation: Huguenot Families, Faith, and the King's Will.* Oxford: Oxford University Press, 2017.

– "'The Pains I Took to Save My/His Family': Escape Accounts by a Huguenot Mother and Daughter after the Revocation of the Edict of Nantes." *French Historical Studies* 22, no. 1 (Winter 1999): 1–64.

Lüthy, Herbert. *La banque protestante en France de la Révocation de l'Édit de Nantes à la Révolution.* 2 vols. Paris, 1952.

Lyotard, Jean-François. *The Postmodern Condition: A Report on Knowledge.* Translated by Geoff Bennington and Brian Massumi. Minneapolis, MN: University of Minnesota Press, 1984.

Mahmood, Saba. *Politics of Piety: The Islamic Revival and the Feminist Subject.* Princeton: Princeton University Press, 2011.

Mandrou, Robert. *Introduction to Early Modern France, 1500–1640.* London: Edward Arnold, 1975.

Marfleet, Philip. "Refugees and History: Why We Must Address the Past." *Refugee Survey Quarterly* 26, no. 3 (2007): 136–48.

Matytsin, Anton. "Fictional Letters or Real Accusations? Anonymous Correspondence in the Bayle-Jurieu Controversy." *Societate si politica/Society and Politics* 7, no. 2 (2013): 178–90.

Maugham, Frederic Herbert. *The Case of Jean Calas.* London, 1928.

McKee, Jane, and Randolph Vigne, eds. *The Huguenots: France, Exile and Diaspora.* Brighton, UK: Sussex Academic Press, 2013.

McMahon, Darrin M. *Enemies of the Enlightenment: The French Counter Enlightenment and the Making of Modernity.* Oxford: Oxford University Press, 2002.

McManners, John. *Church and Society in Eighteenth-Century France.* Vol. 2, *The Religion of the People and Politics of Religion.* Oxford: Clarendon Press, 1998.

Mentzer, Raymond A., and Bertrand Van Ruymbeke. *A Companion to the Huguenots.* Leiden: Brill, 2016.

Merrick, Jeffrey. *The Desacralization of the French Monarchy in the Eighteenth Century.* Baton Rouge: Louisiana State University Press, 1990.

Michelet, Jules. *Histoire de France jusqu'au XVIe siècle: Louis XIV et la Révocation de l'Édit de Nantes*. Vol. 13. Paris: Chamerot, 1860.

– *Histoire de France, nouvelle édition revue et augmentée*. Paris: Marpon, 1879.

Mori, Gianluca. *Bayle Philosophe*. Paris: Champion, 1999.

Mours, Samuel. *Essai sommaire de géographie du protestantisme réformé français au XVIIe siècle*. Paris, 1966.

Nelson, William Max. "Making Men: Enlightenment Ideas of Racial Engineering." *American Historical Review* 115, no. 5 (December 2010): 1364–94.

Nicolet, Claude. *L'Idee republicaine en France (1789–1924): Essai d'histoire critique*. Paris: Gallimard, 1982.

Nixon, Edna. *Voltaire and the Calas Case*. London: Vanguard Press, 1961.

O'Cathasaigh, Sean. "Bayle and the Authorship of the *Avis aux réfugiés*." *Studies on Voltaire and the Eighteenth Century* 219 (1983): 133–45.

Paganini, Gianni. "Towards a 'Critical' Bayle: Three Recent Studies." *Eighteenth-Century Studies* 37, no. 3 (2004): 510–20.

Perceval, Émile de. *Montesquieu et la vigne*. Bordeaux: Delmas, 1935.

Perry, Elisabeth Israels. *From Theology to History: French Religious Controversy and the Revocation of the Edict of Nantes*. The Hague: Martinus Nijhoff, 1973.

Pichichero, Christy. *The Military Enlightenment: War and Culture in the French Empire from Louis XIV to Napoleon*. Ithaca, NY: Cornell University Press, 2017.

Pocock, J.G.A. *Barbarism and Religion*. 6 vols. Cambridge: Cambridge University Press, 1999–2015.

– "Conservative Enlightenment and Democratic Revolutions: The American and French Cases in British Perspective." *Government & Opposition* 24, no. 1 (1989); 81–105.

– *The Machiavellian Moment: Florentine Political Thought and the Atlantic Republican Tradition*. Princeton: Princeton University Press, 1975.

Poland, Burdette. *French Protestantism and the French Revolution: A Study in Church and State, Thought and Religion, 1685–1815*. Princeton, NJ: Princeton University Press, 1957.

Pombejra, Dhirvat na. "Seventeenth-Century Ayutthaya: A Shift to Isolation?" In *Southeast Asia in the Early Modern Era: Trade, Power, and Belief*, edited by Anthony Reid, 250–72. Ithaca: Cornell University Press, 1993.

Popkin, Richard H. *The History of Skepticism: From Savonarola to Bayle.* Oxford: Oxford University Press, 2003.

– *The Third Force in Seventeenth-Century Thought.* Leiden: Brill, 1992.

Porter, Roy, and Mikuláš Teich *The Enlightenment in National Context.* Cambridge: Cambridge University Press, 1981.

Probasco, Nate. "Catherine de Medici and Huguenot Colonization, 1560–1567." In *Colonization, Piracy, and Trade in Early Modern Europe*, edited by Estelle Paranque, Nate Probasco, and Claire Jowitt, 41–72. New York: Palgrave MacMillan, 2017.

Quinet, Edgar. *La Révolution.* Translated by Claude Lefort. Paris, 1987.

Read, Charles. "L'Opinion du duc de Bourgogne sur la question protestante et le rappel des huguenots (1710)." BSHPF 41 (1892): 347.

Reboul, Juliette, and Laure Philip. *French Emigrants in Revolutionised Europe: Connected Histories and Memories.* New York: Palgrave, 2019.

Rees, D.A. "Kant, Bayle, and Indifferentism." *Philosophical Review* 63, no. 4 (October 1954): 592–5.

Rex, Walter. *Essays on Pierre Bayle and Religious Controversy.* The Hague: Nijhoff, 1965.

Riley, Patrick. *The General Will before Rousseau: The Transformation of the Divine into the Civic.* Princeton, NJ: Princeton University Press, 1986.

Robbins, Caroline. *The Eighteenth-Century Commonwealthsman.* Cambridge: Harvard University Press, 1959.

Rolland, Pierre. *Dictionnaire des Camisards.* Montpellier: Presses du Languedoc, 1995.

Romane-Musculus, Paul. "L'Église réformé de Pouzauges de l'Édit de Nantes à sa Révocation." BSHPF 125 (1982): 9–46.

Root, Hilton L. *Peasants and King in Burgundy: Agrarian Foundations of French Absolutism.* Berkeley: University of California Press, 1987.

Rosanvallon, Pierre. *The Demands of Liberty: Civil Society in France since the Revolution.* Translated by Arthur Goldhammer. Cambridge: Harvard University Press, 2007.

Rosenblatt, Helena. "The Christian Enlightenment." *The Cambridge History of Christianity*. Vol. 7, *Enlightenment, Reawakening and Revolution, 1660–1815*, edited by Steward J. Brown and Timothy Tackett. Cambridge: Cambridge University Press, 2006.

Rosenwein, Barbara H. *Emotional Communities in the Early Middle Ages.* Ithaca, NY: Cornell University Press, 2006.

Sahlins, Peter. "Fictions of a Catholic France: The Naturalization of Foreigners, 1685–1787." *Représentations* no. 47 (1994): 85–110.

Sauter, Michael. *Visions of the Enlightenment: The Edict on Religion of 1788 and the Politics of the Public Sphere in Eighteenth-Century Prussia.* Leiden: Brill, 2009.

Schwab, Richard N. "Un encyclopédiste Huguenot: Le chevalier de Jaucourt." *BSHPF* (April–June 1962): 45–75.

Schwab, Richard N., Walter E. Rex, and John Lough. *Inventory of Diderot's Encyclopédie.* Vol. 223. Oxford: Oxford University Studies in the Enlightenment, 1971.

Scoville, Warren C. *The Persecution of Huguenots and French Economic Development, 1680–1720.* Berkeley: University of California Press, 1960.

Scott, James C. *Domination and the Arts of Resistance: Hidden Transcripts.* New Haven: Yale University Press, 1990.

Scott, Joan Wallach. "The Evidence of Experience." *Critical Inquiry* 17, no. 4 (Summer 1991): 773–97.

Serna, Pierre. "Every Revolution is a War of Independence." In Hunt, Desan, and Nelson, *The French Revolution in Global Perspective*, 165–82.

Sheehan, Jonathan. "Enlightenment, Religion, and the Enigma of Secularization: A Review Essay." *American Historical Review* 108, no. 4 (October 2003): 1061–80.

Sher, Richard B. *The Enlightenment and the Book: Scottish Authors and Their Publishers in Eighteenth-Century Britain, Ireland, and America.* Chicago: University of Chicago Press, 2006.

Siegelberg, Mira L. *Statelessness: A Modern History.* Cambridge: Harvard University Press, 2020.

Smiles, Samuel. *The Huguenots in France after the Revocation of the Edict of Nantes: with a visit to the country of the Vandors.* New York: Harper & Brothers, 1874.

Soguk, Nevzat. *States and Strangers: Refugees and Displacements of Statecraft.* Minneapolis: University of Minnesota Press, 1999.

Sorel, Albert. *Montesquieu.* Paris: Librarie Hachette, 1887.

Sorkin, David. *The Religion Enlightenment: Protestants, Jews, and Catholics from London to Vienna.* Princeton: Princeton University Press, 2008.

Spieler, Miranda F. "The Legal Structure of Colonial Rule during the French Revolution." *William & Mary Quarterly* 66, no. 2 (2009): 365–408.

Stanwood, Owen. "Between Eden and Empire: Huguenot Refugees and the Promise of New Worlds." *American Historical Review* (December 2013): 1319–44.

– *The Global Refuge: Huguenots in an Age of Empire.* Oxford: Oxford University Press, 2020.

Stepan, Alfred, and Charles Taylor, eds. *Boundaries of Toleration.* New York: Columbia University Press, 2014.

Tawney, Richard Henry. *Religion and the Rise of Capitalism.* New York: Brace & World, 1926.

Taylor, Charles. *Modern Social Imaginaries.* Durham, NC: Duke University Press, 2004.

– *A Secular Age.* Cambridge: Harvard University Press, 2007.

Teller, Adam. *Rescue the Surviving Souls: The Great Jewish Refugee Crisis of the Seventeenth Century.* Princeton: Princeton University Press, 2020.

Terpstra, Nicholas. *Religious Refugees in the Early Modern World: An Alternative History of the Reformation.* Cambridge: Cambridge University Press, 2015.

Tinsley, Barbara Sher. "Sozzini's Ghost: Pierre Bayle and the Socinian Tradition." *Journal of the History of Ideas* 57, no. 4 (1996): 609–24.

Ther, Philipp. *The Outsiders: Refugees in Europe since 1492.* Princeton, NJ: Princeton University Press, 2019.

Tocqueville, Alexis de. *L'Ancien régime et la Révolution.* Paris, 1856.

– *The Old Regime and the French Revolution.* New York: Dover, 2010.

Toews, John E. "Intellectual History after the Linguistic Turn: The Autonomy of Meaning and the Irreducibility of Experience." *American Historical Review* 92 (October 1987): 879–907.

Trevor-Roper, Hugh Redwald. *Religion, the Reformation and Social Change.* New York: Macmillan, 1972.

Tricoire, Damien, ed. *Enlightened Colonialism: Civilization Narratives and Imperial Politics in the Age of Reason.* New York: Palgrave MacMillan, 2017.

Utt, Walter C., and Brian E. Strayer. *The Bellicose Dove: Claude Brousson and Protestant Resistance to Louis XIV, 1647–1698.* Brighton: Sussex Academic Press, 2003.

Van der Linden, David. *Experiencing Exile: Huguenot Refugees in the Dutch Republic, 1680–1700*. Surrey, UK: Ashgate, 2015.

– "A Tearful Diaspora: Preaching Religious Emotions in the Huguenot Refuge." In *Feeling Exclusion: Religious Conflict, Exile, and Emotions in Early Modern Europe*, edited by Charles Zika and Giovanni Tarantino, 44–62. London: Routledge, 2019.

Van der Lugt, Mara. *Bayle, Jurieu, and the* Dictionnaire Historique et Critique. Oxford: Oxford University Press, 2016.

Van Kley, Dale. "Christianity as Casualty and Chrysalis of Modernity: The Problem of Dechristianization in the French Revolution." *American Historical Review* 108, no. 4. (October 2003): 1081–1104.

– *The Religious Origins of the French Revolution: From Calvin to the Civil Constitution of the Clergy, 1560–1791*. New Haven, CT: Yale University Press, 1996.

Van Ruymbeke, Bertrand. "Minority Survival: The Huguenot Paradigm in France and the Diaspora." In Van Ruymbeke and Sparks, *Memory and Identity*, 1–25.

Van Ruymbeke, Bertrand, and Randy J. Sparks, eds. *Memory and Identity: The Huguenots in France and the Atlantic Diaspora*. Columbus, SC: University of South Carolina Press, 2003.

Viner, Jacob. *Religious Thought and Economic Society*. Durham: Duke University Press, 1978.

Vovelle, Michelle. *Piété baroque et déchristianisation en Provence au XVIIIe siècle*. Paris: Éditions du Seuil, 1978.

Weber, Max. *The Protestant Ethic and the Spirit of Capitalism*. Chicago: Taylor & Francis, 2001.

Werner, Michael, and Bénédicte Zimmermann. "Beyond Comparison: *Histoire croisée* and the challenge of reflexivity." *History and Theory* 45, no. 1 (2006): 30–50.

Wood, Dennis. *Benjamin Constant: A Biography*. New York: Routledge, 2002.

Woodbridge, John Dunning. "An 'Unnatural Alliance' for Religious Toleration: The Philosophes and the Outlawed Pastors of the 'Church of the Desert.'" *Church History* 42, no. 4 (1 December 1973): 505–23.

Wright, Johnson Kent. *A Classical Republican in Eighteenth-Century France: The Political Thought of Mably*. Stanford: Stanford University Press, 1997.

Yardeni, Myriam. "Naissance et lessor d'un mythe: La Revocation de l'Edit de Nantes et le decline économique de la France." BSHPF 139 (1993): 191–206.

– *Le Refuge protestant.* Paris: Presses Universitaires de France, 1985.

– *Repenser l'histoire: Aspects de l'historiographie huguenots des Guerres de religion à la Revolution française.* Paris: H. Champion, 2000.

Zurbuchen, Simone. "Jaucourt, Republicanism, and Toleration." In Laursen, *New Essays*, 155–70.

Index